TONGUE OF FIRE

BY DAVID McKNIGHT

CHAPTER 1

As the thrumming of the car's engine drew nearer, Paul Connelly's gut tightened. It was late July and the season opener was six weeks away, but old habits refused to die. The car passed without incident, and the coach relaxed his tensed muscles and unleashed a stream of pent up air. He reminded himself, the honks and the hand gestures didn't usually start until *after* the first loss of the season. He was safe, for now.

He stepped gingerly across the street, down the sloped parking lot, and up to the door of the boys' locker room. He fished a fistful of keys out of his pocket, gave the handle a quick jiggle, and then let himself in. For the first time in two months, the pungent odor of the boys' locker room assaulted his nostrils, bringing with it a terrifying rush of memories of his four bitterly disappointing seasons as head coach of the Mayfield Mustangs.

The coach produced another key, jiggled a second handle, and then stepped into the tiny eight by eight cubicle that had been his refuge for much of the last four years. He surveyed his office. Everything was exactly where he left it when school had let out two months earlier. To one side there was a basket of worn, leather footballs. From the corkboard hung a lonely press clipping and a well-worn whistle. Other than the weekly dusting by the school janitor, the room appeared to have been largely undisturbed.

Yet, Paul couldn't shake the sensation that something *was* amiss. Something in the room was chipping away at his precarious sense of calm. He scanned the room one more time, and that's when he saw it. At the base of the phone on the corner of his desk he saw an ominous, pulsing red light. Someone had called. Already. Two-a-days were still a week away, yet the messages were already starting to arrive. This was unexpected, and very unsettling.

In the course of the last four years, messages left at his extension rarely brought good tidings. Paul had fielded messages from concerned citizens, anxious school board members and angry parents. These last ones proved to be the most vexing. When a child's playing time didn't rise to the level of his perceived talent, Paul received a message. In the last two years the messages had begun to arrive in flurries. Each new week brought with it another disgruntled parent, another angry phone call.

What the parents never fully understood, however, was the central tenet of Paul's coaching philosophy: playing time in football had as much to do with moral rectitude as it did athletic prowess. This had been acceptable at first, especially given the circumstances surrounding Paul's hiring. But as the losses piled up, the parents grew impatient, and then hostile.

But opening night *was* over a month away, and depth charts had yet to be defined. So, who could it be? Dread and curiosity battled within him until the latter prevailed. Paul pushed the button.

"Coach Connelly, this is John Peterson calling from Thousand Oaks, Oregon. We've never met, but I do have an application pending in your principal's office to teach an Italian pilot program at your high school. Your school is one of five that is currently considering my application. Anyway, I'm calling because my son Jacob is a quarterback and I wanted to get a sense for your offensive scheme should we end up in Mayfield. You can reach me at 555-255-8329. I look forward to the chat."

As Paul listened to the message he absently scribbled the details on a post-it note. When he was done, he surveyed it quickly and then dropped it mercifully into his desk drawer.

Ok, so add parent-turned-agent to the growing list of calls he now had to field as head coach of the Mayfield Mustangs. Paul knew exactly where this conversation was going: roll out the red carpet, rearrange your depth chart and adopt the West Coast Offense for the express purpose of accommodating my son's golden arm. No, this was a return call Paul could pass on. He'd talk to the guy if and when the kid actually showed up on the practice field. In the meantime, Paul had enough on his mind. He had a team to assemble and, with a little luck, a winning season to engineer.

A shadow moved into John's periphery. He turned to see Stan Carraway standing in his doorway.

"Getting a jump on the season, I see."

"You know me. I just couldn't wait until next week," Paul said, standing and grabbing the outstretched hand of the school's athletic director.

"Good man," Stan said, the broad smile slowly fading from his face. "I saw you walk in this morning. Thought maybe we could have a little chat before two-a-days started and things around here got really crazy."

"Uh, sure, what's on your mind?"

Stan's forgoing of any small talk or pleasantries gave Paul an uneasy feeling. They hadn't seen each other in months yet Stan's visage was ominously devoid of warmth.

"Listen, I just wanted to keep you in the loop here about some exchanges I've been having with some of the school board members."

"Ah yes, my fans on the school board."

"Come on Paul. You know they unanimously approved your hire four years ago."

"Uh-huh."

"With the incident, and then the firing, they were about to deep six the whole program. The only reason it's still around is because of you. You were the compromise."

"I know, I know, bring in the former pastor, and make him your football coach. It placates the public, and keeps the players out of the headlines."

"Exactly. What you did when you came on is the reason we still play football here at Mayfield High. And for that, we all owe you a debt of gratitude. But, I have to tell you, memories are starting to fade. You've kept these kids out of trouble, which is great. But people are starting to wonder when you're going to actually turn this ship around."

Paul glared at his athletic director.

"Are you one of those people Stan?"

"Listen Paul, I'm one of your biggest fans. Have been since our playing days in college. But, I can only get your back for so long. If you have another losing season, I may be the guy that goes down with you. So, at the instigation of the school board, we've…started looking around."

"You're looking around?" Paul said, his chin jutting out defiantly.

The question was met with stony silence.

"Stan, are you actively searching for my replacement?" Paul pressed, anger rising in his voice.

After a few more moments of awkward silence, Stan took a deep breath. "Yes, Paul, we are considering someone else, but there have only been preliminary discussions."

"Who Stan?"

"They've only been preliminary."

"Who?" Paul demanded, this time more forcefully.

"Chan Yarber over at Lincoln Central. He retired last year and the word is he's looking for a challenge. A project. Somewhere he can go and start over. Build a program from the ground up."

"Chan Yarber? You've got to be kidding me Stan. Tell me you're not talking to Chan Yarber."

Chan Yarber had won multiple state championships over the last 20 years at Lincoln Central. But, in Paul's mind, his methods had always been questionable. Recruiting was illegal in high school, but Chan knew how to finesse all of the gray areas in the system.

"Well, Chan Yarber is a proven coach," Stan said. "And frankly the school board likes him."

"How about you Stan? Where are *you* on this?"

"He's a nice guy, Paul, and a good coach. But, to be honest, I'm not quite ready to pull the trigger. What I *can* tell you is that keeping your players out of trouble is no longer enough for you to keep your job. You've had four years to turn things around. Sooner or later, you have to start winning games. I can only get your back for so long before it's *my* neck that's on the line. I'll keep Yarber on the outside for as long as possible, but it wouldn't hurt if you could pull together some sort of winning streak to start off your season."

"Alright, Stan. I get it. This is a warning shot across the bow. Get the program on track or the jig is up."

"In so many words, yeah."

"Great. Nothing like starting your season with a guillotine hanging over your head."

"Come on Paul, you know I like you, right? This isn't personal."

"Sure."

"If I didn't like you, you'd just show up one day with a pink slip posted to your door. I'm here because you're a friend, and I care about you. Just get things rolling. You're running out of time."

"Fine Stan, I'm on it."

Paul was growing impatient with the tenor of the conversation.

"Good enough."

With that, Stan tipped two fingers to his temple, skimmed off a salute, and then slipped around the corner.

Paul sat alone in his office, a crampy dread stabbing away at his stomach. So, the day of reckoning had finally arrived. Even in high school football, chronic losing was not without its consequences. The honeymoon was over, and now they expected results.

Sadly, his prospects were no better this year than they were last year. Last year's team had won two games against eight losses. His offense had graduated ten seniors and this year's likely starting offense consisted of two seniors, five juniors, and four sophomores. In another year maybe they'd season into a middle of the pack team, but this year was expecting too much too fast. The learning curve was too great.

Amid the angst of all these swirling thoughts, he whimsically pulled open his desk drawer and stared down at the post-it note. He studied it for a while before grabbing it and pulling it out.

"Jacob Peterson," he read aloud. "Thousand Oaks, Oregon."

Just for kicks, Paul pushed a button on the computer below his desk and the monitor before him fired to life. He quickly pulled up the Google search engine and started to type: Jacob Peterson Thousand Oaks Oregon. He clicked search and then watched the results pour onto his screen. He clicked on the first link that he came to and started to read.

Thousand Oaks Loses Star Quarterback

"July 17th, Thousand Oaks, OR—Athletic Director Tom Jenkins from Thousand Oaks High School has confirmed that Jacob Peterson, the returning junior quarterback for the Loggers, is moving out of state for reasons incident to his father's change of employment. This is an enormous loss for the Logger program given the quarterback's play in his first and, apparently, only season at Thousand Oaks. He started all 13 games last season passing for 3300 yards and 35 touchdowns with only 3 interceptions. After transferring to Thousand Oaks following his freshman year, he was to be the face of the program for the next three years. No word yet on who his replacement will be. Head coach Ralph Johnson could not be reached for comment."

Paul stared at the screen, reading and rereading the article, checking the names and facts against the scribbles on his post-it note. He then clicked on all the other links, soaking up the information, and confirming all of the statistics that had been referenced in the first article.

"You have got to be kidding me," he said, shaking his head in wide-eyed disbelief.

There was no doubting it now. Jacob Peterson wasn't just a star. He was easily one of the top-rated quarterbacks in the nation. Even as a sophomore, his stats were doubtless turning the heads of every college in the country.

Paul paused to consider what was, perhaps, the most important statistic of all: the one in five chance this kid could end up in his huddle. He suddenly felt a kernel of faith germinate deep within him. And Paul knew exactly what the Bible said about faith without actions.

Suddenly energized, Paul printed out the first article, folded it and then stuffed it into his pocket. The wheels of Paul's mind were now spinning into motion. He had another idea. This time, he did a Google search on Italian pilot programs. Within a few clicks he discovered that in Roanoke, Virginia, an Italian pilot program had been successfully voted into existence by the school board. Paul's eyes lingered over an especially useful section of the article.

"Jackpot," he said.

Paul grabbed a notepad and started writing furiously, a feverish excitement building within him. Within minutes he was running out the door. He sprinted down the hall, through the gymnasium, and then up the stairs that led to the school's administrative offices. Once on the main level, he tore down the hallway, garnering a concerned look from a janitor as he whizzed past.

He slid to a stop in front of a glass door that led to an open cluster of offices. He slipped past a protesting receptionist and hurried down the hall to a door marked Principal Skinner. Once at the door, he collected himself, moderated his breathing, mopped his brow, and then knocked lightly.

"Come on in," came a friendly voice from the other side.

Paul pushed the door open and let himself in. There, sitting on the other side of the desk behind a huge stack of manila folders was Mike Skinner, the principal of Mayfield High School. He met Paul with a broad smile.

"Well if it isn't Coach Connelly," he said cheerfully.

Winning record or not, Mike Skinner was a big fan of Paul Connelly. After the incident involving Coach Bellamy and the "Mayfield 8", Paul had quickly restored order to the troubled program. Given carte blanche authority, Paul dismissed the serial offenders outright, while burying others deep in the depth chart. In Paul's first full year as head coach, his house cleaning efforts had single-handedly guaranteed them a losing season. Four losing seasons later, Principal Skinner still owed Paul Connelly a debt of gratitude. Regardless of wins and losses, he'd kept the team out of the headlines in the wake of the biggest public relations crisis in the school's history.

"Gearing up for a winning year my friend?"

"We just may be," Paul said. "We just may be."

"Sounds terrific. What can I do for you Paul?"

"Say, I was just wondering if you had made any final decisions on an application for a John Peterson. I believe you're considering him for an Italian pilot program."

Skinner frowned, drawing his eyebrows together as he struggled to recall the name. He began rifling through the folders in front of him, and finally pulled one out. He opened it up and pushed it up to his nose.

"Ah yes. John Peterson. You know, we *had* been considering this one quite strongly, but at the end of the day the school board just couldn't convince themselves that Italian was a particularly useful language. Why, what's it to you?"

"Well, I've been researching it, and I think you'd be surprised at its practicality. Apparently, it's the seventh most spoken language in the country. There's a huge Italian immigrant population in the U.S., including the grandparents of quite a few of our students. Also, I don't know if you know this, but we still carry on substantial commerce with Italy as it relates to food, furniture, clothing and other manufacturing. Actually, I think it'd be a real boon to the school."

"Um, ok," the principal said suspiciously. "And you care about this why?"

"I don't know…Italian just strikes the right balance between pragmatic and exotic. Maybe it's just the romantic side of me coming out."

"Now I've officially heard everything. You don't have a romantic bone in your body. Seriously, what's his name?"

"What's whose name?" Paul said, playing coy.

"You know, John Peterson's son. What's his name?"

With a look of sheepish resignation, Paul pulled the folded article out of his hip pocket, threw it across the desk at the principal, and then slumped into a chair. Mike Skinner picked up the piece of paper, unfolded it and began reading. After 30 seconds, he looked up at Paul who sat grinning in the chair opposite him.

"So, a sudden, burgeoning interest in Italian, huh? This sounds more like a sudden infatuation with a quarterback. And by the looks of these stats, I don't know if I can blame you. But think about what you're asking me to do here Paul."

"Look Mike, my neck is on the chopping block here. If I can't get things turned around, I'm on the next train out of town. You know that just as well as I do. This kid could save our season."

"No, no Paul. I get it. Thirty-three hundred yards. Thirty-five touchdown passes. Total game changer. But add a language program with questionable utility just to get a quarterback? That seems like putting the cart before the horse, doesn't it?"

"I know it does," Paul admitted. "I just thought that maybe if you were still, you know, on the cusp of making a decision, that this little tidbit of information might push this guy over the top."

"I don't know Paul. I can take this to the school board, and I do have clout, but what you're asking me to do is unprecedented."

"Listen, all I'm saying is if the program is a good fit for what you're trying to accomplish at this high school, that it comes with an ancillary benefit. That's all."

"Paul, I appreciate you bringing this to my attention. I'll take it under advisement."

Paul walked out of the principal's office with the sinking feeling that his chances of landing Jacob Peterson were now substantially lower than one in five. But of one thing there could be no doubt: Jacob Peterson was the key to Paul's football season. At this point, he could only wait, hope and try to suppress the rising feeling that his future as coach of the Mayfield Mustangs was no longer in his hands.

CHAPTER 2

"You know, you can't blame them for how they feel."

John Peterson looked over at his wife Sarah and mustered a half smile.

"Three towns in three years in three different parts of the country. That'd be tough even for a military family," she said.

"I know, and I accept full responsibility for it. If I could do it all over again, I would. Things *will* go differently this time."

"You promise John? I just don't know if the children can be uprooted one more time. It would devastate them."

"Yeah, I promise. As long as we follow our plan, we won't be looking for another home for a long, long time."

"You *really* think so?" she said, her voice thick with skepticism.

"Absolutely. And to convince you of my new found resolve, I've got something for you."

John reached into his pocket and pulled out a folded piece of paper and tossed it onto his wife's lap.

"What's this?" she said, eying it suspiciously.

"Take a peek. I've already had talks with the real estate agent. I think we can actually afford to get into this place."

Sarah unfolded the paper and scrutinized the picture before her.

"Are you serious?" she said, excitement building in her voice. "You want to buy a house?"

"I think it's the right thing to do. I want to show you and the kids that I'm committed to change. This is my way of showing you that things are going to be different."

For the first time in over 48 hours a smile spread across Sarah's face.

"We would love a house," she said, pulling the picture to her chest and wrapping it in an embrace. "I think a home is just what our family needs."

"Good, because I have a good feeling about this place. I think we're really going to love it here."

Just then, as if on cue, they heard a sputter, a series of dissonant clanks and then a violent shimmy. John quickly maneuvered their 2003 Suburban over to the side of the road as a steady billow of steam shot out from under the hood. John pulled to a stop then inclined his head to the wheel in frustration. When he lifted it up, he saw a large sign mocking him off in the distance. It said: "Welcome to Mayfield."

"How's that for irony," he muttered.

By this time, sleepy heads had started to pop up in John's rearview mirror.

"What's going on?" rumbled a deep, adolescent voice from the back of the car.

"I don't know Jake. Whatever it is, it didn't sound good," John said. "Beyond my sad mechanical skills for sure. I'll have to go for help."

"Just use your cellphone. Call AAA," Jacob said, as if it were the most obvious solution in the world.

"The cellphone stayed in Oregon, Jake. I'm going to have to hoof it."

John turned to his wife. "Do you think you can manage the troops until I get back?"

"How long do you think you'll be gone?" she asked, a touch of worry in her voice.

The twins were starting to squirm fitfully in their car seats. This didn't bode well for a prolonged delay on a hot summer morning. John saw Sarah's brow wrinkle with concern.

"I don't know. It can't be too much further. According to the friendly sign there, we've practically arrived."

John turned towards the tangle of children in the back two rows. "Jacob, will you help your mother keep a handle on things?"

"I guess," he muttered under his breath.

John suddenly remembered the grudge Jacob had been nursing since the news of their move had broken two days earlier. He'd taken it right on the chin. Of all of his children, Jacob stood to lose the most.

John opened the car door and felt the stifling heat of the late July morning blast him in the face. As he stepped out of the car, the hot air enveloped him, instantly bathing him in a sticky film of sweat. He looked both ways and, seeing no cars in either direction, began trudging towards the welcome sign that leered at him off in the distance.

"Welcome to Mayfield," he mumbled to himself in a bemused tone. "That's a good one."

Within a few minutes, he passed the sign and stepped into the Mayfield city limits. There were still no signs of life. All he could see were massive walls of trees rising up on either side of the country road. In the stark heat of the midmorning sun, he was suddenly grateful for tall, leafy trees. He kept trudging forward, the sweat now starting to well into puddles under his arms, and on the small of his back.

After another half mile, John suddenly saw the trees open into a massive clearing. Rising before him, as a beacon to passing cars, was perhaps the largest marquee John had ever seen. It simply said:

PASTOR LESTER LE HAYE WELCOMES YOU

John's eyes followed the long, narrow road that led past the marquee and into a massive parking lot that was teeming with cars. John gave a sigh of relief. Civilization at last.

As John turned down the road, his eyes were suddenly drawn to the focal point in the midst of the clearing. Out of the vast ocean of cars rose an enormous, sprawling edifice. Judging by the smell of the fresh asphalt, and the newly laid sod, the building was only recently completed. Its most prominent feature was a gigantic, shiny cross affixed to a steeple that rose high above the tree line, heralding the church's arrival to a population in a three county radius.

The size and aesthetics of the massive church combined to take John's breath away. Given the number of cars surrounding the building,

John estimated that at least a quarter of Mayfield's population was in attendance. He looked down at his watch: 9:05 a.m. The sermon was likely just getting underway.

Within minutes, John was pulling open one of the mirrored glass doors at the base of the enormous stone façade. As he stepped into the cavernous foyer, he felt a refreshing blast of cool air wash over him. He inhaled the frigid air for a few seconds before scanning the room for evidence of a courtesy phone. As he searched the room, he became aware of a voice issuing through the crack in the folded double doors off to his right. Indeed, the sermon was under way. And, judging by the congregation's reaction, Pastor Le Haye was starting to build momentum.

Curiosity suddenly piqued, John abandoned his search for a phone. He slipped through the door, and saw open up before him an impressive configuration of seats that gave him the impression of a tiny football stadium. Seats sloped halfway up the walls on three sides and were met by an enormous stage on the fourth. There in the middle of the stage stood, presumably, Pastor Le Haye himself. As he spoke he slammed his fist down upon the shiny glass pulpit behind which he stood. Each new hammer of the fist elicited more and more approval from the congregation. John couldn't resist the allure of what was coming next. He began to listen.

"I love the Lord," the pastor said. " I looooove the Lord, and I praaaaise his name. My brothers and sisters, God is great. He shines down upon us and pours out his blessings. If you ask him for bread, will he give you a stone?"

"No!" they all shouted in unison.

"Oh no. That's not the God that I know. If you knock, it shall be opened. Praaaaaise Jesus!"

Lester Le Haye was clearly a gifted orator. The tone, the affectation, the charisma—he had it all. The cadence of each well-chosen word was calculated to whip his congregation into a frenzy.

John listened, nearly entranced, for almost ten minutes. The exuberant parishioners were now clapping, swaying, and praising Jesus amidst a chorus of hallelujahs. From what John could tell, there did not appear to be any real doctrinal meat to the pastor's sermon, but there could not be any question as to the crowd's enthusiasm for what they were hearing.

As John basked in the glow of Pastor Le Haye's oratorical gifts, suddenly, as if emerging from a trance, he remembered why he was there.

Snapping back to attention, he retreated to the foyer, once again scanning for signs of a phone. John could locate no phone, but could see an oblong cast of light thrown against the carpet about midway down the hall. Signs of life. Someone could help.

John hurried down the hall, pausing just outside the open door. The sign to the left of door read: Church Administrator. John mustered a scintilla of courage and walked into the office. Sitting behind a desk was a man in his fifties with glasses and suspenders. Spread open before him was an enormous Bible.

"Hi there," John said gingerly. "Sorry to trouble."

"No trouble at all," the man said with a thin smile. "What can I do for you?"

"Well, my family and I are just coming to town and, wouldn't you know it, our car broke down about a mile east of here. Just looking for a phone to call for help."

The man grabbed the phone on his desk and turned it towards John.

"I'm sorry to hear that. It's all yours."

"Wow, I really appreciate it. You're a real lifesaver."

The man gave a slight nod of the head, and then went back to his Bible.

John began fishing through his wallet searching for his AAA card. Before long, he produced it, and began punching numbers. John relayed his family's location to the agent on the other end and within five minutes was assured that help was on the way. John laid the receiver gently back in its cradle.

"Once again, a real life saver," John repeated.

"Happy to help," the man said managing one final smile.

"Name's John Peterson," he said, extending his hand.

"Buddy, Buddy Holler," the man replied, meeting John's hand.

"This is quite the edifice you have here," John said, looking around, as if the building's immensity could be appreciated from within the spare office.

"Thank you. Thank you very much."

"And quite the preacher. Pastor Le Haye, I presume?" John asked, cocking his thumb in the direction of the assembly hall.

"The one and only."

"Boy can he whip those folks into a lather."

"Yep, that's what we do here, get 'em all riled up. If you need foaming at the mouth, Lester Le Haye's your man."

John detected a sarcastic edge to Buddy's voice. This tone, coupled with Buddy's conspicuous absence from the sermon struck John as odd. The church's chief administrator seemed perfectly content to bury his nose in a Bible while pandemonium broke out in the enormous meeting room down the hall.

John pushed the feeling aside. He'd met his first resident of Mayfield, and from what he could judge, a fairly consequential one. He couldn't let the opportunity pass.

"Mind if I ask a quick question?"

The man peered up at John over the rims of his glasses. "What'd you have in mind?"

"Well, our family is new in town and we'd really like to get involved," John said.

"Involved?" Buddy said, a puzzled look coming over his face. "How do you mean?"

"You know, service organizations, charitable work, any way to lend a helping hand. I imagine you're the perfect person to talk to."

The man locked eyes with John, and that's when he noticed it. There was a sadness, a forlornness in Buddy's eyes that John hadn't seen at first glance.

"There *are* opportunities in town," Buddy said, "but I probably wouldn't be your point man on that. Not really my purview."

"Oh?" John said, making little effort to hide his surprise. "I just thought that maybe, you know, given your position here, that you'd have your finger on the pulse of these things."

"No Mr. Peterson, not really what I do. All we really do here is preach sermons. Lester does his thing, I take care of the numbers, and that seems to keep everyone happy. Try the chamber of commerce in town. They may be able to point you in the right direction."

Now it was John's turn to look puzzled. "Hmm, ok. Tell you what, why don't I leave my name and address in case something *does* come up."

"Suit yourself," Buddy said.

Buddy shoved a pad of paper and a pen across the desk at John.

"Perfect," John said, tearing off a sheet of paper and starting to scribble. "Listen, no phone yet, but this is our address. If you hear of something, anything, send us a notice, or drop by. We really would love to pitch in."

Buddy took the slip, scrutinized the address, and then slipped it into the top drawer of his desk.

"Will do."

"I appreciate it," John said, as he turned to leave.

"Say, you folks by chance Christian?"

This strange postscript to their conversation stopped John in his tracks. "Yes," he said, turning and meeting Buddy's eyes once again. "Yes we are."

"Well, if you and your family are looking for a congregation, you're welcome to try us out next Sunday. There's plenty of room."

Now *this* was unusual. Here was a man that didn't appear to have the least interest in the worship services, yet here he was inviting them to have a listen.

"We'd like that sometime. Won't be this Sunday, though. If you'll believe it, I've been asked to speak in my own congregation. Haven't even attended yet, and they've already pegged me for a sermon."

Buddy's eyebrows arched upward in surprise. "Why, are you clergy?" he asked.

"I am," Paul said. "It's a lay clergy, but I do hold the priesthood. I preach every now and then, whenever they ask me to."

Buddy seemed briefly intrigued by this arrangement.

"I'll be darned. Well, come back any time. You're always welcome."

"Pleasure to have met you Mr. Holler."

Their hands met one final time.

As John walked down the hall towards the enormous foyer, he was struck by the oddness of the exchange. Something didn't add up. Pastor Le Haye's strategy appeared to be, whip every one into a frenzy, pass the dish, and then call it a day. Buddy's strategy seemed to be, mind his own business, and stay as far away from the pastor as possible. The stark contrast between the two rooms was unsettling.

First a broken down car at the city limits, and now an undeniably strange encounter at the town's newly christened mega church. John was natively optimistic, but these two strange omens weighed heavily upon him as he began the long, hot journey back to his family.

CHAPTER 3

The next day, Buddy Holler sat at his desk staring at the screen before him, scrutinizing the rows of figures and subtotals. As his eyes scanned the rows of numbers, Buddy felt a wave of serenity settle over him, vanquishing the dread that had gnawed at him since the church's grand opening a month earlier. Cash flow, as it turned out, would not be the source of stress Buddy thought it would be when they had broken ground. Not if things continued at this pace.

He clicked the mouse and his printer roared to life. He felt compelled to share the good news, even if it meant wandering over to Lester's side of the church. He grabbed the charts from the printer, stepped out of his office and into the broad corridor that adjoined the administrative and pastoral echelons. He felt a sweet peace consume him as he strode down the hallway, the warm sheets of paper sending a tingly sensation up his arm.

As he approached the pastor's office he found the door open and lights on, but no immediate sign of Lester. He was likely out prowling the campus, examining the as yet unexplored nooks and crannies of their shiny, new edifice. Buddy turned to leave, but as he did, a glint shimmered in the corner of his vision. His eyes scanned the room and quickly honed in on the carpet by Lester's desk. What he saw there paralyzed him.

Extending from behind the desk was a pale, Rolex-clad hand. Buddy's mouth dropped open as the terror rose in his throat. His limbs seized up, a subconscious repudiation of what lay before him. Within seconds, however, adrenaline overrode everything and his legs jerked into motion. Buddy ran over to the desk and saw sprawled behind it the lifeless form of Pastor Lester Le Haye.

He dropped quickly to his knees and put his ear to Lester's mouth, listening for signs of breath, feeling for a pulse. There was no sign of either. Buddy marshaled every bit of courage to beat down the anguish that was rising within him. He'd spent a lifetime crowding emotion out of his life. Now would be no different. He steeled himself, and then stoically, mechanically began to pump Lester's chest. After eight vigorous pumps to the chest, he tilted Lester's chin, opened the airway, and exhaled deeply into his lungs. Then he listened again for signs of breathing. Still nothing. He repeated this process twice more, each time crashing down on Lester's chest with greater intensity, his pulse pounding in his temples.

"Don't do this to me," he breathed between clenched teeth, driving down on Lester's chest time and again. "Not now," he said frantically, droplets of sweat cutting a clean line down his cheeks.

And then, all at once, he collapsed onto Lester's motionless chest, crushed by the realization that his efforts were in vain. The tears began flowing, slowly at first, but then in torrents. Buddy lay sprawled across Lester, his head bobbing up and down as the sobs rolled forth. He had arrived too late. Lester Le Haye was gone. And the last girders of reason that held Buddy's world together came crashing down.

• • •

Buddy allowed himself to mourn the loss of the church's principal revenue source for approximately 24 hours before once again erecting the pillars of reason that held his world together. With substantial obligations now bearing down on him, he didn't have the time for a protracted grieving process. The congregation would now look to him for leadership and, frankly, this terrified him. Over the last 15 years he had thrived in his role behind the scenes, the voice of reason that propelled the work forward. Now, as the sole remaining principal of Living Christ Ministries, the future viability of the ministry fell squarely on him. The logistics of growing and running an operation of this size was not what filled him with terror. This was what he was born to do. What he could not reason himself around, however, was the impossibility of his most pressing task: finding a replacement pastor whose talent and magnetism could rise to the level of Lester Le Haye.

Of more immediate concern, however, was what he would do when 1200 parishioners converged on his campus for Sabbath worship, just four short days hence. Who would preach the sermon? Who would stir the souls of their parishioners? More importantly, who would harness the spiritual energy necessary to keep the money flowing? It didn't have to be another Lester, at least not immediately. Just someone who could buy Buddy some time.

Buddy sat in his tiny office awash in fear and uncertainty. The peace he'd felt just 48 hours earlier had evaporated. Spurred by the tide of disquiet that was now consuming him, he reached into his desk, pulled out the thin Tri-County yellow pages and flipped to Christian Churches. His eyes slowly scanned down the page. Besides Living Christ Ministries, there were six other churches listed.

More than I expected, he thought, taking courage.

Buddy had never bothered sizing up the competition. A visitor need listen to Lester only once before becoming a parishioner for life. It had simply been that easy. Over the years, the other churches had served as a feeder system for their exploding congregation. Buddy had assumed these good folks had come from somewhere. Sizing up the list of churches that lay before him, he now understood where. He swallowed thickly as he contemplated what he was about to do.

He dialed the first number. It was Abundant Grace on Pines Road on the south side of town. The phone rang three times, and then picked up.

"Pastor Flynn," came the voice on the other end.

"Pastor Flynn. Buddy Holler over at Living Christ Ministries, how are you?"

"I'm fine Mr. Holler. What do you need?"

The voice sounded detached, impartial. Buddy's heart fell, but he pressed forward.

"I'm sorry to bother you this fine summer morning."

Buddy paused, waiting for the perfunctory "No bother at all", but it never came.

He forged ahead.

"Anyway, I imagine you've heard by now of the tragic death of Pastor Le Haye?"

"Yes, brain aneurism. Just awful. My deepest sympathies to you and your congregation."

It was an apology that was strangely devoid of feeling. Buddy's hope again began to wane, but he persisted.

"Thank you. Thank you very kindly. Listen, Pastor Le Haye's unexpected death has put us in a bit of a bind for Sunday's sermon. I know it's last minute, and a terrible imposition, but I was wondering if there was any way you might see clear to favor us with some words of inspiration this Sabbath."

Buddy's query was met by an awkward silence. After an uncomfortably long pause, Pastor Flynn finally spoke.

"Look Mr. Holler, you have my deepest condolences. I can't imagine what you're going through. But, if it's all the same to you, I'm going to have to pass. It's really tough to break away on Sundays. As you can imagine, it's our busiest day."

"Of course it is, of course," Buddy replied. He paused, considering a different tack. "What if we could keep it under 30 minutes, and throw in an honorarium for your trouble?"

"Look Mr. Holler." The "Mr." title had a cold, distancing affect. "I'm going to cut to the chase here, lest I waste any more of your time. You and the late Pastor Le Haye have been a thorn in my side for the last 15 years. Do you know what it's like to pour your soul into missionary outreach and member retention, only to see your efforts neutralized by the pied piper at the local mega church?"

Pied piper? The words stung. Deep within Pastor Flynn lurked a current of antipathy that Buddy had failed to anticipate.

"Uh, no. I don't suppose I do," Buddy replied. A prickly heat rose within him as he felt his fight or flight engage.

"When your members show up on Sunday, and there's no Lester Le Haye preaching another empty sermon, no charisma forcing open their wallets, you'll be just another church. The playing field will be level, and frankly…"

Buddy cut him off. The conversation was spinning violently out of control.

"I think I get the picture Pastor. The answer's no. God's blessings upon you and your congregation."

Buddy hung up the phone, wincing as he did so. He sank into his chair, reeling and shell-shocked. He had not been prepared for the caustic, hateful tenor the conversation had taken on. Had Living Christ Ministries really engendered such unbridled contempt in Mayfield's community of churches? He eyed the list of remaining churches warily. If Pastor Flynn's verbal lashing was any sign of things to come, this was not going to be a pleasant day.

Buddy spent the balance of an hour talking to four more pastors whose antipathy for Lester Le Haye was exceeded only by their enthusiasm for reclaiming their lost membership. As the last conversation drew mercifully to a close, Buddy reclined deeply in his chair, lines of exasperation creasing his brow. He pressed both hands over his closed eyes, drawing them slowly downward, exhaling deeply.

He rolled his chair backwards, and rose before his desk. As he did, his eyes fell upon the lone remaining name on the list. Not surprisingly, it was another name he didn't recognize. After the carnage of the first five phone calls, it was a call he wanted to put off. But as he thought about the proximity of Sunday's sermon, he collapsed backwards into his chair. He lifted the receiver one last time. The phone rang six or seven times before Buddy hung it up, satisfied he'd suffered enough for one day.

As Buddy drove home, his mind started to synthesize all of the bits of reality that had started to take up residence in his brain. It's what Buddy did. It was a process that made him feel alive, somehow in control. Just like every other time, he would create order from chaos. He would have to. He had no other choice.

Chapter 4

Pastor Ethan Reddick sat in his tiny office and studied the statement sprawled across the desk before him. Twelve months ago the balance had read $63,000. After the down payment on the church, a modest outlay for a pulpit, chairs and other furnishings, and finally a monthly draw to keep his small family afloat, the balance now read $12,000.

Ethan saw a shadow move in his periphery and turned to see his wife Jenny standing in the doorway, their four month old Ian in her arms.

"Well aren't you a sight for sore eyes?" Ethan said.

"Now why would your eyes be sore?" she said with a laugh. "Tough day at the office?"

"If only you knew," Ethan said darkly.

The smile slowly faded, her eyebrows drawing together.

"If only I knew what Ethan? What's going on?"

Ethan slid the statement across the desk. She picked it up and started to read.

"Twelve thousand dollars?" she gasped. "That's what's left of your school loan?"

"I just thought we'd be self-sustaining by now," he said, shaking his head. "I thought a pure, undefiled, Bible-based message was just what this town needed."

A storm of emotions spread across Jenny's face as she studied the statement in her hands.

"You know Ethan, this isn't what I signed up for. When you said God told us to drop out of divinity school and start our own ministry, this isn't how I saw it playing out. If God sent us here, then where are all the congregants? Why's all the money drying up?"

Ethan sat there, staring back at his wife, answers eluding him.

"How much time does this give us?" Jenny said.

"Well, between the mortgage on this place, our draw, and other miscellaneous expenses associated with the ministry, I'd say we've got... about two months."

"Two months? And then what Ethan? What happens when the money's gone?"

"Do you really want to have this conversation now?" he asked, a pleading look on his face.

"What happens when the money's gone?" she repeated, the panic ringing in her voice.

Ethan took a deep breath before answering.

"We default on the church, we get evicted from our apartment, and we sell all of our assets for a fraction of their worth. Then, right around that time, the first payment on the school loan comes due. So, take the $63,000 we had when we got here, and add to it the $62,000 we spent our first three years in divinity school. Take your total and then amortize a payment."

Jenny's hand drew up to her face as if to restrain the tears, but they came all the same.

After a few moments of tortured sobs, she returned her gaze to Ethan.

"So, I guess that means you won't be coming home for dinner tonight?" Jenny said, dabbing at her nose with a tissue.

"Jenny, darling, you know I can't."

"Just this once Ethan. One hour with your family couldn't possibly hurt."

"Sweetheart, you know there is nothing I want more than to be with you and the baby, but missionary work is our only way out of this mess. Early evening is my only window."

Jenny glowered at Ethan through eyes full of tears.

"I don't buy it Ethan. You've been knocking doors for months with nothing to show for it. Is this really what God wants?"

"Look sweetheart, God's still at the helm. He's just testing our faith. If we can endure it well, he will reward us. I'm sure of it."

"He's testing our faith by leading us over a financial cliff?" she said, her eyes spreading wide. "That's not the God I know," she said, turning to leave. "I'll leave the light on."

• • •

As Ethan angled his car away from the church, his foot moved reflexively to the brake. He closed his eyes, bowed his head, and then uttered a brief prayer.

"Heavenly Father, please bless me and guide me as I seek out the hearts in whom the truth of your gospel will find purchase. In Jesus' name, Amen."

Ethan's eyes stayed closed as he listened for a whisper or a flash of insight. But nothing came.

"Come on God, where are you?" he muttered.

Suddenly, in a flash of revelation, he saw a row of tract homes on the north side of town. He knew exactly where it was; he'd knocked all those doors before. Why the Lord was sending him there again, he didn't know. But given the circumstances, he was in no position to argue.

His car lurched out of the driveway and within minutes, he was pulling up to the curb on Everett Drive. Before getting out, he bowed his head and listened for any final, last minute instructions. Hearing nothing, he got out of his car and walked up to the first house.

Ethan knocked for an hour and a half without a sniff of success. It was the same old story. *We have a church. We aren't religious. Who are you again? I don't think I've ever heard of your church.* But Ethan bore it all in patience. He politely answered their questions and then asked questions of his own, hoping to spark some discussion that would lead somewhere, anywhere. But today did not appear to be his day. Doors were slammed, responses for the most part were curt, and his message seemed to fall on deaf ears.

Troubled, Ethan thought back to the flash of insight he had received in the gravel parking lot of his church. He'd gone exactly where he'd been directed. He'd knocked every door. Well, every door but one. He stood in front of this last house, weighing the prospect of a final, fruitless encounter.

Masking his dejection, Ethan turned up the walk, scaled the steps and rang the doorbell. Within seconds, a man opened the door and stepped onto the porch.

"What can I do for you?" he said.

"My name is Ethan Reddick. I'm the pastor at the Community Church of Christ over on Merchant Street."

Unexpectedly, the man's eyes flickered to life. "Sure, I know who you are. I know exactly who you are. What brings you to these parts?"

"Well, I'm just out and about, sharing a brief Bible-based message with the folks in your neighborhood. Can I ask sir, are you a religious person?"

A smile tugged at the corners of the man's mouth and then he chuckled. "Why yes, you could say that."

"And do you believe in the Lord and Savior Jesus Christ?"

"With my whole soul."

Ethan was quickly warming to the conversation. Finally, someone who was willing to engage him in a gospel dialogue.

"Do you mind if I ask your denomination?"

"It's nondenominational. But Jesus Christ is my personal savior. I'll just leave it at that."

The man was beginning to smile. Ethan didn't know quite what to make of it.

"Very good," Ethan said approvingly. "And do you have a church that you're currently attending?"

The man's smile broadened. "Yes, you could say that."

"And is your perspective on Jesus Christ broad enough to accommodate an alternate, Bible-based view of the gospel?"

"Yes, yes it is. But before you get too far down the road here Pastor, do you mind if I ask *you* a few questions?"

Ethan's face registered surprise at the sudden role reversal, but at this point, he was happy just to be talking.

"Sure," he said. "Fire away."

"Have you ever heard of a church called Living Christ Ministries?"

"Oh sure, new chapel on the east side of town? Grand opening about a month ago?"

"That's right, you know the one. Well, that's my church."

Ethan was undeterred. Most people he talked to belonged to *some* church.

"And how long have you been worshiping at Living Christ Ministries?"

"Sorry Pastor, maybe I should clarify. I don't just attend Living Christ Ministries. I own it."

Ethan's face deflated like a three day old balloon. He thought this was going somewhere, but the man was merely indulging him.

"The name's Buddy," the man said, holding out his hand. "Buddy Holler."

Ethan grabbed the extended hand.

"An honor to meet you Mr. Holler."

"Call me Buddy. Say, now that you've extended me an invitation to your services, I'd like to go you one further. How would you like to join *us* on Sunday?"

Ethan flashed a kind smile. "That's very nice of you Mr. Holler, but that's quite impossible. I've got a congregation of my own. They're expecting me. I've got a sermon to preach."

"Alright then," he said chuckling. "Why don't I clarify my invitation." Buddy paused for a second, his face turning grave. "I'm not sure if you're aware Ethan, but our pastor, Lester Le Haye, died suddenly and unexpectedly, two days ago."

Ethan's jaw fell loose.

"No, no, I hadn't heard. I'm…I'm terribly sorry."

"So, as it turns out," Buddy continued, "Living Christ Ministries is in a bit of a jam. We're expecting a full turnout on Sunday. I've called every church in town, and there isn't a pastor out there who wants to guest preach. Not a single one."

"Not a one?" Ethan gasped. "Seems like the perfectly Christian thing to do…given the circumstances."

"Under ordinary circumstances, that might be the case," Buddy said. "But Lester Le Haye was no ordinary preacher. The success of his preaching over the years has devastated a lot of these congregations. There aren't many pastors in this town that will miss Lester Le Haye."

Buddy stared glumly at his feet, contemplating this stark reality. After a few moments he looked up, meeting Ethan's gaze.

"So Ethan, I'm not just asking you to join us for church. I'm asking you to preach to us. This Sunday, maybe longer. Now, I'll be honest, I don't know you from Adam, and you do look awfully young. But you are in the priesthood, and from the sound of things, you're the only church in town who we haven't managed to alienate. What do you say Pastor, will you do us the honor?"

Buddy's invitation washed over Ethan, paralyzing him. As the silence persisted, Buddy's countenance fell.

"Listen, I understand if you can't do it," Buddy said. "It *is* awfully short notice."

Suddenly, Ethan's eyes spread wide, as if emerging from a trance. "Wait, wait, no! I mean yes! I'm absolutely interested."

Buddy's eyebrows sprang upwards in surprise. "Great. Outstanding. We start at 9:00 a.m. I'll need you to speak for 20 minutes. I'll throw a few extra congregational hymns into the mix. That way, we don't baptize you by fire. We'll start you small, and see how you do."

Ethan nodded silently, now wary of talking any more than was required. The invitation had been extended. There was no need to give Buddy any reasons to revoke it.

"Oh, and as long as you're here, I think I should warn you that you can expect at least 1200 people, maybe more given the death of Pastor Le Haye."

"Twelve...hundred?" Ethan stammered.

"At least. Also, as you prepare your sermon, I want you to think about a few things. They *will* be looking for comfort, but that's just a small part of it. There are a lot of churches to choose from Ethan. They'll be trying to figure out if Living Christ Ministries is still where they want to be on Sundays. You know what that means?"

"Uh, no, Mr. Holler. What does that mean?"

"Ethan, it means if you've got some whiz-bang, hair-raising sermon in a file back in your office, I need you to dust it off, and come loaded for bear. I need you to speak with the tongue of fire. Can you speak with the tongue of fire Ethan?"

"Tongue of fire?" Ethan asked.

"That's right Ethan. This is a fickle congregation with a low threshold for lackluster sermons. Your goal is to make sure that each one of those souls is still in their seats come next week. Do you think you can manage that?"

Ethan tamped down the tide of anxiety that was rising within him and snapped back to attention. "I won't disappoint you Mr. Holler," he said, pumping Buddy's hand earnestly. "I'm your man."

"I'm sure you'll be great," he said smiling. "We'll see you Sunday".

Ethan floated back to the sidewalk, lost in a surreal daze.

This is my chance, he thought. *This is what I've been waiting for. God has finally heard my prayers. Now come on Ethan, try not to blow it.*

CHAPTER 5

"You're going to drive me to my first practice, Dad?" Jacob said, his face twisting in anguish. "For crying out loud. It's my *first* day. You're killing me."

"Jacob, we don't have a fleet of cars. We have one car, in questionable repair, and your mother has errands to run. So, if you're ok with it, I will happily save you the trouble of having to walk to practice and drive you myself."

"Dad, what good's a driver's license if I never get to use it?"

"Your time will come Jacob. Just not today."

Jacob glowered at his father, his arms pressed tightly against his chest.

"Come on, let's go. If we keep arguing the point, you'll be late for practice," John said.

Jacob was now staring at the carpet, shaking his head in disbelief. Suddenly, he pulled open the front door, stormed through it and slammed it behind him.

John cast a bewildered glance at Sarah who stood drying dishes in the kitchen.

"Just remember John. This is not about the car," she said.

"I know it's not. And I'll make it right. I've promised you that."

John followed Jacob out the front door, and then slid into the car next to him. The tension in the car was thick and palpable. Jacob's hands were tucked tightly into his armpits, his glance averted, his countenance hard and unyielding.

John let Jacob brood on his side of the car for the first mile or so before finally breaking the silence.

"So, looking forward to your first day of practice?"

"How would I know?" he mumbled. "I don't know the first thing about this team."

"Well, I *can* tell you that these guys need you. Two and eight last year. Ten wins total in the last four years. They're primed for a guy like you to come in and shake things up. They could use a game changer."

"Are you *serious*?" Jacob groaned. "Two and eight? How can I change anything if my offensive line is collapsing all around me?"

"Look, Jake it won't be like that. You've had success everywhere you've played. You make everyone around you better. You know that. Why so down in the mouth?"

"Because for once Dad, for once I'd like to be at the same school for two consecutive years. Any idea what it's like to have to learn a new offense, compete for a starting position, make new friends, year after year after year? It's getting old Dad."

"I told you I'd make it right Jake. I told you this time was going to be different. And I'm standing by my promise."

"Did that coach even call you back?" Jacob grumbled.

John was silent for a moment, his eyes scanning the horizon as the street signs whizzed past them.

"No, he never called back. But, you know, he's probably slammed. Coaches get crazy busy this time of year."

"Perfect," Jacob said. "They don't even know I'm coming."

"Yeah, maybe not. But they'll know who you are by the end of today. You can take that to the bank."

In a few moments John saw the high school approaching on the right. He turned into the back parking lot and squealed to a stop in front of the boys' locker room.

"Well, this is it," John said, mustering all the excitement of which he was capable. "First big day. Knock 'em dead."

Jacob pushed the door open with all the enthusiasm of a death row inmate.

"Yeah, see you around," he growled, slamming the door behind him.

• • •

When Jacob stepped into the locker room, he was met by an eerie silence. Where was everyone?

"Hello?" Jacob said. The sound of his voice echoed off the walls of the barren locker room. No answer. He *had* gotten the right day, *hadn't* he? This *was* the boys' locker room, *wasn't* it? His eyes continued to scan the room for signs of life. Before long he spotted a projection of light cast against the floor on the far side of the locker room. He moved towards it, his nerves buzzing to life.

Jacob stepped up to the door, the bottom half of which was closed creating a countertop. He poked his head through the opening at the top, half expecting to see a short order chef flipping burgers inside. In the back of the room, he spotted a balding, gray head hunched over a box of maroon shirts.

"Excuse me," Jacob said.

The man jerked up, startled by the sound of Jacob's voice.

"Oh, scared me," the man said in a raspy voice. "Didn't hear you walk in. What can I do you for son?"

"Well, I'm new in town, and I'm here for two-a-days. Is this the right place?"

The man let out a chuckle.

"Right place. Wrong time. Practiced started an hour ago. If you hurry out there, there's still time. Just don't mind Coach Connelly when he sees that you're late. He'll get over it. He always does."

Late? How could he be late? His dad had specifically told him 9 a.m. Jacob looked up at the clock that hung on the far wall. It read 10 o'clock. How could it be? His heart sank as he realized their blunder. They now lived in a different time zone. This was *perfect*. It was just the impression he needed to make on his first day of practice.

The man's eyes began to scan Jacob's tall frame, as if sizing him up.

"I'd say extra large on top, large on the bottom, and what do you think for helmet size, 7 1/4, 7 3/8?"

"Uh, 7 3/8 would be perfect," Jacob said

"Name's Doc," the man said as he handed Jacob a stack of school issue over the counter. I'm the equipment manager here…among other things. Forty three years strong."

"Nice to meet you Doc. My name's Jacob Peterson. I appreciate your help."

"Say, what kind of player are you, offense, defense? What's your pleasure?"

"Uh, quarterback. I play quarterback."

"I see," the man said, his face screwing up into a smile. "So, you want to be a quarterback, do you?"

"Uh, yeah, that was the plan."

"Just be careful out there Mr. Peterson."

"Careful? Why's that?" Jacob said, worry creasing his brow.

"You'll be competing with a boy named Trevor Bickle."

"That's ok. I'm no stranger to competition."

"This time it's different Jacob. Trevor Bickle just happens to be the son of one Jasper Bickle, president of the local school board. It's supposed to be a balanced committee, but if you ask me, Jasper calls all the shots. He's the one that decides if Coach Connelly gets to keep his job."

Doc gave Jacob one last smile and then returned to his pile of boxes in the back of the room.

Doc's last words had cut through Jacob like a knife. From what he could tell, the deck was stacked impossibly against him. He was a new transfer and they'd given the coach no warning of his arrival *or* his track record. What was worse, the son of the school board president was firmly entrenched in the starting role. And then, the cherry on the sundae: he was an hour late to his very first practice.

Jacob strode out of the locker room, his plastic cleats clicking on the pavement as he walked. Once on the grass Jacob jogged towards the practice field where players in maroon jerseys gathered at various stations.

As Jacob stepped onto the practice field, he spotted a quarterback hovering near midfield. He was taking snaps from an imaginary center and throwing passes to a line of receivers on either side of the field. Jacob jogged over.

"Hi, I'm Jake. Mind if I join you?" he said, marshaling his friendliest demeanor.

The boy sized him up and then scowled.

"Suit yourself," he muttered, making no effort to hide his contempt.

"Alrighty then," Jacob said under his breath. "Welcome to Mayfield."

Jacob picked a worn leather ball off the ground, spun it around in his palm, and then strode up to the imaginary line of scrimmage.

He made eye contact with the receiver off to his left, signaled a slant pattern, and then barked a signal. The receiver fired out of his crouch, made a few stutter steps and then broke towards the middle of the field. Now in a three step drop, Jacob held the ball by his right ear, waiting and timing. Zing. The ball shot towards the receiver as if from a cannon. The receiver stuck up his hands just in time, but to not avail. The blistering pass tore through his hands like a rock through rice paper, careening off his face mask and shooting straight up into the air. The receiver let out a yelp of agony, quickly doubled over in pain, and began kneading his hands.

With the first pass, helmets had whipped around. With the second pass, he had their rapt attention. The next receiver stepped tentatively up to the line of scrimmage off to Jacob's right. Jacob flashed the sign for "go" and once again strode up to center.

"Hut," he barked.

At Jacob's signal, the receiver tore off down the side line, building speed as he went. Jacob made a five step drop this time, and with a smooth flick of his wrist, launched the ball deep down the field. A dozen heads traced the ball as it flew in a long, broad arc, landing safely in the receiver's arms nearly 65 yards down field.

The other receivers erupted in a chorus of gasps. They turned to Jacob, appraising his tall, wiry frame, their eyes full of wonderment.

• • •

Paul Connelly was standing on a tackling sled barking at five beefy linemen when he heard the commotion from the other side of the field. He turned just in time to see a tall, lanky figure launch a crisp, arcing spiral 65 yards down the sideline, and into the hands of Donavan Dooley.

His jaw went slack, as he struggled to compute what he'd just seen. With seemingly little effort, a quarterback, wearing Mayfield issue no less, had launched a tightly wound spiral *65 yards* on the fly. Who was this kid? And what could he do if he actually broke a sweat? Excitement and curiosity surged within him as he leaped off the sled and jogged towards the burgeoning crowd of players that had gathered at midfield.

As Paul approached, he was heralded by a growing chorus of whispers. He picked his way through the crowd until he was within arms length of the quarterback. Paul extended his arm, grabbed the player by the facemask and yanked him close.

"What are you doing on my practice field son?" Paul demanded.

"Just trying to compete sir."

Paul looked into the boy's eyes as if searching his soul.

"You realize I already have a quarterback don't you?"

"Yes sir."

"And that my players make a habit of coming to my practice on time."

"Yes sir. I apologize sir."

"Dagummit, will you stop calling me sir. I'm your coach, and you will address me as such."

"Yes Coach."

"Coach Connelly."

"Yes Coach Connelly."

"Alright, now we're getting somewhere. Now I have a good mind to make you run hills for being late to my practice. You want to give me any reasons why I shouldn't?"

"It was a time zone change, sir. I forgot to adjust my watch when we came to town. It's my fault."

A glint of light flickered in Paul's eyes. Time zone change? His mind latched on to this little detail.

"Time zone?" he said. "What's your name boy?"

"Jacob Peterson."

At the mention of the name, Paul's heart leaped into his throat, his legs nearly collapsing beneath him.

"Jacob *Peterson*?" he asked in disbelief. "Jacob Peterson, of Thousand Oaks, Oregon?"

Now Jacob looked confused. "That's right, Thousand Oaks, Oregon."

"Jacob Peterson, whose dad teaches Italian?"

"John Peterson, that's right."

Praise Jesus, he thought. *Praise God in Heaven*! He exerted every ounce of energy he could muster to suppress the wellspring of joy that was rising within him.

"Very good Peterson. Tell you what," he said with a smile, "we'll save the hills for later. How's about you carry on with your throwing while I stand here and observe."

"No problem Coach Connelly."

"Alright, everybody back up, give the man some room. Receivers, back to your stations. I want to see sharp, crisp patterns. No banana routes. No lollygagging. Sharp and crisp. Sharp and crisp. Bickle, you can stand down for the time being."

Trevor's face screwed up with anger as he receded into the crowd of players.

For the next 30 minutes Jacob connected with receiver after receiver on slants, posts, corners, and down out and ups, all with breathtaking velocity and silky, pinpoint precision.

As Paul silently observed Jacob's passing exhibition, he began to calculate the vast implications. They had been projected to once again finish in the back of the pack, owing mainly to their porous defense and a quarterback position largely devoid of talent. With Jacob's arrival, however, defense no longer mattered. With Jacob running his offense, they would simply outscore the opposition. Jacob's arrival was an act of Providence that would completely alter the course of their season. Inexplicably, Principal Skinner had decided to act on the John Peterson file, without alerting Paul. No matter. Jacob Peterson was in Mayfield. His team had prospects. The conference championship was now within reach. In 35 short minutes, Jacob Peterson had changed *everything*.

CHAPTER 6

B uddy had been on edge all week, ever since that woefully impulsive decision to put the future of his church in the hands of a young, unproven pastor from an unknown, fledgling congregation. It was Sunday morning, and he sat in his office, haunted by the reality of how little he knew about Pastor Ethan Reddick. Did he have a track record? What if the guy couldn't deliver? First he'd start hemorrhaging congregants, then cash flow. The stakes were unbelievably high. Without the cash flow, the ministry and the shiny new chapel were unsustainable. A number of apocalyptic scenarios began to dance through his mind.

Then his thoughts turned to the devastating impact financial insolvency would have on his personal life. He immediately erected a wall against this kind of thinking. The consequences for his church were severe. But the implications for his personal life were unthinkable.

He had to somehow divert his thoughts or the whole day would become some sort of a horrible, self-fulfilling prophecy. He looked around his office for a diversion, anything to disrupt this bleak progression of thoughts. At wits end, he picked up his phone, entered a password, and listened for new messages. There was only one.

"Hello Mr. Holler. John Peterson here. We met last week in your office. I was just following up with you on those service opportunities.

Last time I saw you, I left an address, but no phone number. We do have a phone now, so here's the number: 555-271-1562. Once again, if anything pops up on your radar, don't hesitate to give me a call. We'd love to lend a hand. Take care."

I can't believe this guy, Buddy thought. Talk about tenacity. Buddy absently hit the delete button and then laid the phone back in its cradle. When was this guy going to figure out that Living Christ Ministries is not about service? People come here to worship because of its reputation for dynamic sermons delivered with the tongue of fire.

Buddy chuckled. *Tongue of fire.* That had been Lester's calling card for so many years. At some point, without even realizing it, Buddy had simply appropriated it. Tongue of fire was now code for that rare quality in a preacher to persuade a congregation to open their wallets and "give 'til it hurts". And right about now, Buddy was having serious questions about Pastor Ethan Reddick's ability to summon such a gift.

By 8:45 a.m. Buddy had managed to stave off all visions of imminent destruction, and work himself into a reasonably calm state of mind. Buddy heard a quick rap on the door, and then saw the door swing open. Standing before him was his guest preacher, the impossibly young Ethan Reddick.

Buddy masked his concern, rose from his chair, and met Ethan with a hearty handshake.

"Hello Pastor. Are you ready to do this thing?"

"Yes sir. I sure am," Ethan said enthusiastically. "I'm locked and loaded, tongue of fire at the ready."

Buddy smiled. Just hearing that phrase somehow spoke peace to his soul. Lester's tongue of fire got people in the seats and kept them there. If Ethan could summon even a fraction of Lester's abilities, then maybe they'd live to preach another week.

"Now that's what we like to hear. Tongue of fire. I'm excited already," Buddy managed.

For the next few minutes, Buddy reviewed the agenda for the meeting, previewed the announcements, and then explained the mechanics of Ethan's entrance.

"No seats on stage," Buddy explained. "So, once I'm finished with announcements, details of Lester's funeral and the like, then I'll introduce you. You'll enter stage left, I'll greet you with a warm handshake, and then I'll exit stage right. Does that sound workable?"

"Sounds real good Mr. Holler. Real good."

At 9 a.m. sharp, Buddy Holler strode up to the pulpit, cleared his throat, mopped his brow with a handkerchief, and welcomed nearly 1,300 parishioners to the worship services of Living Christ Ministries. He began by relating the tragic circumstances of Pastor Le Haye's death and announced the details of his viewing and funeral service. After a rousing congregational hymn, Buddy once again stepped up to the pulpit.

"My good brothers and sisters," he began. "There is no way to replace Pastor Le Haye. He could call down the powers of heaven and fill our hearts with God's awesome power. We were all eyewitnesses. Now that he's gone, however, someone must fill this pulpit, and take up his mantle. It will take months to find a pastor whose zeal for God's word approaches our dear Pastor Le Haye. Until we do, my brothers and sisters, we will be blessed to hear from fine pastors who will guest preach on a weekly basis. To that end, I have invited to be with us today Pastor Ethan Reddick of the Community Church of Christ, here in Mayfield. My brothers and sisters, please extend a warm welcome to Pastor Reddick."

A tepid applause rose up from the congregation as Ethan entered stage left, shook Buddy's hand, then strode towards the microphone. Settling in at the trademark glass pulpit, he peered out at the vast assembly of worshipers. The butterflies reprised themselves as an enormous knot formed in his throat. After a period of awkward silence, Ethan cleared his throat, placed a large, worn leather Bible onto the pulpit, and pulled it open.

"My good brothers and sisters of Living Christ Ministries," Ethan began. "I am both saddened and humbled by the circumstances that require my being here today. The death of Pastor Le Haye was both tragic and unexpected. We all mourn his passing. It is at times like these, however, that we must look to the scriptures for both meaning and solace. For it is only as we search God's word, holy and undefiled, that we find the answers to life's most pressing questions. For example: 'Why did you lose your dear pastor, Lester Le Haye?', 'Why would God call home one of his anointed servants?', 'Is death really the end, or is it merely a marvelous beginning?' The answers to life's most troubling questions are all here for the taking. We need only sup from the pages of these holy words. And so today, brothers and sisters, I will take you on a journey through holy writ wherein the glorious answers to life's most enigmatic questions are both propounded and elucidated. Let us begin by consulting the words of the Apostle Paul. Please grab your Bibles and turn with me if you will to 1 Corinthians 15, verse 55."

Buddy stood off stage, trickles of sweat already streaming down his temples. He peered from behind the curtain, appraising the vast congregation. Not a soul stirred. No one reached for their Bible. He doubted if there was a single parishioner among the vast assembly who had even brought a Bible. Yet Ethan was about to take them on an arduous journey though the Old and New Testaments in search of the answers to life's most troubling questions. A flame of panic flickered within him, lapping at the small kernel of hope he'd managed to preserve until now.

After five minutes, Buddy began to notice it. The members of the congregation were shifting uncomfortably in their seats. It wasn't that what Ethan was saying was untrue, or even misguided. It was clear that he had a marvelous command of the scriptures. But that's not why they had come. They had come in search of whatever it was Lester had been giving them every Sunday for the last 15 years. They were looking for the *tongue of fire*. And this strange and awkward navigation through the Bible was anything but Lester Le Haye. The ethereal heights to which he climbed with his soaring rhetoric stirred the soul. The contrast between the two styles was perhaps too great. The congregants were perhaps too aware of the passing of time.

Obscured by the curtains to the right of the stage, Buddy squirmed nervously. He too felt the contrast, and it terrified him. Soaring rhetoric was the catalyst that kept their church solvent. What he saw playing out before him was just the opposite. The doors to the assembly hall's exits were sealed shut, yet the energy in the room was somehow seeping out. He glanced uncomfortably at his watch as the bile began to lap at the back of his throat.

Another week of this and we'll be done, he thought. The members whose primary allure was Lester's magnetism would be gone, and with them their tithing contributions. What would remain would be a small residue of its most devout parishioners. A nice nucleus, but certainly not enough to sustain the day to day operations of the church. As much as he hated to admit it, Buddy *needed* Lester Le Haye. Or someone just like him.

Two hours later, Buddy sat in his office, still dazed and reeling at the unmitigated disaster of Ethan's sermon. Buddy's worst fears about Ethan had proven all too real. The only preacher in town that they hadn't managed to offend just so happened to be the dullest preacher in town. Now it all made sense: impossibly young, zero name recognition, knocking doors to build his congregation. Why hadn't he seen it? Young Ethan Reddick was *not* the answer to saving his congregation. He probably couldn't even save his *own* congregation. In one lusterless sermon, Ethan had shown the denizens of Mayfield what they could expect from future sermons at Living Christ Ministries. No, Ethan Reddick was *not* the answer.

Buddy reclined in his office chair, exasperated, evaluating his dwindling alternatives. Perhaps, with the passage of time, the five other pastors' hearts would soften. But venturing afresh into the lion's den was not a chore Buddy would relish.

With next week's sermon drawing closer by the hour, he gathered his courage, pulled open his desk drawer and reached for the Tri-County Yellow Pages. As he did, something caught his eye. There, tucked beneath some pens, was a scrap of paper. He grabbed it, pushed it up to his nose, and scrutinized it from behind the rims of his glasses. On the scrap of paper was written the name and address of John Peterson: preacher, humanitarian, and Christian disciple extraordinaire. Not only was John Peterson in the priesthood, but he was tripping all over himself to lend a hand. He was tall, handsome, seemed to have a warm, friendly presence about him and, for the love of Pete, he wasn't an adolescent.

Buddy suddenly kicked himself for having erased the phone message. Without a phone number, he'd have to make an appearance in person. He grabbed the scrap of paper, stuffed his keys in his pocket, and raced out to the parking lot. He *had* to find John Peterson.

CHAPTER 7

Had it really come to this? Buddy ran the largest church in three counties and was now racing around Mayfield desperately seeking someone, anyone who was both qualified *and* willing to address his congregation. Increasingly, however, *qualified* was up for negotiation. Buddy tossed the scrap of paper onto the passenger seat and threw his car into gear.

He pulled onto Colfax Road, and followed it north. As he turned onto Mill Road, he saw open up before him a sprawling apartment complex. He grabbed the address and confirmed the final coordinates. Taking cues from the rudimentary map posted at the entrance of the complex, he steered around to the back of the complex and pulled into an open spot in front of #121C.

As he stepped gingerly up the walk, he could feel his heart churning away in his ribcage. He paused briefly at the door, inhaled deeply, and then rapped three times. Beyond the door, Buddy could hear the banter of small children, a chaos of movement and then the sound of footsteps. The door opened, and Buddy looked down to see a small girl, no older than seven or eight.

"Hello," she said, in a conversational tone, as if they'd been friends for years.

"Well, hello there. And who might you be?"

"I'm Hannah. Who are you?"

"My name's Buddy. It's nice to meet you Hannah," he said, mussing the hair on her head.

Buddy was grateful for this interaction. Friendly banter with an eight year old was just what he needed to soothe his frazzled nerves. He could feel his heart rate slow from a gallop to a trot.

"Nice to meet you Mr. Buddy."

Buddy chuckled, then continued. "Listen Hannah, I'm really glad I met you. You seem like a very nice young lady. Is your daddy around by chance?"

"Yes he is," she said matter of factly. She continued to stand there, her smile unabated, making no effort to retrieve her father. Buddy looked over her shoulder and saw a swarm of children bustling about in the narrow confines of the living room.

"Would you mind letting him know that I'm here?" he added.

"Ok," she said. Apparently that was all the prompting she needed because she twirled about, pranced off in the opposite direction, and disappeared into the thicket of children.

"Daaaaaaddy!" came a voice from somewhere within. "There's somebody hear to seeeeee youuuuuu!"

In a few moments, Buddy saw John Peterson rounding the corner. He was even taller than he had remembered.

"Well, Mr. Holler," John said, extending his hand. "To what do I owe the honor?"

"Hello John," Buddy said smiling nervously and meeting John's hand.

John looked over his shoulder, appraising the tempest of movement behind him. "I'd invite you in but...you know...I think you get the idea."

"No problem John. And please, call me Buddy. We can chat right here on your doorstep."

"Great, what brings you to these parts?"

"Well, I don't know if you remember the conversation we had the day you rolled into town."

"Oh sure. Every word."

"Good...great. Listen, I wanted to take you up on your offer to render some service. That offer still on the table?"

"Absolutely," John said enthusiastically. "Tell me what you had in mind. We'd be happy to chip in."

"Well, actually, this doesn't have so much to do with your family as it does with you. I would be requiring *your* services. Your family is welcome to come and lend moral support, but specifically, this is a service that you and only you can perform."

"Um, ok." John looked surprised, but intrigued. "How can I help?"

Buddy hesitated, wondering how to begin. "Since I saw you last, there have been some, how do I put this, developments over at Living Christ Ministries."

"Oh?" John said, surprised.

Buddy's face was lined with gravity.

"You may not have heard. About two days after you and I met, Lester Le Haye passed away."

John's jaw dropped, his eyes widening into saucers.

"Oh, Buddy, I'm terribly sorry."

"Yes, very tragic and very unexpected. Subarachnoid hemorrhage. Brain aneurism, basically. The good news is he died very quickly."

John's eyes conveyed sadness, his head shaking subtly in disbelief.

"Anyway, my purpose in being here is not to burden you with sad news, but to ask for your help. As you can imagine, given Lester's oratorical skills, we've never had a hard time attracting members."

"So I noticed," John said.

"Truth is, most of our congregants have come to us from other churches here in town. To put it mildly, the pastors from these churches are not exactly tripping over each other for the chance to guest preach in our chapel. In fact, now that Lester is gone, they're looking to make up for lost time."

John's eyes narrowed as he processed Buddy's news.

"So, to say the least," he continued, "finding someone to fill in has been a challenge. We tried a young kid this morning, but frankly, it was an unqualified disaster. In the aftermath of the sermon, I suddenly remembered our conversation. I thought maybe you could help."

"Buddy, you know I'm happy to help, but what exactly are you asking me to do?"

"John, I'm going to be very direct. We're the largest church in three counties. We've built this congregation on powerful, dynamic sermons.

If I can't find a compelling preacher by next week, it could sink us. I'm afraid the bleeding has already started."

Buddy took another deep breath.

"John I'm asking you to preach."

"You're asking me to *preach*?" John said, his eyes spreading wide.

"Look, you said you wanted to serve. So, now I'm asking. Will you preach at Living Christ Ministries on Sunday?"

"But Buddy, you don't know anything about me."

"I know enough John. You're Christian, you're part of a lay clergy, and you preach sermons. In fact, if memory serves, you were slated to preach one this morning. That's all I really need to know."

John reeled back, collapsing against the door behind him. His hands drew up to his face, masking the horror that had spread across it.

"I don't know Buddy," he said dropping his hands to his sides. "I never say no to the opportunity to serve, but you don't know a thing about my church, our doctrines, or our beliefs. I *have* been known to preach, but I don't know if what I have to say would be the best fit for you and your congregation."

"John, I appreciate what you're saying, but I'm all out of options. There isn't a soul in this town who's willing to preach to my congregation."

"What about guest preachers from out of town?" John countered. "Surely with a congregation as big as yours, an outside preacher would jump at the opportunity."

"I'm afraid that's impossible," he said flatly.

"Impossible? Seems like the perfect solution."

Buddy's hands drew up to his temples.

"I keep forgetting," he said with a touch of impatience, "you're new in town."

"What does that mean? What am I missing here?" John asked.

Buddy winced as the memories came rushing back.

"About three years ago, there was an exposé on national TV called 'The Business of Saving Souls'."

John's eyes widened.

"The lead reporter on the story contacted me telling me he had sources that claimed we were mismanaging our tithing receipts."

"Mismanaging?" John asked.

"You know, using tithes and offerings in ways other than advertised. Of course I vehemently denied everything and invited a third party audit. A team of accountants came in and spent a whole week tearing through our records. Turned the whole place upside down."

"What'd they find?"

Buddy's mouth curled into a frown.

"As it turns out their sources were right. Something *was* amiss. Lester had been skimming revenue for years. Now the whole country knows."

"From what I can see, your congregants don't seem to mind."

Buddy smiled grimly.

"With Lester's charisma, none of that mattered. Our congregation rallied around him, convinced that it was all some sort of conspiracy cooked up by jealous pastors. But the fact is, Lester did exactly what he was accused of doing. Things were never the same between us."

"I'm sorry Buddy. I really am."

"Anyway," Buddy said, snapping back to the present, "you've told me you're Christian and that you're willing to pitch in. What do you say? Will you preach?"

John looked over his shoulder at the closed door as if fearful of eavesdroppers. He then looked down at the ground, taking a sudden interest in a spot on the pavement about six inches in front of his toes. Finally, his head rose, and he met Buddy's gaze.

"Alright," he said, "I'll do it. But on one condition. This is a one off deal. I'm only doing it to buy you some time. By next week, I need you to have someone else in there. I'm just a stop gap. A temporary sub. Is that something you can live with?"

A smile creased the bottom half of Buddy's haggard face.

"You've got yourself a deal, my friend. John Peterson," he said, using his hands to mimic a Las Vegas marquee, "One Day Only."

With agony lurking just beneath his stoic features, John met Buddy's hand one last time. As he watched him walk slowly towards his car, Buddy suddenly stopped and turned back.

"I almost forgot to ask. What do I call you, you know, when I introduce you? Pastor? Reverend?"

"Brother," he responded. "Brother John Peterson would be just fine."

"Brother John it is," Buddy said with some satisfaction. And then he walked down the sidewalk, slipped into his car, and drove out of sight.

John stood at the door of his apartment, trying to discern if what had just happened to him had been real or only imagined. He spent the next several minutes leaning against his door, hands on his knees, trying to fathom the terrifying consequences of what he had just agreed to do.

After a few minutes, he turned around, faced the door, and with all the solemnity of a condemned man at the gallows, pushed it open and stepped back inside.

Reeling and dazed, he was impervious to the commotion as his children bandied about in their spare, 1200 square foot apartment. Buddy's request, and his subsequent acceptance, had inured him to his surroundings. He rounded the corner and saw Sarah sitting at the kitchen table, a magazine lying open before her.

"Visitors already?" she asked. "That certainly didn't take very long."

John stood there, eyeing her warily, a lump forming in his throat. After a period of silence, she looked up.

"You alright, hon? You don't look well."

He took a deep breath and then collapsed into the chair opposite her.

With no answer forthcoming, Sarah began to press. "What's going on John? Who was at the door?"

Finally John broke his silence. "Do you remember the man I told you about, the one that runs the huge church on the edge of town?"

"Where you found the phone the day we broke down? Sure, I remember him."

"Well, before I left, I pressed him on some service opportunities. You know, our family plan? Well, at the time, he seemed utterly uninterested in helping. Not his thing. Not what they do."

"Ok."

"Well, he just showed up at our door. Sounds like he wants to cash in on my offer."

"That's great news. So, why do you look like your dog just died?"

"How do I explain this?" John said, grimacing, searching for the right words. "When I was about to leave his office that day, he stopped me. He wanted to know if we were Christians. I told him yes. Then he asked if we'd like to come to their church some time. I told him we'd be happy to. But then I added that it wouldn't be that Sunday because I had to preach a sermon in my own church. Surprised, he asked me if I was a pastor. I told him no, but that I did hold the priesthood."

"Alright," she said, "nothing scandalous so far."

"Well, the plot thickens. Two days later something happened. Remember the flamboyant pastor I told you about?"

"Sure, lots of charisma, empty message."

"That's the one. He just died of a brain aneurysm."

Sarah let out a gasp, her hand drawing up to her mouth in horror.

"Ever since, this guy Buddy has been combing the town trying to find someone to guest preach."

"Well, that shouldn't be too hard, right? What pastor *wouldn't* want to preach there?"

"That's what you'd think. Apparently, over the years, their ministry has managed to draw away congregants from nearly every congregation in town. Throw in a financial scandal that played out on national television and, voilà, the pool of substitute preachers dries right up. So, the long and the short of it is, this guy's got a 1200 person congregation, and no one to preach to it."

"Ok," Sarah said, worry sounding in her voice for the first time.

"So, ten minutes ago, he showed up on our doorstep and said he needed a favor."

This time Sarah didn't answer him. Her arms were now crossed, her visage hard and devoid of warmth.

"He asked me if I'd preach to his congregation."

"Tell me you said no John. Tell me you declined," she said frantically.

John simply sat there, helpless and resigned as his wife combusted before his very eyes.

"You said yes," she exclaimed, her eyes wide and furious.

"Yes Sarah. I told him I'd do it."

"So you didn't tell him then. Are you telling me he doesn't know?"

For a split second, John looked confused. "What doesn't he know Sarah? What didn't I tell him?"

"You know, the most damning detail of all. That we're Mormons."

Chapter 8

"No Sarah, I didn't. I gave him every opportunity to find out. He just didn't seem to care. The only things that seemed to matter is that I believe in Jesus, I hold the priesthood, and I can preach. The poor guy's at the end of his rope."

"I don't care if he's at the end of his rope John. What about our plan?"

"The plan hasn't changed. The plan is why I qualified my acceptance."

"What does *that* mean?" she said crisply.

"I told him I'd preach to his congregation only if it were a one shot deal. I'd do it this Sunday, but only to help buy him some time. Don't worry hon, under no circumstances will I preach two weeks in a row."

Her mouth rose in an angry smile that bordered on hostile.

"Don't you get it John? It doesn't matter how many times you preach. It flies in the face of everything we agreed upon. You know, *the plan*? Move to a new town, fly below the radar, and engage the community through service, not religion."

"I know, I know. And that still *is* my plan. Even if the entire town of Mayfield rises up against us, I *will* do things differently. I'll deflect their criticisms. I won't battle it out in the public arena. I'll turn the other cheek."

"Exactly, because when you answer their attacks, they only redouble their efforts. The last two schools didn't drop you because you don't have a good program John. Your program's a stroke of genius. It's exactly what these schools need. They dropped you because you're a Mormon, and your battles were spilling over into the community. An aggressive defender of the Mormon faith is not what they were looking for. They just wanted Italian John. Just Italian."

"And that's exactly why I told him that this is a one-time deal."

"But John, if you preach to them, and they get so much of a whiff that you're a member of the Mormon Church, things are going to get nasty. When it all hits the fan, and it will hit the fan sooner or later, we risk a public ostracism that might be greater than the one we're probably already in line for. You and I can deal with it. We've dealt with it before. But, I'm worried about our seven children, five of whom will be attending public schools in a very small town. You have to call him back John. You have to tell him no. We can't risk it. Not in our third city in three years. There's just too much at stake."

John's arms were now folded against his chest, his eyes narrow, his mouth a tight line.

"Look sweetheart, this guy really is in a bind. I told him when we first met that we wanted to help, to get involved. How does that make us look if, in his moment of dire need, we join the ranks of everyone else who has kicked this guy to the curb? That's not what we're about. That's not what we believe."

Sarah was now shaking her head in disbelief.

"I can't believe it. We've been here one week and we've already scrapped our plan. John, you and I agreed that if we were going to uproot everyone again, that we would do it the right way. Stay out of the spotlight. Avoid contention. Agree with our enemies in the way. Preaching a stealth Mormon sermon to the largest congregation in Mayfield is not my idea of sticking to the plan."

"Look, I just don't think I can retract my offer. He's got nowhere else to turn. I feel *compelled* to help."

She stewed in silence, her eyes dark and brooding.

"Look Sarah, there's no denying what's at stake here. And because there's a down side, a fairly severe down side, I'll make you a commitment. Before I make any final decisions, I'll take it to the Lord in prayer. But, if

I do take it to the Lord in prayer, are you prepared to live with the answer that I get?"

"There's no way *He* would agree to this," she huffed.

"Sarah, if I take it to God in prayer," he repeated, "are you prepared to live with the answer?"

She covered her face with her hands and groaned in disgust while she weighed his proposal. After a few moments of tense silence, she spoke.

"Ok John. I can live with it. But it better be the most overwhelming manifestation you've ever received. I mean, we're talking angels, visitations, the whole nine yards. Anything short of that, and you're calling that man back."

The faintest trace of a smile pulled at John's lips.

"Alright young lady, you've got yourself a deal." He took her hand in his, caressed it briefly, and then gave it a tender kiss.

• • •

Sarah was already deep in sleep when John knelt beside his bed that night. He laid out his case in prayer for the better part of 15 minutes before finally rising and pulling back the covers.

As he lay in bed, eyes fixed to the ceiling, sleep evading him, he began to listen for his answer. But instead of hearing that quiet whisper of confirmation he had sought, something terrifying happened. Slowly, but steadily, his limbs grew heavy, and then unresponsive.

Affixed to his bed, like a butterfly pinned to a board, he prayed with renewed fervor. Amid the terror of his frightening paralysis, he tried to parse out a whisper, a thought, an answer. Instead of clarity, the storm in his mind began to rage even more violently, muddling his thoughts and filling his chest with a dense blackness.

Somewhere near midnight, as John's anguish reached its apex, he felt a tiny flame begin to gnaw away at the tendrils of energy that held him fast. It built slowly at first, but then quickly radiated upwards to his chest, extending to his arms, and finally enveloping his legs. As it did, the strings of tension began to dissolve. His body was slowly consumed by an intense heat that enlivened his soul and quickened his faculties. The storm of muddled thoughts had suddenly yielded to peace and clarity.

Clearly, some sort of heavenly communication was taking place. But what was the message? As he lay there in stunned wonderment, he heard a quiet voice. It was a small voice, almost imperceptible, but it was a voice nonetheless. The voice simply said, "Preach my gospel."

CHAPTER 9

Ethan Reddick was greeted Monday morning by a flashing red light at the base of his office phone. *Who could this be?* Ethan thought, as nerves and excitement battled within him. Although Ethan extended the offer for spiritual counseling to his congregation at every turn, no one had ever called. The town of Mayfield sat by idly while a vast spiritual resource languished in their midst. This reality had lodged in Ethan's chest, growing and festering with each passing week. But all that would change after what had taken place at Living Christ Ministries. There can be little doubt that Ethan had spoken with the tongue of fire. Having made his mark on a regional stage, the citizens of Mayfield had finally taken notice. Ethan Reddick had arrived.

With a nervous burst of energy, he extended his arm and pressed play.

"Hi Ethan," came the voice from the speaker. "Buddy Holler over at Living Christ Ministries. Listen, I just wanted to call and say that I appreciate all the effort you put into your sermon on Sunday."

Ethan felt another burst of excitement. He hadn't seen Buddy after the meeting. Now would come the congratulatory phone call. And, more than likely, a follow up invitation.

The message continued: "I know that we had originally talked about possibly having you back, but we're probably going to be moving in a different direction. So, anyway, thanks again for stepping in at the last minute. Good luck to you and your congregation."

Ethan dropped the receiver and slumped into his chair, the blood slowly draining from his body. Wings of darkness encroached on his vision as he felt himself sink into a deep, black chasm. He sat there for ten minutes, chin pinned to his chest, his eyes staring blankly at the receiver that now dangled from its cradle, suspended midway between his desk and the floor. How could it be? This was not how it was supposed to unfold. God had directed him to Buddy Holler's house for the express purpose of preaching to his congregation. He had aligned his will with God's and delivered the sermon he had been asked to preach. It had been pure and undefiled. How could Buddy not see that? This was some sort of terrible mistake. Had Buddy been blinded by an adversary intent on frustrating God's grand designs? If so, Buddy could be made to see the truth.

Impelled by anger and confusion, Ethan suddenly picked up the phone and began feverishly punching the numbers for Living Christ Ministries. He would let Buddy know about God's plans for them. Buddy *needed* to know. The phone rang twice, and then suddenly, on an impulse, Ethan slammed the receiver back down in the cradle. *Don't be rash*, he thought. Don't tinker with God's timeline. This relationship may yet work, but Buddy's heart would need to soften. That could take time.

Instead, Ethan punched the button again. After listening to Buddy's message a second time, he sat in his chair puzzling over one particular phrase. Buddy had simply said, "We're probably going to be moving in a different direction." Different direction? Had he already found another guest preacher? Hadn't Buddy exhausted all of his resources by the time Ethan had knocked on his door? What other options did he have? Curiosity began to mount within him, slowly crowding out the other competing emotions. Ethan's replacement would be preaching to Buddy's congregation in six short days. Who had Buddy chosen? There was only one way to find out. It was time for Ethan to pay Living Christ Ministries another visit.

CHAPTER 10

"What's that smell?" said 12 year old David Peterson, holding his nose high in the air and giving a sniff. Rachel's hands flew up to her forehead creating a loud smacking sound.

"Oh no, what have I done!" she said, her voice laced with dread.

Rachel, 14, sprang from the sofa and dashed into the kitchen. She was greeted by pillars of smoke billowing from the oven door, filling the kitchen with an opaque mist that left her gasping for air. She pulled open the oven door, and then threw open the kitchen windows in an attempt to create a cross draft. She quickly grabbed a dish towel from the drawer beside the sink and began waving it frantically at the smoke detector on the wall above her.

"Come on, work with me, work with me," she pleaded, flapping the towel vigorously in the hopes of staving off the inevitable, shrill alarm. Within two minutes she reappeared in the family room, the offending sheet of scorched cookies in hand. She looked confused and mildly put out.

"It *was* 22 minutes, right?" she asked no one in particular. "Or was it 12?"

Her curiosity piqued, she disappeared back into the kitchen in search of the cookbook. In another moment she emerged, sputtering and gasping for air.

"Yeah, it was 12 minutes," she said flatly. "Overshot it by, oh, about 10 minutes. Cookies anyone?"

Clouds of smoke had now begun to waft into the family room, engulfing the family in a milky haze. Within seconds, the twins, Joseph and Sadie were coughing and sputtering as their lungs strained for air.

"I think they're perfect...," Jacob said, breaking the silence, "hockey pucks."

"Jacob!" snapped Sarah. "Enough already. As if you've never made a mistake."

The sharpness in Sarah's voice cast an instant pall over the room. Jacob's mouth hung open, stunned at the unexpected rebuke. The rest of the children stared into their laps, not daring to meet their mother's gaze. Rachel stood transfixed, mouth likewise agape, the tray of burnt cookies threatening to slip out of her hands.

"Ok, then," John said, sensing the mood change. "Tell you what, given the unfortunate turn our refreshments have taken, I move we adopt Plan B."

"Plan B?" asked Jacob timidly, still bristling from the exchange.

"I always have a Plan B waiting in the wings for moments such as these. Plan B," John said, pausing for dramatic effect, "is a family trip to the ice cream parlor down on Main Street."

The room suddenly erupted in a chorus of cheers, vanquishing the air of hostility that had threatened to derail the evening.

"Nice job Sis," David said wryly. "You can burn my cookies anytime."

Within ten minutes, the Petersons were cruising past the menagerie of shops and boutiques in the heart of Mayfield's business district. John pulled into an open space in front of Molly's Ice Cream Shoppe, and idled the engine.

"Alright, everyone out," John ordered.

"Why aren't you parking?" Jacob asked, panic in his voice. "You guys *are* coming with us, right?"

"Too rich for our blood," John said. "Mom and I are going a few blocks down the street for frozen yogurt. We're a little more metabolically challenged than you young upstarts. We'll circle back in a few."

"Whoa, whoa, whoa. Wait a second here. You don't expect me to handle these hooligans by myself do you?" Jacob said, a stunned look on his face.

"Into your hands we commend our progeny."

"Come on Dad, you know I need reinforcements. You've seen what these guys are capable of."

Jacob gave them a long, pleading look, but could sense that no reprieve was forthcoming.

"Fine, how long are you guys going to be?" Jacob huffed.

"Relax, we'll be back lickety-split," John said.

"Uh, ok. I hope you know what you're doing," Jacob said, his face dark with dread.

With all the gravity of a soldier mustering for battle, Jacob opened the door and stepped onto the sidewalk. Turning, he poked his head back into the car and said, "Alright everyone, time to unload. We will proceed in an orderly fashion. And when we're inside, no one touches a thing. Not a solitary thing. Got it?"

His orders were met by a chorus of groans and protestations. One by one, the remaining six Peterson children spilled out of the car and onto the sidewalk. Jacob then marched them towards the door of the ice cream parlor which David opened with a jingle.

Once his siblings were safely corralled within the confines of the parlor, Jacob let out a small sigh of pent up air. As he relaxed, he was struck by the strangeness of his parents' decision. Yogurt? Since when did they eat yogurt? Metabolically challenged? Yeah right. Jacob immediately suspected a deeper motive. His mom *had* been acting more and more strange of late. Frankly, the rebuke had stung him, but not surprised him. The tension between his mom and dad had been mounting all week. Something had wedged its way between them and he couldn't quite put his finger on it. Their quest for yogurt had very little to do with calories and waistlines. His mom and dad needed to sort some things out.

His quiet reflections were suddenly shattered when Sadie and Joseph made a B-line for the buckets of penny candy, intent on their plunder. Jane, in the meantime, had been drawn to a tub of fluffy stuffed animals. In the blink of an eye she was sifting through the tub, its contents spilling over onto the floor.

Jacob's hands flew up to his head, pulling at his hair in exasperation. He quickly gathered the twins in his muscular arms, each of whom now held fistfuls of tootsie rolls.

"No, no, not good, nooooot good," Jacob said, as tootsie rolls spilled out of their clenched fists and across the floor of the shop. He put them both down, emptying their fists of any surplus rolls and then began making large sweeping motions on the floor, trying to corral the candy into a pile before him.

As Jacob busied himself with the cleanup from their first pillaging, the twins were racing towards a different bucket, this one full of Hershey's Kisses. Their shiny metal wrappers had overwhelmed their meager capacities to resist. No sooner had Jacob restored the tootsie rolls to their home than he noticed the calamity that was about to unfold at the bucket of Hersey's Kisses.

"You gotta be kidding me," he said, racing across the floor and whisking the twins into his arms before they could reach their intended target.

Jane, after much winnowing, had in the meantime found the object of her affection.

"Ooooh, a fluffy liiiion," she said, holding up her prized find for all to see.

Holding a twin under each arm like sacks of flour, he lumbered over to the disaster that was unfolding all around Jane.

"Jane, remember what I said. No…touching…anything," Jacob hissed from between clenched teeth.

Jane simply looked up at Jacob and extended her arm, showcasing the lion she had successfully exhumed from the tub of stuffed animals. The satisfied look on her face bespoke the thrill she felt at her new find.

He now turned his sights on his remaining siblings. "David, Rachel, Hannah, are you ordering?"

"Yes master," David said, in the mocking tone of an automaton.

"Come on guys, let's get it done, preferably before you turn this place into rubble."

After restoring a semblance of order, Jacob collected himself, took a deep breath and then focused his attention on the vast array of flavors before him. As he looked through the glass at the buckets of ice cream below, he became dimly aware of a figure standing on the opposite side of the counter. His eyes slowly rose until they rested on the girl in front of him. She had brown, shoulder length hair that framed a stunningly beautiful face. Her crystalline blue eyes left Jacob gasping for breath, while a strange wave of fire swelled in his chest. He blushed, suddenly realizing that the breathtaking creature before him had beheld the entire tumultuous scene from the minute they'd walked through the door.

"So," she said, a playful smile coming across her face, "is this your brood?"

A horrified look came across Jacob's face.

"Uh, no. I mean yes. I mean, no they're not mine—they're my brothers and sisters…sadly." He managed a weak smile. Wow, he was really blowing it.

"That was quite the performance," she said giggling. "You managed to avert a major catastrophe."

"This isn't the half of it," Jacob said, recovering, warming to her smile. "Had I not employed my blazing speed and cat-like agility, this whole place would have been destroyed. Utterly and completely. No survivors. You owe me big time."

"Is that right?" she said, her mouth broadening into a smile.

"Oh yeah, you only saw a brief glimpse of the destruction these children are capable of."

"Wow. I feel like I'm living on a sense of borrowed time. I don't know how to thank you."

"Tell you what, if you can get me and my brood lined up with some ice cream before my mom and dad come in, and keep what happened here a secret just between us, then consider the debt repaid."

"You've got yourself a deal," she said, her eyes lingering on his dark, handsome features.

The children made their orders and after a flurry of scooping from the girl behind the counter, they all sat in metal chairs contentedly licking their cones. All except for Jacob. He still stood at the counter, far more taken by the dispenser of the ice cream than the ice cream itself.

"So, I don't believe I've seen you around town," she said.

"Jacob. Jacob Peterson," he said with a smoldering smile. "We're new in town."

He reached across the counter and grabbed the petite hand that was now reaching towards him. He suddenly felt her warm hand in his, her soft, supple skin sending a warm tingle up his arm.

"Ashley Hudson," she said, making no effort to reclaim her hand. Their eyes held each other fast, neither one averting their glance. Jacob felt more fire spreading through his chest when he suddenly heard the jingling of the parlor door. Their hands instantly retracted in a subconscious effort to conceal their prolonged hand shake. They turned their heads and saw a couple step through the door. His mom and dad had arrived. At precisely the wrong time.

"Remember," he said under his breath, "our little secret."

She smiled and blushed, her eyes twinkling. "Our little secret," she whispered.

CHAPTER 11

A brooding tension filled the car as the Petersons made their way across town towards Living Christ Ministries on Sunday morning. Amid the chaos of preparation that had engulfed their tiny apartment that morning, Sarah and John had managed to spend most of the time avoiding each other. Forced into close proximity by their car ride, the disquiet had finally begun to flare.

"You're sure you received a confirmation on this?" Sarah finally blurted.

"Sweetheart, I told you, it was as clear as any manifestation I've ever received. I'm supposed to do this today. I *am* on God's errand."

"I still don't understand this. Why God would want you to preach at this church after all we've been through is beyond me."

"I know it is Sarah. But we're just going to have to have a scintilla of faith on this. Sometimes God asks us to do things that defy reason. But that doesn't make them wrong."

"A scintilla of faith?"

"Yeah, about a mustard seed's worth. That's all he asks of us."

"You didn't just use the collective 'us' did you? You and I both know you mean *me*. You think *I* need to show more faith. That's what you're saying, isn't it?"

John could feel the tension ratchet up a couple notches. This was not the spirit he wanted to bring to the most consequential sermon of his life.

"Look, God has asked me to do this. The answer was unmistakable. But, regardless of whether you think it came from God, there's no turning back now. Buddy Holler is relying on me. I gave him my word. Let's just make the best of it."

"Fine," she said, her tone curt, her eyes dark and cold.

Within minutes they were pulling into a front row parking spot at Living Christ Ministries.

"Wow, this doesn't look like 1200 people to me," John said scanning the sparsely filled parking lot. John got out and puzzled over the scant number of cars. Where *was* everyone? John shrugged it off. He'd been asked to deliver a single sermon. The number of people who would actually end up hearing it was inconsequential.

• • •

As John yanked open the shiny glass door at the base of the building, he felt an explosion of nerves that started in his gut and shot upwards into his chest. The magnitude of what he was about to do was beginning to settle over him. He was no longer a missionary in Italy, divinely called, impervious to rejection, and insulated by thousands of miles of land and water. He was about to preach to community members, colleagues, his future students and their families. This wasn't a lonely doorstep in a far off land. This was a real sermon with real-life consequences. He followed his family through the door, past the foyer and into the vast, airy assembly hall. It was there that John's suspicions were confirmed. The meeting was slated to start in only ten minutes, but the congregation was sparse at best. The attendance wasn't anywhere close to what Buddy had predicted.

John led his family towards the front of the chapel where he spied a large swath of open seats.

"Look, Buddy wants to meet for five minutes or so. Can you take it from here?"

"Fine."

Her tone was icy, her eyes narrow and reproachful. John felt a small tinge of regret welling with in him, but he pushed it aside. Now was not the time for misgivings.

"Good enough. See you afterwards."

He bent over and gave her a quick peck on her forehead. Her eyes looked straight ahead, refusing to requite his show of affection.

John hurried into the foyer and made for Buddy's office. When John walked in, Buddy was sitting at his desk, the Bible sprawled open before him.

"Brother John…right on time," Buddy said rising and extending his hand.

"Hello Buddy. A pleasure to see you again," John said, meeting Buddy's hand.

"The pleasure's mine. Listen I really appreciate you pinch hitting like this. It means a lot."

"I'm happy to do it," John said, forcing a smile.

"Say, we won't be at full capacity today. You may have noticed it on the way in. They're not exactly jockeying for parking spots out there."

"Maybe not, but it's not quite 9 a.m.," John said, trying to strike an optimistic tone.

"I appreciate the positive attitude, Brother John, I really do. But unfortunately, I've put you in the difficult position of having to stop the bleeding."

"Stop the bleeding?" John said.

"That's right. I was hoping these folks would overlook last week's transgression. They didn't. So, you're the tourniquet. There's a lot riding on the sermon you deliver here today."

John felt a small ball of acid gurgle in his stomach, gnawing at his tenuous sense of calm. Things were much worse than he'd been lead to believe. From all accounts, the congregation had experienced an attrition of nearly half in only one week. And now, he was being asked to staunch a massive hemorrhage. *He* was. John Peterson.

He looked down at the sermon in his hand, and smiled at the irony. He was about to preach a Mormon sermon, not in an attempt to convert others to his own church, but in a last ditch effort to save the membership of the largest Christian church in town.

"No worries," John said, feigning confidence. "I'll see what I can do."

Buddy gave a half smile but, he didn't seem optimistic. He seemed rattled. Here was a man who was drowning, grasping for a lifeline. And for today, that lifeline was John Peterson.

CHAPTER 12

When Ethan Reddick arrived at Living Christ Ministries at 8:58 a.m., his heart fell into his stomach. What had once been an assembly hall brimming with congregants was now a half-filled room with waning energy. He suddenly felt a surge of shame swell within his breast. Is this what his sermon had wrought? As his self-doubts amplified, he saw a window of reality open up before him. The problem wasn't with Buddy *or* the congregation. Ethan Reddick was the problem.

Ethan hadn't spoken with Buddy after his sermon. Buddy had simply scurried out through a side door and disappeared from sight. There were no thanks, no commendations. In the afterglow of his sermon, Ethan had simply brushed this aside. Surely Buddy was attending to the prodigious duties of his ministry. They could always chat later. As Ethan stared at the empty seats before him now, everything began to add up. First, his chronic failure to build his own congregation. Then Buddy's hasty escape after his sermon. Then the phone call. The truth opened up a fresh chasm of pain deep within him.

Suddenly anxious to conceal his identity, Ethan quickly ascended the empty bank of seats that rose up behind him. Once safely ensconced on the top row, he began to survey the decimated congregation. The change in attendance from last week to this was breathtaking. His inadequacies as a preacher were far more profound than he could have ever imagined.

Just then, Ethan saw a man settle in at the shiny glass pulpit. It was Buddy Holler. He looked out over the congregation as if appraising its sparseness. He shuffled a few papers, cleared his throat and began to announce the program. After a lackluster hymn from the anemic congregation, Buddy returned to the pulpit.

"Today we are blessed to have in our midst a member of a lay Christian clergy in a neighboring county. John Peterson and his family have recently moved in on Mill Road. Although not yet a member of our congregation," Buddy said with a chuckle, "John has been kind enough to be today's guest preacher. His wife Sarah and their seven beautiful children are seated before me in the congregation."

The mention of seven children elicited a series of gasps and whispers from the congregation. Buddy smiled as if to say, "I know what you mean," and continued.

"I hope you have a chance to speak to *all* of them and extend them a special hand of fellowship."

With that, Buddy turned and walked off the stage. Entering from the left was a tall man with dark hair and handsome features, probably around 40. He strode confidently across the stage and settled in at the pulpit.

As the man began speaking, Ethan tucked his arms tightly against his chest, jutting his chin out in subconscious defiance of Buddy's decision. Ethan *was* curious about John Peterson, but there was no getting around the fact that he'd been weighed, measured and found wanting. Buddy's call had festered in his subconscious all week, gnawing away at his dwindling hope.

John Peterson was hardly two minutes into his sermon when something strange happened. Ethan began to feel something he hadn't felt in a very long time. It wasn't just charisma. There was no denying that John Peterson was very charismatic. It wasn't just his way with words. There was no question he had a penchant for the turn of the phrase. It was the words themselves. They seemed to be invested with…some sort of power.

Ten minutes into the sermon, Ethan suddenly realized that the feelings of inadequacy and confusion that had raged within him for nearly a week had all but disappeared. John Peterson's sermon wasn't just inspiring, it was…purifying. Ethan suddenly felt as if his whole world had been set aright.

Ethan's gaze drifted to the other congregants scattered about the hall. Their attention was likewise rapt, their expressions solemn. They too seemed to be entranced by the curious sermon that was rolling out across the chapel.

Who is John Peterson? Ethan suddenly wondered.

By the time the sermon finished, Ethan was leaning forward in his chair, a strange fire burning deep within him. Whatever it was that radiated from that pulpit, it was unlike anything he had ever felt. John Peterson's sermon possessed some power of which Ethan's own sermons were strikingly bereft. Of course this man had been asked to preach. He had the tongue of fire.

Suddenly Ethan made a snap decision. Whatever John Peterson possessed, and however he came by it, Ethan had to have it. Had his cataclysmic failure of the prior week been part of some grand design? Had it been necessary in order to ensure his presence in the chapel today? Surely *this* had been God's plan. God had broken him down, only to build him up again. And John Peterson was just the man God had chosen to do it.

Ethan stayed in his seat, watching as the enraptured congregation slowly filed out of the assembly hall. Within ten minutes, the hall was empty and Brother John stood in front of the pulpit chatting with a small group of people huddled around him. Judging by the number of children, it was no doubt Brother John's family. Ethan quickly descended the steps and strode towards the family huddled at the front of the chapel.

As he drew closer to the group, he saw heavy creases lining John's forehead. As John's eyes shifted to Ethan, John's wife likewise became aware of his approach. She turned her blonde head to reveal stunning features, and haunted green eyes. Deep within her eyes, Ethan could sense an undercurrent of sadness. And that's when Ethan realized that all was not well with the John Peterson family. But that wasn't going to stop him now. Things might not be well with this family, but things were likely to get much worse with his own. There was a window of opportunity here, and he needed to act before it slammed shut.

"Mind if I have a word before you go Brother John?" Ethan said, extending his hand.

Brother John's eyes darted quickly to his wife and then back to him.

"Um, sure, what can I do for you?" John said, grabbing the outstretched hand.

"We'll be out in the car," the woman said crisply, and began shepherding her children towards the exit.

"My name's Ethan Reddick. I'm the pastor over at the Community Church of Christ, here in town. I'm probably better known as the guy who completely laid an egg here last week."

John flashed an empathic smile.

"Nice to meet you. Didn't go so well, huh?"

"That's the understatement of the year. I preached straight from the good book for about 20 minutes. I thought it had gone well. Really well, actually. But the day after, I got the 'Thanks, but no thanks' from Mr. Holler. Didn't quite rise to the level of lingual combustion, I suppose."

"I'm sorry to hear that Ethan. I really am." John paused, searching Ethan's face. "What is it I can do for you?" he said finally.

"Look, I'm afraid that what happened here last week is merely a symptom of a larger problem. My livelihood depends on my being able to keep people in their seats. But my chapel's like a revolving door. People show up. People leave. I do missionary outreach. More people show up. And then more people leave. It's a vicious cycle and it's sinking my ministry. Not to mention what it's doing to my home life."

"I see," John said, nodding. "So, how can *I* help you?"

"Well, during your sermon, I realized something. *You* have what *I* need. If I could preach half the sermon you just preached, all my problems would go away. You sucked me in from word one and kept me riveted until that final Amen."

Ethan paused while he gathered his courage.

"Brother John, I'll never build a congregation if I can't learn how to preach. I think God sent me here today because *you're* supposed to teach me how."

John's eyebrows shot upwards.

"Me?"

"Absolutely," Ethan replied. "Whatever you have going on—I need it. I've got to harness it, internalize it, and unleash it on my own congregation. That's the only way my little ministry is going to survive. That's the only way I can save my family."

"Look…it's Ethan right?

"That's right."

"Look Ethan. I'm flattered that you liked what you heard here today. But I've got a lot on my plate right now. I'm adjusting to a new town, I've got seven kids going in a million different directions, and I still haven't unpacked the boxes in my living room. It just isn't good timing."

A look of surprise came over Ethan's face. But then it hardened with resolve.

"Look Brother John, I'm totally flexible. Work me in however you can. I'll do it on your terms. I'll do whatever you ask of me. Squeeze me in an hour here, an hour there. I'll come over and personally unpack your living room for you. Tell me what I need to do to earn a bit of your time."

"Look Ethan, it's not about earning any of my time. I've got complications in my life you couldn't possibly comprehend. I'm not opposed to lending a hand, but it's just not a good time. I understand your plight, and I feel your pain. But, I'm just not the right guy for the job. I hope you understand."

John extended his hand one last time. "It was a pleasure to meet you Ethan. I hope things work out for you and your family. I really do."

Ethan met John's hand in stunned silence. As John turned and walked out of the hall, Ethan could only watch in shock. Brother John's words and his actions seemed strangely out of step. Ethan was teetering on the brink of insolvency, his marriage was unraveling, yet Brother John was utterly unmoved. Of one thing Ethan *was* sure. If he had any hope of saving his family and floundering ministry, he had to get through to John Peterson.

CHAPTER 13

"Dagnabbit, Dooley! If it touches your hands, you catch the ball!" Paul yelled.

Donavan Dooley stood in the middle of the field, hands on his hips, eyes studying the turf in front of his feet. After muttering a few choice words to himself, he began the long slog towards the hills at the northern end of the practice field.

Jacob had been warned by the other players about Coach Connelly's system. You drop a pass, you run the hills. You fumble the ball, you run the hills. Ten times up, ten times down. Only upon completion of the hills could you return to the huddle. Backups would fill in until the penance had been paid. In order to ingratiate himself to his new teammates, Jacob had taken just a little of the zing off his passes. The last thing he needed at this early stage was extra hills for his teammates because of an over-exuberant arm.

Paul Connelly was now standing in front of his offensive huddle, arms crossed.

"I will not tolerate fumbles and dropped passes. If you're going to be on this offense, I demand your full concentration. Now Peterson, this is what I want to see. I want a 929 waggle, x post, y corner."

"Uh coach," Jacob said. "Who's filling in for Dooley?"

Paul whirled around, head on a swivel, scanning the field. Donavan Dooley was halfway over to the hills, intent on paying his penalty, no different than in seasons past. Coach Connelly put his fingers up to his mouth and let out a loud, shrill whistle.

"Dagummit Dooley, quit horsing around and get your tail side back in this huddle. We're trying to run a practice here."

Donavan stopped in his tracks, whirled around, and began a slow jog back to the huddle. Jacob looked into the facemasks of his teammates and saw a look of sheer surprise written across their faces.

"Can't remember him ever doing that," muttered Chad Cogan, the team's fullback. "Last year, that would have been ten hills for sure."

Jacob puzzled briefly over the sudden change in policy, then stepped back into the huddle.

"Alright, guys we've got a 929 waggle, x post, y corner on two, on two, ready break."

The huddle broke and Jacob strode up to the line, assessing the defense and barking signals. After taking the snap, he rolled out to his left, planted, then launched a perfect, arcing spiral deep down the field and into the outstretched hands of Donavan Dooley.

"That's it Peterson," Paul yelled. "That's the read I'm looking for. Nice square shoulders. Weight evenly spread on both feet. Very well done. You see that Bickle?"

Since his demotion, Trevor Bickle had been relegated to outside linebacker. He glared back at his coach from the defensive side of the ball, as his hands balled into fists.

"That's the type of execution I was looking for all last year. Roll out, plant, then hit the receiver in stride, just over the outside shoulder. Well done Peterson," Paul said, tapping him on the helmet. "Well done."

Jacob shot a quick glance at Trevor and saw a face that was red with rage. It was one thing to be replaced by the new kid in town. It was quite another to have the head coach use the new kid as his training manual.

"Nice throw Peterson. Good catch Dooley. Alright, this time I want to see the same thing to the other side, 121 waggle."

Jacob relayed the play and the team broke their huddle and lumbered up to the line. As Jacob scanned the defense, he could feel Trevor's eyes burning holes into the side of his helmet. An unexpected chill shot up his spine, making the hairs on the nape of his neck stand on end.

"Hut," Jacob barked.

The ball slapped his hands and he rolled quickly out to his right. Scanning the field, he spotted the tight end Bobby McSwain streaking across the field on a back corner post. Jacob stopped, planted, then cocked his arm back to throw. As he did, he suddenly felt a bone-jarring impact. The next thing he knew he was flying through the air, nearly parallel to the ground. In another instant, he came crashing down on the unforgiving turf under the crushing weight of his assailant. He lay on the ground, gasping for air, the field swimming in double vision. Then he heard a shrill whistle.

"Bickle!" Paul screamed. "Off my practice field! Now! You're going to run hills 'til you drop, boy. And once you drop, I'm going to scrape you off the grass and make you run some more. Now get out of my sight!"

Trevor pushed himself off the ground, pausing long enough to flash Jacob an insidious smile. He then began a slow, deliberate trot over to the hills.

Paul now towered before the residue of the defense, his face red with anger.

"No one, and I repeat no one, lays a hand on this quarterback. Is that crystal clear? Is there any part of this message that needs to be clarified? The quarterback…is not…to be touched."

Paul then walked over to Jacob who lay prostrate on the field, a glazed look in his eyes. "You alright, son?" he asked, grabbing Jacob by the forearm and pulling him off the ground.

"Yeah, I think so," Jacob said, wincing in pain. Though, he could have sworn he heard something crackle as the coach yanked him up.

"That was inexcusable," Paul growled. "I will not risk injuring my quarterback on the practice field of all places. It won't happen again."

"I'll…be alright," Jacob said tentatively as he limped back to the huddle.

Off in the distance Jacob could see Trevor inching his way up the hill on the north side of the field. It *was* reassuring to know that his coach was intent on protecting him. But with a jaded Trevor Bickle prowling around on the defensive side of the ball, one thing was clear: the practice field was anything but safe.

Chapter 14

John Peterson sat in the Suburban in front of his apartment, gearing up for another tense exchange with his wife. The few words they'd spoken since Sunday had been harsh and terse. He needed more time to let things air out. The preaching episode was now behind them and, in time, things would return to normal. He hoped.

Pushing the front door open, he saw Rachel sitting on the couch reading. The apartment was strangely silent.

"Hey Rache," John said, smiling. "Where is everybody?"

"Well, Mom's taking a little catnap while the twins sleep. Jacob's still at practice. Jane and Hannah found some neighbor kids to play with, and David's out back, doing whatever it is that 12 year olds do."

"Gotcha," he said, setting his bag down and unlacing his shoes.

"Oh, before you get too settled, that guy from the church stopped by, Mr. Holler."

"He did?" John said, his eyes widening.

"Yeah, said he needed to talk to you. Sounded urgent. Said he'll be over at the church until about seven if you could stop by."

"Um. Ok. Did Mom see him?"

"No, she was asleep the whole time."

"Thank goodness," John muttered under his breath.

John tied his shoestrings and headed back out the door, his thoughts racing. Why would Buddy stop by his apartment? He'd fulfilled his commitment. There were no loose ends.

• • •

John pulled open the shiny glass door at Living Christ Ministries, and made for the familiar square of light about midway down the hall off the main foyer. Once there, John stepped into the doorway and saw the administrator sitting at his desk, Bible sprawled before him, deep in study.

At John's appearance, Buddy rose slowly from his chair, a tentative smile on his face.

"Brother John. Thanks for stopping by."

John stepped into the office and met Buddy's outstretched hand.

"Not a problem at all," John said, flashing an uncomfortable smile of his own. "So, what's going on? My daughter said you wanted to see me, and that it was urgent."

Buddy chuckled softly and waved his hand at John.

"Did I say urgent? Urgent is an awfully strong word."

John felt his tensed muscles release as he slipped into the guest chair opposite Buddy.

"Well, what is it I can do for you Buddy?"

"Well, seems you created quite a stir with your sermon on Sunday," Buddy said, settling into his own chair.

"Oh?" John said, trying to mask the dread in his voice.

"I thought you might like to know that in the 24 hours since your sermon, my phone lines have been jammed. On Monday alone, I received 95 phone calls from members of my congregation."

John's heart skittered and then leaped into his throat. This was precisely what he had been afraid of. Someone in the congregation had discovered what he had foolishly hoped would never be revealed: the identity of his religion. And the news had quickly spread. He braced himself for what was sure to be a stinging rebuke.

"Do you know why they were calling, Brother John?"

"Uh, no, but I imagine that you're going to tell me," he said, his voice faltering.

"They were all calling about the same exact thing. How do I put this...?"

Buddy's eyes fell to the Bible in front of him, his eyebrows drawing together. Acid began to churn in John's stomach.

"Well, the long and the short is, they loved your sermon on Sunday. They all want you back. Whatever it is you're selling, they're buying. I don't think I've ever seen anything quite like it. Don't get me wrong. Lester Le Haye was a master. But your abilities may go beyond even Lester. It wasn't just your charisma, or your presence. You had that, of course, in spades. It was your words. They were imbued with some sort or power. The way these folks tell it, they didn't just hear your words. They felt them. They internalized them. Your sermon made them want to do better. Be better. Whatever it is you brought with you on Sunday, these folks want more of it. They want more Brother John."

"Want more of *me*? You mean, like another sermon?" John said in shocked disbelief. "You know that's impossible Buddy. You and I had a deal. This was one time only. I couldn't have been any more clear on that point."

Buddy immediately raised both hands as if to parry John's hasty refusal.

"I know John. I know that's what we agreed upon. But the response has been overwhelming. Your words touched souls in there on Sunday. You transformed that assembly hall. They're all coming back, and from the sound of it, they're bringing friends."

John was shaking his head as his face drooped into a frown.

"Buddy, if you had any idea of the turmoil your first invitation created in my life, you wouldn't be asking me to do this."

"Yeah, I guess I still don't understand the sticking point there, but..."

John cut him off. "Maybe, just maybe, if I walk out of here today, and never come back, I can steady the boat and repair the relationship with my wife. She was totally against this. She begrudgingly relented only after I prayed about it and got God's approval. But for her, it was always a one-time deal."

Buddy's eyes suddenly widened.

"So, you're telling me that God approved of you preaching to my congregation?"

"That's right. It was a very clear manifestation. Couldn't quite convince my wife of that, but to me it was clear as day."

"And when God gave you this response, what did he say?"

"He simply said 'Preach my gospel.'"

"Ok. And when he said 'Preach my gospel.', did he put any time parameters or constraints upon it?"

John squirmed in his seat as he considered where Buddy was heading with this. After an uncomfortable pause, John said, "Uh, no. There were no time parameters. He just said 'Preach my gospel.'"

A faint smile dimpled the corners of Buddy's mouth.

"Don't you see John? God's behind all of this. I could see that the moment I heard you preach. The dozens of phone calls I received? Those folks could see it too. God gave you an open-ended invitation to preach here because this is where He needs you. Do you really think it's a coincidence that your car just happened to break down right down the road from our church? In God's plan, there's no such thing as coincidence."

John sat in his chair, a dark cloud gathering about him. There was no denying the open-ended nature of his confirmation. But what Buddy was asking him to do was impossible. With luck, and another couple of weeks of major reparations, his wife's frazzled nerves would be restored, and their relationship set aright. To accept another invitation to preach would take them back to square one…or worse.

"I'm sorry Buddy. This just isn't going to happen. My top priority is my family. I wish I could help you."

John rose from his chair and extended his hand towards Buddy. Buddy likewise rose, only his hand did not extend. Instead it went up to his chin as he appraised John one final time. After an awkward moment, John's hand fell back to his side.

"You know John. You've got some things to sort through here. You've got an incredible amount of talent and, heaven knows, this congregation needs you. But I can't impose my paradigm on you. In the end, you've got to figure out God's will on this."

"I appreciate your perspective Buddy."

Buddy came around the desk and put his arm around John's shoulder as they walked together to his door.

"You're a good man Brother John. I can sense it. But listen to God on this one. I think he's trying to tell you something."

"Thank you Buddy. And again, I appreciate the opportunity. It's been….interesting."

John stepped through the door, turned and began walking down the long dark corridor towards the church's foyer. As he made his way down the hall he was stopped by the sound of Buddy's voice.

"One more thing," Buddy said.

John stopped in his tracks. "What's that?" he said, turning his head.

"Matthew 6: 31-33."

John paused, and looked at the empty space above his head as if trying to place the scripture. He could not.

"Got it," John replied, and then continued down the hall and out the door.

• • •

Out in the parking lot, John leaned against his car, reflecting upon the exchange as Buddy's scripture reference resounded through his mind. He quickly pulled out his smartphone, tapped the Gospel Library icon, and pulled up Matthew 6: 31-33. He began to read: "Therefore take no thought, saying, What shall we eat? or, What shall we drink? or, Wherewithal shall we be clothed? (For after all these things do the Gentiles seek:) for your heavenly Father knoweth that ye have need of all these things. But seek ye first the kingdom of God, and his righteousness; and all these things shall be added unto you."

After reading the verses, John re-read them for good measure. They were verses with which he was very familiar. In fact, he'd quoted them frequently on his mission. But why was *Buddy* referencing them *now*?

As the words echoed through his mind, John felt a subtle lightness begin to suffuse his being. After another 30 seconds, he began to feel as if gravity had relinquished control of his body. John suddenly realized that the disquiet he had felt in Buddy's office had simply disappeared. Peace and calm now filled the void. But why?

As he stood reflecting upon the singularity of the experience, the words of the final verse flashed through his mind: "But seek ye first the kingdom of God, and his righteousness; and all these things shall be added unto you."

"But seek ye first the kingdom of God…and all these things shall be added unto you," he repeated out loud. What *exactly* was Buddy driving at? For the next several minutes he stood there, leaning against the car, puzzling over Buddy's intent.

And then, all at once, it hit him. Of course! God's original mandate had been simple and direct. He'd been told to "Preach my gospel." By referencing this scripture, Buddy was simply imploring John to surrender to this injunction. If John did that, God's promise was that everything else in his life would fall into place, even his relationship with Sarah. That was the answer!

John turned his eyes upon the enormous edifice before him, scanning upwards until they rested upon the enormous, shiny cross at the building's apex. And that's when he made the connection. This was the tabernacle within which he would carry out the very thing he had been commanded to do: preach the gospel of Jesus Christ. Was this not the very purpose for which he had consecrated two years of his life in Italy?

Propelled by a wave of euphoria, John sprinted back through the glass doors, down the hall, and into Buddy's office. Buddy looked up with a jerk, startled by the figure charging into his office.

"Brother John? Everything ok?"

"Never better Buddy, never better. I'll be here on Sunday. Let everyone know. I'm coming back."

The look of surprise on Buddy's face had no sooner appeared than John was spinning about and charging back through the door. Buddy sat in his chair too stunned to move. After a few moments of paralysis, his cheeks lifted into a smile. He picked up the phone and started punching numbers.

"Yeah Fred. I'm going to need you to drop by the chapel after all. Yeah, that's right. The sooner the better."

• • •

As John pulled open the apartment door, all was quiet. Rachel was still sitting on the couch, engrossed in a book. As he stepped through the door, she looked up and smiled.

"Everyone still doing what they were doing?" John asked.

"For the most part," she replied. "Except for Mom and the twins. She woke up about ten minutes ago and took the twins with her to visit another sister in the ward."

John was a little crestfallen. He had hoped he could speak to Sarah right away. The sooner he could explain what God had told him, the better. He would have to allay her fears, but after a second manifestation in as many weeks, there could be no doubt he was doing God's bidding.

Anxious to make headway on his sermon, John made his way towards the tiny desk in their cramped bedroom. Just as he pulled open the door, he heard a ping. He dug into his pants pocket and pulled out his smartphone. The script at the bottom of his screen signaled the arrival of a text message. He pressed a button and saw it was from Sarah. He punched a few buttons and within seconds, he saw a picture fire onto his screen. It was a picture of the enormous marquee outside of Living Christ Ministries. In huge, black, two foot letters, John could read a message. It said:

THIS SUNDAY
BROTHER JOHN IS BACK!

At the very bottom of his screen, he could see the brief text that accompanied the picture. It simply read: "John, what have you done?"

CHAPTER 15

The wave of spiritual energy John had been riding suddenly collapsed beneath him when he saw those five stark, pixilated words. In an instant, all the dark and foreboding thoughts, formerly vanquished, came rushing back.

"What *have* I done?" he wondered aloud.

How could he have been so reckless? How easy would it have been to simply confer with Sarah before giving Buddy the final ok? Of course she was furious. He felt a film of sweat lace out across his forehead as he contemplated damage control. But then he caught himself. There was no denying that he'd received a second spiritual confirmation. It had been as clear as day. God had revealed his will, and John was simply obeying. *Seek ye first the kingdom of God.* Of course he had done the right thing. Even if the timing of the marquee was unfortunate and mismanaged, it didn't change the broader picture: God had given him a task to perform. And he would answer the call. Sarah would need time. But she *could* come around. She would *have* to come around.

• • •

John sat on his bed, his mind racing, bracing for Sarah's arrival. Within ten minutes he heard the faint jingling of keys. He peeked out of the bedroom and saw Sarah step through the front door, Joseph and Sadie under foot. He ventured gingerly out of the bedroom and into the hallway that adjoined the living room. From there, he padded past Rachel and into the kitchen. There he saw Sarah, back turned, removing dishes from the cupboard.

"I'm sorry you had to find out that way," John said softly.

He was met with silence. Sarah continued about her activity as if John had said nothing at all. As if he simply weren't there.

"I wanted to be the first to tell you. I had no idea about the marquee. I mean, I must have gotten your text 20 minutes after I left Buddy's office. And when I left Buddy's office the marquee was…"

"Just drop it John. I have nothing to say to you."

Her words pounded into John's chest with a blunt trauma that left him breathless. The emotional alienation of last week was trying, but this would prove to be far worse. He stood in the kitchen doorway, a surge of heat rising within him, anxious to say something, but fearful of making things worse. She continued about her activity in silence, the angst in the room ratcheting up by the second.

John stepped gingerly across the kitchen and put his hand on Sarah's shoulder. The instant he did so she whirled around. And that's when he noticed it. Her eyes were red and puffy. She'd been crying.

"John. I have nothing to say to you right now," she said, a raw rage in her voice.

He winced, as if he'd been struck.

"But Sarah, you have to let me explain."

"John, it doesn't matter what you say. It's obvious you're not interested in my input. You've made it clear that when it comes to making decisions about the welfare of this family, you're flying solo."

John cringed. In 18 years of marriage, he couldn't remember an exchange like this. And then he knew there would be no winning Sarah over. There would be no persuading or compromise. There was only retreat.

"Good enough sweetheart. When you're ready to talk, I'm ready to listen. Until then, I'll give you some space."

John treaded quietly out of the kitchen. He walked past Rachel who sat pinned to the sofa, her body frozen in place, her eyes wide, fixed to an invisible spot on the opposite wall.

Once in his bedroom, he sat down at his desk, anxious to chip away at the Sunday deadline that was now looming over his head. But the words didn't come easily. A maelstrom of thoughts bandied about in his head, none of which was fodder for an inspirational sermon. He tried to brush it all aside. His marriage would not right itself before his Sunday deadline. He would have to forge ahead, buoyed by his faith and the hope that his second revelation in as many weeks had, in fact, come from God.

CHAPTER 16

"No John, we won't be coming with you. The children are coming with me, to our church where they belong," Sarah said, her voice hard and bitter.

"You're not coming to my sermon?" John asked, stung by Sarah's sudden proclamation.

"John, I'm not going to keep my children out of church, just so you can preach your sermons. God wants *our* family to go to *our* church. I mean, how much longer can this go on?"

Her tone suggested the matter was not up for discussion. Her first words to John in nearly a week had served only to push them further apart.

"Uh, anyone mind giving me a ride?" John said.

"Jacob can drop you off. I'm sure one of your fawning congregants can bring you home."

Her words were cold and defiant. John felt all prospects for an uplifting sermon slipping away.

"Um. Ok then. Well Jake, we better get a move on it. Don't want to be late."

• • •

As Jacob pulled to a stop in front of Living Christ Ministries, his mouth gaped open.

"Dad, this is an absolute madhouse. What's going on here today?"

"Uh, that's a really good question," John said, his eyes scanning the parking lot.

"Are all these people here to see *you*?"

"Uh, yeah, that…would appear to be the case."

"Dad, do you have any idea what you're doing? You're about to preach to a packed house of non-Mormons. Dad, there's got to be half the town here today."

John gave the parking lot another appraising glance. "Yeah, you might be right. A little better than last week, huh?"

"Uh, Dad," Jacob said, worry in his voice. "They don't know you're Mormon, do they?"

John fell silent as he watched a small family pull one of the shiny glass doors open and step through it.

"No Jake. They don't. They don't know the first thing about me or our religion."

"Yeah, well I hope you know what you're doing here. Things are going pretty well for me right now, and I'd kind of like to not crash and burn at this point."

"I know Jacob. I don't want any of us to crash and burn. But Heavenly Father has asked me to do this. We just have to trust that He is running the show."

"Alright Dad. I'm counting on you to not mess up my life."

"It's all going to work out. Trust me on that. Now get outta here. Oh, and thanks for the lift."

As John stepped through the glass doors, he was met by a wave of energy that set his nerves atingle. Inside the cavernous foyer, masses of clamoring congregants were pressing towards the doors of the assembly hall. John stepped into the crowd and, after five minutes of herding, made it into the chapel. Halfway down the aisle, he stopped and scanned the congregation, soaking in the wildly electric ambience. It was now 8:50 a.m., and congregants were already vying for the few remaining seats in the very top rows. A nervous sweat broke out across his forehead as he contemplated what he was about to do. John Peterson, the only

Mormon Elder in the town of Mayfield, was about to preach before a capacity crowd at the largest church in three counties. And they didn't have the faintest clue of who he really was.

He continued down the aisle, and then worked his way over to the door on the left side of the stage. Halfway there, he felt a small tug on his elbow. He turned and saw a teenage girl with braces and pig tails smiling before him. He didn't recognize her.

"Hey, you're Brother John, aren't you?"

John was still getting used to the "Brother John" title after a lifetime of Brother Peterson.

"Yes, yes I am," he said meeting her outstretched hand.

The young lady squealed with delight and then started clapping her splayed fingers together and jumping up and down. Amid all the commotion, other congregants had turned and begun to take notice. Soon, heads were turning and fingers pointing. Slowly a rumble of excitement began to build throughout the assembly hall.

Embarrassed at the sudden attention, John released the girl's hand, gave a quick wave to the crowd, and then hurried towards the door to the left of the stage. He yanked it open, slipped through it, and pulled it shut. As he leaned his back against the inside of the door, he could hear his pulse pounding in his ears. What was *that* all about? His reception in the assembly hall was more befitting a celebrity. Maybe even a rock star. All this after a single sermon? John said a silent prayer of thanksgiving that his wife had opted out this morning.

After a few anxious moments alone backstage, John saw the door pull open. Buddy Holler stepped through it, a broad grin on his face.

"Can you believe this crowd? I've never seen anything like it. Lester could fill them up, but never anything like this. It's like sardines out there. God bless you John. I think our financial concerns just may be over."

John's face tightened. He then shot Buddy a withering glare.

"But you know that's not why I'm here, right Buddy? This isn't about filling the coffers of Living Christ Ministries. It's about helping people and doing the right thing. You do know that, don't you?"

Sensing John's umbrage, Buddy went into damage control. "Of course I do John. That's why we're here. We're here to lift souls. Forgive the administrator side of me coming out there. Force of habit I guess."

"No worries," John said. "As long as we don't lose sight of why we're here."

"Of course," Buddy assured. "We're in the business of saving souls."

John winced again. It was an unfortunate use of words, especially given the ministry's financial scandals. Buddy Holler was turning into a true enigma. Every time John felt like Buddy was coming into focus, his words somehow betrayed him. Here was a man who, most days, sat sequestered away in his tiny office studying his Bible. Yet, he couldn't manage to tear his attention away from the financial component of the ministry. Not for a single minute. John thought about it for a moment and then shrugged off the apparent contradiction. He had bigger fish to fry. Like somehow meeting the exalted expectations of 1,500 congregants waiting just beyond the curtain.

• • •

When John concluded his sermon, he was met by a deafening chorus of Amens from the congregation. His marriage was starting to unravel yet, miraculously, God's power continued to sustain him. He gathered up his notes, grabbed his Bible, and then worked his way towards the safety of the offstage enclave. But before he could take five steps, he found himself thronged on all sides by congregants who were frantically shouting his name and shoving their hands in his direction.

Some, he would learn, were there to lavish him with praise. Others just wanted to shake the hand of Mayfield's rising star. Many had come laden with heavy burdens. These he greeted, hearing of their struggles, and imparting words of comfort and counsel. With each new tale of spiritual woe, John became more acutely aware of the painful inadequacies of Lester Le Haye's ministry. They had been drawn in by Lester's magnetism, yet they had left his chapel bereft of the spiritual direction they so earnestly sought. The evidence was standing all about him, clamoring for a moment of his time, a consoling word. Lester could preach a rousing sermon. John had seen that first hand. But, with each new tale of spiritual bankruptcy, John became more and more convinced: Lester Le Haye had not fed his sheep.

CHAPTER 17

"Once again, you delivered the goods."

The assembly hall was now empty, except for the owner of the voice coming from somewhere near the back of the chapel. John turned towards the sound and saw a familiar face walking slowly towards him.

"Hello Ethan," John said awkwardly.

Ethan's face broke into a smile as he approached and extended his hand. John met his hand tentatively, and managed a halfhearted smile of his own.

"Not only does he preach with the tongue of fire, but he ministers. An example worthy of emulation."

"What can I do for you Ethan?" John said, not giving an inch.

The smile disappeared from Ethan's face. He was suddenly all business.

"Listen, I feel like we got off on the wrong foot last week."

"Look Ethan, I understand what you're trying to do," John interrupted. "I understand the position you're in. I'd really love to help. But like I told you, the timing couldn't be worse."

Ethan persisted. "Come on Brother John, hear me out here. Look, I've got a 2,000 pound anvil hanging above my head, and the rope's starting to fray. God talked to me. He told me you could help. It was as clear as day. Haven't *you* ever received a revelation Brother John?"

John froze. He had, in fact, received revelations. It was just those revelations that had turned his world upside down. He paused for a moment, considering Ethan's words.

"Yes Ethan, I have received revelations. What's your point?"

"Look, I don't mean to be a pest, but when God asks me to act, I do it. That's the story of my life. If you tell me no this week, I'll just be back next week. You're going to have a hard time shaking me Brother John."

John was beginning to chafe at Ethan's stubbornness and persistence. All he needed was a young kid pounding on him week after week. He had to get out of there. He had to get home. Home. His thoughts turned suddenly to Sarah. She would not be pleased with how things had gone today. The more he thought about it, the more Ethan seemed like a welcome reprieve.

"Alright Ethan. What exactly do you want from me?"

Ethan's eyes lit up. "Ok, great. For starters, I'm preaching in about half an hour. If you could just come have a listen, maybe we could establish some sort of baseline. You know, so you can figure out what it is you have to work with."

John thought about it for a moment. "Alright Pastor," he said, relenting. "I'll come have a listen, but on one condition."

"Anything Brother John."

"I'm going to need a ride home afterwards."

A wide smile spread across Ethan's face.

"*That* I think I can manage."

• • •

Within a few minutes they were pulling into the gravel parking lot at the Community Church of Christ. As John got out of the car, he surveyed the small, spare building. In the bright light of the midmorning sun, the building's dilapidated condition was evident. The siding was split and corroding in spots and the roof's shingles hung limply out of alignment.

"Well, this is where it all happens," Ethan said as they got out of the car.

As they stepped through the front door, John could make out the rudiments of a very makeshift chapel. Folding metal chairs were arranged in two sections, each no more than seven or eight across and five deep.

A spindly wooden pulpit stood before the chairs, behind which hung a rudely framed portrait of Jesus.

The size of the chapel and its modest furnishings were faintly reminiscent of the meetinghouses John had attended in Italy. He suddenly grew nostalgic as he regarded the lone families scattered throughout the mostly empty chapel.

While Ethan busied himself in his office, John settled into an aisle chair on the back row. As he sat there musing over the similarities between this chapel and those from his mission, he could practically hear the words: "Anziano Peterson, I know it's last minute, but we need your help. Fratello Rizzo was supposed to speak, but he is not here. Can you speak for 15 minutes on tithing?"

Every worship meeting he attended was another opportunity to hone his craft. He quickly grew accustomed to extemporizing before tiny congregations of Italian saints. It was within those tiny chapels that he forged the skills he now brought to bear at Living Christ Ministries.

By 10:55 a.m., a total of three small families had settled into the modest grouping of chairs. John honed in on a young woman juggling a baby on her lap. She sat by herself, her sad features drawing her face out. John quickly surmised that this was Ethan's wife and baby. So, figure two other tithe-paying families in the congregation. It was suddenly looking very grim for the future of Ethan's ministry.

At 11 a.m., Ethan stepped through the door at the back of the chapel and strode down the center aisle and up to the pulpit.

"Brothers and sisters," he began. Ethan seemed to cringe as his voice echoed off the walls of the embarrassingly empty chapel. Such a formal tone before such a scant congregation seemed strangely out of place. The size of the congregation seemed more like a small gathering of friends than a church service.

"I welcome you to our Sabbath day worship service here at the Community Church of Christ," he continued.

After a few brief announcements, an opening hymn and a prayer, Ethan shuffled a few papers nervously before him, and began to speak. John looked around the chapel, gauging the room's energy as Ethan began. The ten or so congregants sat listlessly, shifting uncomfortably in their hard metal chairs, steeling themselves for what was about to unfold.

Ethan spent the next 30 minutes dividing his time between four parables from the New Testament. From the outset, one thing became very clear to John. Ethan had a marvelous command of the scriptures. His commentaries were both insightful and relevant. Yet, while doctrinally sound, they utterly failed to inspire. Most sermons, by dint of their reliance on scripture, could score *some* points with the congregation. This piece of work had failed to do even that.

At 11:40 a.m., the meeting came mercifully to a close, and the families began a slow, death march out of the chapel. When the room was finally empty, Ethan walked slowly towards John, his head hanging in defeat.

"You see what I mean?" he said, in a tone of resignation. "What's your diagnosis?"

"Have a seat," John said, motioning to the empty chair in front of him.

Ethan grabbed it, spun it about so it was now facing John and then collapsed into it.

"Why don't we start with the positives?" John began.

Ethan's countenance seemed to brighten a shade. "Ok," he agreed.

"Your talk *was* scripturally based. That's a solid foundation of which you need not be ashamed. You have an outstanding command of the scriptures and their meaning. That's another point in your favor."

John paused, a look of hesitation crinkling his eyes.

"Go ahead John, lay it all out there. I can't fix it unless you tell me what's broken," Ethan pressed.

John nodded his head in assent. "Alright then. Here goes. It's not so much what you are doing as what you aren't doing. For starters, let's talk about the elements of a good sermon."

With this, Ethan plucked a small notebook and pen from his breast pocket, and trained his focus on John.

"First of all, I want you to see in your mind's eye the most memorable sermon you've ever witnessed."

Ethan looked up into the air as if watching a movie unfold in his mind.

"Alright," he said, "I'm there."

"Ok, so you're watching the one that touched you the most, the one that really moved you."

"Even as we speak. Happened about two and a half hours ago."

John blushed for a second and then continued. "You're very kind. Ok, so what was it about my sermon that made an impression on you?"

"I don't know. It just seemed to suck me in."

"Great. So, the first rule of a good sermon is that if your congregation is asleep, they won't hear your message. "

"Right."

"That's our first problem. The way you structured today's sermon, it pains me to say, was utterly sleep inducing."

Whatever trace of light that had accented Ethan's face was now swallowed by a look of complete resignation.

"To that end," John continued, "you have to realize that you've got about 30 seconds to make your case to the congregation that your sermon is worth staying awake for. I don't care what you do, you've got to convince them that it's worthwhile for them to not tune you out."

The look on Ethan's increasingly malleable face had transformed into one of resolve. His brow was furrowed, his hand scribbling feverishly on his pad. "Go on," Ethan said, suddenly a picture of focus and concentration.

"Second, I'm grateful that you appreciate the importance of using the scriptures in your sermons. There is no question that you know your stuff. Scriptures by themselves, however, do not a sermon make. Scriptural references need to be coupled with a few other very important ancillary tools. What are we talking about here? Analogies, stories, personal experiences. All indispensible cogs in any good sermon."

"Keep going," Ethan said, a trail of ink streaming across his notebook. "This is good stuff."

"Your real problem seems to be, and excuse me if I'm being overly candid, is that all you do is read scriptures and make personal commentary. This is the number one recipe for losing your congregation. I've seen it in my own church a hundred times."

"Instead of starting with the scriptures, why not start with an experience, a story or even an analogy? Give them something they can sink their teeth into, something they can relate to. Once you've got their attention, then you can start expounding on scripture. The whole goal is to leverage these tools so that, by the time you introduce your scripture, they're viewing it through a whole new window of understanding. But it's a window of your creation, Ethan."

"I'm with you, I'm with you," Ethan said, flipping his first page and starting on his second.

"Put differently, think of your stories, experiences and analogies as fertilizer for their spirits. Once their spirits have been sufficiently fertilized, only then can you sow the seeds of scripture with any degree of success. By spending the first portion of your sermon on things they can actually relate to, you provide them a prism through which to interpret the scripture in a way that will be meaningful to them."

"Ok, so be generous with the stories, analogies, and personal experiences. Got it," Ethan said.

"Third, you might want to liven things up with a bit of humor. Now, there's a fine line here that you have to be very careful not to cross. Humor is good, but this is not stand-up comedy. There's a time and a place for that, and it's not on Sundays from the pulpit.

"What we're looking for are accents of humor. Spice it up just enough to keep their attention, but not enough to compromise the spirit of the meeting. Because, at the end of the sermon, if your congregants are not feeling the Holy Ghost, they won't be motivated to change their lives. And, at the end of the day, isn't that what we're all about?"

"That's *exactly* right," Ethan said, looking up from his pad. "That's why I'm here. That's what it's been all about since the beginning. Changing lives. I just can't change lives if I can't get people in the seats."

"And keep them there," John added. "Now, I want to ask you a question. About how many congregants do you think show up at Living Christ Ministries every week?"

"I don't know, twelve, maybe fifteen hundred?"

"And how do you think they were able to attract these numbers over the years?"

"That's what I'm trying to figure out," Ethan said wistfully.

"When you drive around Mayfield, do you see any billboards advertising for Living Christ Ministries?"

"No, not a one."

"Then how do they fill that place up?"

Ethan frowned for a second and then spoke.

"It's got to be word of mouth. Friends bringing friends. Family bringing family."

"That's exactly right," John said. "If you follow the formula I showed you, you're going to start filling this place up. It won't happen overnight, but it will happen. People will hear you and they'll start spreading the word."

Ethan was nodding his head, hanging on every word.

"Ethan, you're a great guy. You're young, you're energetic, and I can tell that you really want to make a change in people's lives. You're great with people and you love Jesus. The only missing element is a good sermon. And, unfortunately, when you're trying to fill a chapel, that's the one thing you cannot afford to go without. Get that down and this ministry is going to start growing."

Ethan's face had the appearance of one having a revelatory experience. He seemed to be emerging from a deep, dark dungeon into the vast, liberating light of truth.

"This is exactly what I needed to know," Ethan said. "I don't know how to thank you."

"I do," John said. "Incorporate everything we talked about today into next week's sermon."

A huge smile spread across Ethan's face. "Brother John," he said, extending his hand, "you've got yourself a deal."

Chapter 18

"I know today's our anniversary John, but I'm just not in the mood to go out," Sarah said flatly.

"Are you serious? We haven't missed celebrating our anniversary in 18 years," John replied.

"Yeah, well, I don't know what to tell you. I'm just not at a place where I feel like we have anything to celebrate."

Sarah was drying dishes in the kitchen, her back turned to John. Two more days had passed in silence since their tense Sabbath day exchange. Somehow, some way, John had to break through to her. He reached out his hand to touch her shoulder and found, to his surprise, that she didn't pull away. It was the first time they'd touched in over a week. He felt that familiar energy crawling its way up his arm as his touch lingered. As his hand loitered on her shoulder, she slowly turned around to face him.

Her eyes were red and puffy as if she'd been crying all week, yet her eyes were dry. The redness had taken up permanent residence on her visage of late. Sarah seemed to be in a near constant state of mourning. He felt a bolt of pain as he considered that *he* was the source of her sadness.

Sensing her acquiescence, he slowly pulled her in. He gently interlocked his hands around her slender waist, studying the delicate features of her face.

"Listen, it'll be just you and me. I've got something I want to show you," he whispered.

After meeting his penetrating gaze, she averted her glance.

"John, I…"

Before she could utter another word, he planted a soft kiss on her lips.

Their heads now touching, John strived to regain eye contact.

"I'm asking you on a date Sarah. Just you and me."

She suddenly broke his grip and turned around, and he felt the icy wall once again rise up between them.

"Fine. But I don't want to be out all night," she said, her words short and clipped.

Despite her icy response, John couldn't suppress the wellspring of joy that was rising within him.

"No problem. A quick dinner and I'll whisk you right home."

John walked out of the kitchen, an extra spring in his step, his soul infused with a fresh, sunny optimism.

• • •

John had been surveying the acceptable dining establishments in Mayfield for a few days. Even before Sarah's acceptance, he had settled upon a venue. At 6 p.m. sharp, John nosed their car into the parking lot at Funicelli's Trattoria Italiana. He had wooed Sarah over vintage Italian cuisine 18 years earlier. It was time to dig into his old bag of tricks.

The maître d seated them at a candlelit table in a secluded corner of the restaurant. After taking a few bites of grissini, John grabbed Sarah's hands. Her hands felt cold and unyielding as he enveloped them in his own. He could tell he still had a ways to go.

"Listen, I've been praying about this whole preaching thing, and I've come to a decision."

"Go on," Sarah said, her voice still devoid of emotion.

John released her hands and then stuffed his own into his back pocket and pulled out a piece of paper. He unfolded it and then laid it out before her.

"Any idea what this is?" John asked.

She scrutinized the sheet before her, trying to make sense of the vast sea of words and numbers.

"Why don't you just tell me John," she said. He could sense he was already losing her.

"This, my love, is a loan approval. Remember the house I showed you when we first came to town?"

"Uh-huh," she said, her eyes slowly coming to life.

"Well that house can be ours. All I need is the ok, from you."

Her eyes met his briefly, but then returned to her hands.

"I just don't know how this is going to work, John. With you preaching, there's still so much danger. We can't risk buying a house at this point. If we buy a house and then your little secret leaks out, it could ruin us."

"That gets me to my next point," John said. "I've decided…"

Just then a young lady in her late teens stepped up to their table.

"Buona sera. Mi chiamo Roxanne and I'll be taking care of you this evening. Can I start you off with any beverages, or perhaps a wine list?"

John looked up at her and said, "I think a couple of waters with lemons will probably do the trick."

As John's eyes met Roxanne's, her eyes flickered with recognition. Suddenly an enormous smile spread across her face.

"Brother John. Is that you?"

"John Peterson," he said, meeting her outstretched hand. "And this is my wife Sarah," he said motioning across the table.

"Oh…my…gosh," she said, shaking Sarah's hand briefly and then returning her gaze to John. "I can't believe you're in my section! That sermon you gave on Sunday just sent shivers down my spine. I've never, ever thought about charity that way."

"Well I'm so glad you liked it Roxanne. It's our anniversary and we have a special thing for Italian food. We're glad you're waiting on us."

"Well I'll be sure to take really good care of you then," she said, batting her eyes and trying to suppress a giggle.

After briefly looking over their menus, they placed their orders.

"Be back in a few," Roxanne chirped as she twirled about and bounced off towards the kitchen.

"What was *that* all about?" Sarah asked, her tone suspicious.

"Don't know," John said coyly. "She…must have liked my sermon."

"John, that didn't look like someone who liked a sermon. That looked like a 13 year old girl who just met Justin Bieber."

John tried to stifle a smile but failed. "I don't know what to tell you. She must have really, really liked it."

"Hmm," she said, still perplexed.

Within ten minutes Roxanne was back, ebullience undiminished, laden with plates of pasta. She laid the heaping plates in front of them, flashed John one last star-struck glance, and returned to the kitchen.

As John twirled his fettuccini noodles onto his fork, he became dimly aware of another figure stepping up to their table. John looked to his left and beheld a tiny, gray haired woman appraising him, a smile pulling at her mouth. Before saying a word, she reached down and grabbed John's free hand from the table.

"God bless you Brother John," she said, her eyes twinkling. "God bless you."

She looked over at Sarah who by this point had dropped her fork, a dumbfounded look on her face.

"You've got a real keeper here Mrs. Peterson. A real keeper."

Sarah managed a weak smile. "Thank you Mrs..."

"*Ms.* Janice Humphries," she said, turning again to John. "I just wanted to tell you how badly we've needed you at Living Christ Ministries. Lester was nice enough, but he just left so many questions unanswered. When you preach...I feel different. Like my whole world's been set in order. I don't know what Buddy's plan is for a new pastor, but you would certainly have my vote."

"Well, you're very kind Janice," John said, smiling.

"Anyway, I'll let you lovebirds get back to your dinner. Just wanted to say we love you. I speak for more than myself you know."

She gave one last smile, winked at John, and then walked back to a table filled with other gray heads, all of whom were twinkling in John's direction.

"John, what in the world did you say in church on Sunday? And how is it that everyone in this restaurant knows who you are?"

By this time, John's face had flushed bright pink.

"Uh, how do I put this?" he said. "The turnout on Sunday was a little more robust than the week before."

Sarah's eyes bored into her husband. "What are we talking about here?"

John paused, reluctant to ruin an evening that seemed to be trending in the right direction. After playing with his food for another five seconds, he lifted his eyes.

"Um…standing room only?" He grimaced as the words left his mouth, bracing for Sarah's response.

"John, are you serious? The chapel was full…"

"I'm terribly sorry to interrupt," came another voice.

They both turned to see a young mother jostling a baby on her hip.

"Brother John, my name is Heather Dunn. I'm not sure what Mr. Holler's plan is for next week, but I'd be tickled pink if you came back."

Before John could respond, Heather giggled, turned on her heals and hurried to catch her party as they filed out the door.

"John. This is nuts!" Sarah hissed. "Not only does everyone know you, but they worship the ground you walk on!"

The pink in John's face had turned to crimson. "Honestly hon, I… don't know what to say."

As Sarah sat in her chair, she stared off into space, trying to formulate a response. John could feel a prickly heat rising within him as he waited for her next words.

"So, you gave this sermon, you were received to great fanfare, and then what happened?"

"Do you really want to know?" John said, wincing.

After a period of silence, she cracked an almost imperceptible smile that sent a thrill up John's spine. "Yes, I really want to know," she said.

"Uh, well, after I finished my sermon, I closed my scriptures, and began walking towards the exit stage right. Before I had taken five steps, dozens of congregants had rushed onto the stage and hemmed me in. I spent the next half hour meeting and greeting and giving counsel. Much better that you weren't there."

"Why do you say that?" Sarah said with genuine curiosity.

"You know, the more people that know me, the more that hear my sermons, the greater the repercussions once the truth leaks out. Which is why I've made a decision."

"Decision?" she said, her eyes narrowing.

"Before anything cataclysmic happens, we cut our losses. We call it a day before anything really goes wrong."

"Just like that? Finito?"

"That's right. I'm letting Buddy know immediately after my sermon on Sunday."

"Hi there!" It was Roxanne this time. "Just here to see if I can interest you in any dessert before you leave."

John's eyes met Sarah's briefly and then turned back to Roxanne.

"Not tonight. I think we're all set."

John dug his wallet out of his back pocket and produced a credit card.

"Oh no, Brother John. No need for that. Someone from your congregation is picking up your bill."

They turned in the direction Roxanne was pointing and saw an elderly couple sitting across the room. John and Sarah rose from their table, and made their way over to their elderly benefactors.

"You know, that was very kind of you, but not necessary," John said warmly.

"Oh no. It was *absolutely* necessary," the man said. "The spirit you've brought to that church these past two weeks is transforming that congregation. You're a godsend brother John."

"Sent straight from heaven," chimed the man's wife, a glint in her eye.

"Well, you're both very kind for saying so, *and* for picking up our tab. We don't know how to thank you."

"Show up on Sunday, young man, and we'll call it even," the man said with a chuckle.

"You've got yourself a deal. Consider it done," John said, smiling and shaking both of their hands.

John turned and led Sarah past the other tables towards the exit, leaving a trail of turned heads and whispers in their wake. Once out in the cool air of the parking lot, Sarah drew even with John. As she did, their shoulders brushed together. John slowed his gait as if to encourage the close contact. As he did, her left index finger curled onto the fingers of his right hand. This was all the encouragement he needed. He quickly enveloped her hand in his and squeezed tightly. She looked up at him as tendrils of energy shot up his arm.

"Well, Brother John, it looks like you've created quite the stir here in Mayfield."

"Yes, that appears to be the case," he said.

"And you would give up all of that," she said, cocking her thumb back towards the restaurant, "just to make me happy? To let us move into a home? To spread some roots?"

"That's exactly what I'm saying."

"But all the accolades, all the fawning, the rock star status at the mega church? You would walk away from all of that for me?"

"Look sweetheart, this has always been about changing lives. It's nice to be a force for good in this world but if, at the end of the day, I'm not a force for good within the walls of my own home, then what am I really living for?"

"By the way," he said, as he opened her car door, "there's something I want to show you on the way home."

"Oh really?"

"That's right. If we're going to buy a house on Friday morning," he said jingling a set of keys, "I'd kind of like you to see it from the inside."

CHAPTER 19

John heard the light tapping and sprang up in his bed. He looked over at the alarm clock on his nightstand. It read 11:38 p.m. *Who in the world?* he thought. He looked over at Sarah and could sense by her breathing that the knocking had not awoken her. He threw the covers back, jammed his feet into his slippers and then padded lightly out of the bedroom. Once in the hallway he heard the knocking again, this time louder. He pulled up to the front door, and peered through the eyehole. On the other side of the door he could make out a small, female figure. He quickly unlocked the latch, turned the deadbolt and swung the door open.

The woman was short with brown curly hair, no older than forty. She was dressed in baggy sweats and, judging by her swollen eyes, had been crying.

"Brother John?" she said, her voice raspy and cracking.

"Yes?"

"My name is Jackie Williams. I know it's late and a terrible imposition," she said between sniffles, "but I had to talk to you."

John sensed movement off to his right. He turned and saw his bleary eyed spouse walking towards him, clad in her bathrobe.

"Sarah, it's Jackie Williams from...the congregation."

"Well for heaven's sake, invite her in."

"Won't you please come in?" John said, grabbing her by the elbow and pulling her through the door. Sarah led the way into the living room. As they walked past the picture of the temple on the wall to their left, John felt his stomach tighten. He was suddenly horrified by a single, overwhelming fact: evidence of their religion lay everywhere. Jackie fell heavily into the beige love seat while John and Sarah sat on the couch opposite her.

Now ensconced in her seat, Jackie had begun silently appraising a stack of blue books with gold lettering on the table before her. It was the residue from that morning's Book of Mormon study. John felt a flame of terror rise within him.

"I'm sorry," John said hastily. "Let me get these out of your way." John gathered them up and tucked them nervously under his arm. He walked over to the bookshelf and piled them on the top shelf, spines inward.

"No problem Brother John," she said, as if awakening from a temporary stupor.

She had been oblivious. The heavy burdens she was carrying had somehow inured her to the damning clues that lay all about her.

"Now," he said, relief settling across his face, "what can we do for you?"

"I do feel awful coming to your home at such a late hour," she began, "but I just didn't know where else to turn."

"No imposition at all," John assured her. "What's on your mind?"

She stared at her hands for a long, silent moment, and then raised her bloodshot eyes to John's.

"I guess I don't really know where to start."

"Why don't you start by telling me what's troubling you?"

She took a deep breath, as if inhaling a lung full of courage. Then she proceeded. "Well, it's my boy, Scotty. I think…I think I'm losing him. For good this time."

John's eyes narrowed. "Losing him? In what way?"

"Well, it all started when his father died two years ago. First it was the acting out in school. The grades followed. After a while we couldn't seem to see eye to eye on anything. He started staying out 'til all hours of the night. I revoked privileges, the like. Nothing seemed to help. I'd lock him in his room, and he'd sneak out the window. You know the story."

She paused briefly to wipe away tears and blot her nose with a tissue. John sat forward in his chair, nodding attentively.

"Then something changed," she said, pausing to gather her thoughts.

"Go on," John said.

"Oh, about six months after his daddy died, he somehow got it into his head he wanted to be a football player. Peer pressure I suppose. Given what was happening, I assumed any sort of structure would be a blessing. So, that August I started taking him to those two-a-day practices. You know, in that awful heat. And I'll be darned if I didn't start to see a difference. Almost immediately."

"Really?" John said, his eyebrows arching upwards.

"Oh yes. Coach Connelly whipped my boy right into shape. Scotty would come home from practice talking a little more softly. He'd lost that angry edge. He even started obeying his curfew. One day, he brought home a report card that knocked me clean out of my chair. Solid B's across the board."

"You're telling me *football* turned your son around?" John asked, suddenly intrigued.

"There was something about the discipline of those practices that reined him in. Coach Connelly took my boy under his wing. Almost like a surrogate father. Winning record or not, that man is a miracle worker in my book. You met Coach Connelly yet? He's in your congregation you know."

"You mean Living Christ Ministries?" John asked, suddenly surprised.

"Oh yes. Been going ever since he arrived. Don't know that Lester Le Haye was really his style. But, most of his church going players attend. As a former pastor, I guess he just likes to keep his finger on the religious pulse of the team. You know, monitor the message."

"Former pastor?" John said, his eyes spreading wide. The revelations were coming in flurries.

"Don't they tell you anything Brother John?" she said in amazement. "Paul Connelly was the pastor of his own congregation, right up until he became coach four years ago."

"So, what happened? Why the career change?" John prodded.

She lowered her voice to a whisper. "The word is, his wife found favor with another man in the congregation. He was so devastated by her betrayal that he abandoned the ministry. Swore he'd never preach another sermon. Couldn't bear to face his congregation every week. Just threw in the towel. It was a bona fide scandal."

"You are *kidding* me," he gasped.

"Oh no. About that same time Stan Carraway came along and asked Paul Connelly if he was interested in the head coaching position with the Mustangs. They played together in college about 20 years ago. Paul wanted to make a clean break and, for Stan, the timing couldn't have been any better. Given the incident."

"Uh, incident?" John asked.

"Brother John? Surely you know about the incident? It's practically part of town lore."

With each new disclosure, John was feeling more and more uninformed.

"Apparently there's a *lot* I don't know. Please, do proceed."

Buoyed by the prospect of a good story, Jackie's face began to animate.

"Well, it was five years ago. The varsity head coach back then was, of course, Frank Bellamy. In those days, Mayfield was *the* premier football program. A real powerhouse. Hadn't had a losing season in years. Well, one Friday night, after blowing out *another* division rival, Coach Bellamy decided to convene a little celebration at his house. Wasn't the first time, we would later find out. He personally invited 14 or 15 of his top players who, in turn, invited their girlfriends, some of them cheerleaders."

"Go on," John nodded.

"Well, the beer came out and the kegger of all keggers ensued. By midnight, drunken bodies were scattered all over the place. Bellamy, the players, the cheerleaders...all six sheets to the wind. Amazingly, eight of the players and a lone cheerleader were coherent enough to walk over to the high school and hotwire a school bus. That's when things really got interesting."

John looked over at Sarah. Her mouth hung open and there was terror in her eyes.

"After driving the school bus into the next county and doing donuts on the football field of their arch rival..."

"Can you do donuts in school bus?" Sarah gasped.

"Apparently so. It destroyed the field. But that was just the beginning Sister..."

"Peterson. Sarah Peterson"

"That was just the beginning Sister Sarah. After destroying the field, they crashed through a fence, and demolished the ticket box."

She paused for effect.

"Holy smokes," John said.

"It gets better, Brother John. Buckle your seat belt."

"Um…ok."

"After crisscrossing the county a few times, smashing mailboxes and ruining front lawns, someone decided they needed more beer. Only problem is, in these parts, no one sells beers after hours. Didn't stop 'em. They managed to plow the school bus into the Quick Stop over there on Highway 50. No one knows if that was their plan, or if they simply overshot their parking spot. Either way, there wasn't much left of the Quick Stop."

"Are you serious?" John said, now perched on the very edge of his seat.

"Did anyone get hurt?" Sarah said, aghast.

"The players grabbed a few cases of beer and then fled the scene, but they left someone behind. It was the cheerleader. She wasn't so lucky. She got the brunt of the crash. Spent weeks in the hospital with multiple compound fractures and a collapsed lung."

"Ok. So then what happened?" John said, his limbs stiff with suspense.

"Well, the cops investigated and multiple witnesses had them leaving Bellamy's home at the moment in question. The purchase of the alcohol was traced back to Bellamy who was implicated immediately. He pleaded no contest to reckless endangerment of minors and got away with no prison time, but huge fines and community service."

"How did we not know this?" Sarah said, turning to John in disbelief.

But Jackie wasn't done. "For Frank Bellamy, the alcohol was just the tip of the iceberg. When the school board started investigating, they discovered an undercurrent of corruption that went back years. Doctored transcripts, inflated grades, the like. But, most importantly, their investigations revealed that Frank Bellamy was a first rate recruiter. Half his team, as it turns out, didn't even live in the school district. He had been shipping players in from as far as two counties away. *That* was the real scandal. Made national news."

Sarah's face had drawn completely slack.

"Of course, the community was aghast. They demanded justice. The school board fired Frank Bellamy immediately. And, as you know, the pendulum always swings way back the other way. Folks were calling for the death penalty. You know, banish the program. So, in a last ditch effort to save the team, Stan Carraway brings in the preacher, Paul Connelly.

"So Paul comes in and in his first full week totally cleans house. The Mayfield 8, as they came to be called, were dismissed from the team outright. All recruited players were sent back to their home school districts. Paul wanted no part of the corruption of the Frank Bellamy era. He purged every last trace of it from the program. A clean slate. Problem was, he purged the team of every last ounce of talent. And, as I'm sure you're aware, they haven't had a winning season since."

John sat there, his chin pinned to his chest, his body limp.

Jackie continued, somberly this time. "So, as Paul took the reins of the program, he became the father figure for a lot of players including, eventually, my Scottie. He provided male leadership and discipline that many of these boys didn't have at home. People look at his record and laugh. But I'll tell you what, not so much as a J-walking ticket from those players since. Now that's what *I* call results."

"So, sounds like a happy ending. Where's the problem?" John asked.

"Brother John, I'm starting to get a real uneasy feeling. Something's different in that locker room this year. Scottie does tend to get a little rowdy over the summers, but Coach Connelly always finds a way to bring him back down to earth come football season. Well, he's been in two-a-days for nearly three full weeks now, and not only is his behavior not improving, it's getting worse."

"What do you mean?" John asked.

"Last Friday night, he came home at 2 a.m. I'd waited up all night, worried sick. Of course, when he came home, we had it out. I said some things I probably shouldn't have said, and then he stormed out. He didn't come home for two days. When he finally did, he walked straight into his room and slammed the door behind him."

"So who's he running with?" John asked.

"That's the worst part. They're other football players. Scottie doesn't know it, but I see the texts. I know exactly who he's running with."

"His teammates?"

"Yeah, and that's what terrifies me. The discipline in that locker room has dissolved. Now Brother John, I'm not for a minute saying that it's right for a parent to offload the responsibility for discipline to the football coach. I know it's *my* responsibility. It's just, the change has been so sudden. So dramatic."

John cradled his chin, deep in thought.

"I'm sorry to dump all this on you," she continued, "but I didn't know where else to turn. I heard your sermons and you just seemed like someone who could help."

"Jackie, I'm glad you came. And don't ever apologize for coming here. Now, remember, I'm not technically your pastor, but I'll do whatever I can to help."

"God bless you Brother John. God bless you."

"And just so you know, my boy's on that team, and if the train's careening of the tracks, I want to know about it. I'll get to the bottom of this Jackie. I promise."

They rose from their seats and walked over to the door. Before leaving, Jackie wrapped her arms around John and pulled him into an embrace. She then turned to Sarah and grabbed her by her hands.

"Your husband is an angel sent straight from heaven. Thank you for sharing him with our congregation."

Sarah gave John a knowing glance, and then turned back to Jackie.

"I'm glad he's been able to help."

Jackie turned, pulled open the door, and then she was gone. When the door closed, Sarah cast a worried glance at John.

"What's happening John?"

"I don't know. But I have the feeling there's someone who does."

• • •

When John woke up in the morning he walked into the kitchen and found Jacob digging into a bowl of corn flakes.

"Good morning Jake. How'd you sleep?"

"Not bad, I suppose. You?"

"Ok, except I had an unusual interruption."

"Your snoring wake you up again? You know they have procedures that can fix that."

"Nope, nope, wasn't that. And I'm well aware of the procedures. Actually, I got a surprise visit from one of your teammate's mothers. About 11:30 last night."

Jacob dropped his spoon into his bowl, his attention suddenly rapt.

"You know a guy named Scott Williams?" John asked.

"Sure. Starting cornerback. What about him?"

"Well, according to his mother, he's been acting out lately. You know, doing crazy things. Typically Coach Connelly keeps him on a pretty short leash. Not so this year. She thinks the coach's grip might be slipping. What do you think? You notice anything unusual?"

"Unusual? In what way?"

"I don't know, changes in discipline or coaching styles."

Jacob's brow creased as he considered the question.

"Come to think of it, there *was* something a little weird this week."

"What's that?"

"Well, I blistered a pass across the middle to my go-to guy, Donavan Dooley. He's usually pretty sure handed, but he dropped this one. No sooner did he drop it than he started running towards the hills at the far end of the practice field. From what they tell me, this is perfectly normal. When you drop a pass or fumble the ball in practice, you run ten hills, up and down. Well, he got half way over to the hills, and Coach Connelly started yelling at him to get back in the huddle. From the looks on everyone's faces, I could see this was a surprise."

"Has there been any extra running so far this year?"

Jacob thought about it for a moment and then said, "No…not really. Well, wait, there was one specific instance of hills, but it wasn't for dropping a pass or fumbling the ball."

"What was it for?"

"There's this guy named Trevor Bickle. He was the starting quarterback last year. Now he's my backup. Not real happy about it. Plays defense now. Well, we were scrimmaging one practice and he really laid me out. Total blind side hit. You know, the dirty kind. Well, Coach Connelly just went ballistic. I thought he was going to rip the guy's head off. Made him go run the hills until the guy was puking his guts out. He must have gone up and down those hills 30 times before he finally collapsed."

"Um, ok, that's troubling. Any other discipline so far this year?"

"Not so far."

"Would you describe Paul Connelly as a strict coach?"

Jacob scrunched up his cheeks as he considered his father's question.

"Not…exactly," he said. "I mean, he had that one moment, otherwise it's been pretty easy going so far. He just seems to be in really good spirits, all the time. Nothing seems to fluster him. Not fumbles, not dropped passes. I mean, you remember that first day, when we got the time wrong and I showed up an hour late?

"Sure."

"According to the equipment manager Doc, that should have been grounds for a cajillion hills. But no, nothing. Coach just talked to me like he already knew who I was. You sure he never called you back?"

"Yeah, positive," John said.

John stewed over Jacob's words, a deep furrow digging into his brow.

"What's going on Dad? What's this all about?"

"Something's changed in that locker room Jacob, and it's not good."

"What do you mean?"

"From what I can gather, Coach Connelly has always been a firm disciplinarian. That's his bread and butter. His calling card. He'd just as soon lose every game if it meant he could mold his players into men of sound character. Not so this year. Something's different."

"What Dad? What's different?"

"As far as I can tell Jacob, there's only one thing that's changed between last year and this."

"What's that Dad?"

"You."

CHAPTER 20

John closed his third sermon in as many weeks to another enthusiastic chorus of Amens. As he walked offstage, he felt an overwhelming sense of peace that it was all coming to an end. He would break the news to Buddy immediately and then begin to reclaim his life. John found Buddy sitting in a chair behind the curtain stage right, contemplating his cellphone, his eyebrows pinched together. John strode towards him, but before he could reach him, a massive deluge of congregants pushed up onto the stage, blocking his path. John scanned frantically for an alternate route but could see none. As more and more congregants streamed into view, John saw Buddy rise from his chair, hurry down the steps, and break towards the assembly hall exit.

Panic flowered within John as he saw Buddy pull the door open and disappear through it. He would see Sarah in a few short hours and she would be anxious to hear his report. The truce he had struck with Sarah was a fragile one, contingent upon John alerting Buddy of his decision that very day. Failing to deliver on his side of the bargain was not a scenario he cared to envision.

Apologizing profusely, John worked his way through the masses of congregants, shaking hands as he went. When he got to the exit, he threw the door open and scanned the hallway in both directions. There was no sign of Buddy. Wherever he was going, he'd disappeared in a hurry. Suddenly, through the tinted doors off to his right, John saw a shock of grey hair and suspenders disappear into a vehicle. It was Buddy. Wherever he was going, he'd be gone in a matter of seconds.

John threw open the doors and made a mad dash to his Suburban, scanning the parking lot as he ran. As he folded himself into the front seat, John spotted Buddy's car pulling onto the narrow road that connected the parking lot to Highway 2. The Suburban's engine fired to life and within seconds, John was pulling up behind Buddy's red Toyota Tercel.

But Buddy immediately began to pull away and was soon tearing past rows of corn at nearly 20 over the speed limit. John kicked himself for not bringing his cellphone. This frantic high speed chase could be ended with the simple press of a button.

When Buddy crossed the county line, John began to worry. It was strange enough that Buddy had left church before tallying that day's collections. This, John had learned, was the highlight of Buddy's week. All of his activities seemed to build towards that one, glorious moment. Yet, today Buddy had charged right out of the building without giving it a second thought. John's shoe hit the floor as he saw Buddy disappear around the bend.

After another ten frantic minutes of driving, Buddy's break lights sprang mercifully to life. Buddy was turning into the parking lot of a sprawling, institutional structure that resembled a hospital, only smaller.

Buddy parked his car, leaped out and jogged towards the glass doors that opened automatically before him. Fifteen seconds later, John followed suit. Once inside, John scanned the halls in either direction for any sign of Buddy.

"Can I help you with something?"

John turned in the direction of the voice and saw an austere looking woman with tight skin and hair that was drawn back in a bun. She was sitting behind the counter, needling him with a pair of penetrating eyes.

"Um...yeah. A guy with glasses and suspenders just came through here," John said, his breath coming in short, quick hitches. "Any idea where he went?"

"Yes. Yes I do. And you are?"

"John. John Peterson. If you could just tell me which way he went," he said, once again scanning the halls.

"He's in a private room just down the hall," she said nodding her head to their left. "But, you'll need to wait until he comes out. Feel free to have a seat," she said, motioning towards a row of chairs.

John hesitated for a moment and then made a snap decision.

"I'm sorry ma'am. I'm in a bit of a hurry. Could you maybe..."

"Quite impossible sir," she said, cutting him off. "You'll have to..."

Before she could finish, John was already tearing down the hallway. As he passed each room, he slowed to get a glimpse of their occupants. In nearly every room he could make out elderly patients, prostrate in bed, IVs and wires connecting them to life sustaining devices. As John approached the end of the hallway, one thing became very clear. This was no hospital. This was a long term care facility. Yet, it was no ordinary long term care facility. Without exception, every occupant had a network of tubes and wires protruding from their appendages. This detail, added to the strange resistance he got from the receptionist, caused the rhythmic thudding of John's heart to accelerate.

At the end of the hallway, John's eye caught a name on the wall. Next to the last door on the right was a sign identifying the room's occupant: Beatrice Holler.

"Be-a-*tric*-e," John said softly to himself. That was Dante Alighieri's muse in the Divine Comedy. He was well acquainted with that Beatrice. The Beatrice just beyond the door, he surmised, was Buddy's mother. Judging by the speed with which Buddy had abandoned the chapel, something had happened. John felt a surge of shame as he contemplated the lengths to which he had gone to intrude on this intensely private moment. He turned to leave, but as he did, he saw the gatekeeper from the foyer halfway down the hall, closing fast.

Anxious to avoid a confrontation, he poked his head up to the window to see if he could get Buddy's attention. John could see Buddy standing in front of a bed, speaking to a doctor in a white coat with a stethoscope around his neck. As the doctor bent over the still body of Buddy's mother, a crack opened between them, exposing the woman's face. John's mouth dropped open as he beheld the occupant of the bed. This wasn't the face of a frail octogenarian. This woman was no older than Buddy. She had a youthfulness about her sleeping face that took John's breath away. John ducked out of the window and flattened himself against the wall, trying to make sense of what he had just seen.

Within seconds, the door opened and the doctor poked his head out. "Can I help you?" he said, flashing irritation.

By this time, the lady from the front desk had reached them.

"I tried to stop him," she said, "but he just blew right past me."

"I apologize," John stammered as he felt a hot panic rise within him. "I...uh..."

"It's ok Dr. Ignacio. He's a friend," Buddy said approaching the doctor from behind. "Give us a second, will you?"

The look of irritation on the doctor's face melted away.

"Sure thing Buddy. I'll be right down the hall if you need me," he said, turning and brushing past John and continuing down the hall.

"Brother John?" Buddy said, his face awash with surprise. "What's going on?"

"Buddy, I feel very sheepish all of the sudden," John said with an awkward smile. "I was hoping to talk to you after church, but you slipped out on me. I didn't have my cellphone, so I ended up following you. Had no idea you were taking me on a road trip," he said, a poor attempt at levity. "But, I'm intruding. We can chat later." John turned to leave.

"Don't go John. I'm glad you came."

John turned and faced Buddy. Buddy's eyes were grave and forlorn.

"Really, this is a personal matter. I really shouldn't be here," John insisted.

"John, there's something you need to know."

Buddy stepped to the side, giving an unencumbered view of the woman behind him.

"John, this is Beatrice. *My wife.*"

John's whole body went limp.

"Your wife? You're...married?" he said after a moment of stupefied silence.

"I am. I should have told you sooner."

"Buddy, I'm so sorry."

Buddy's mouth hardened into a line. John simply stood there, words eluding him.

"How? Why?" John offered lamely.

"Two years ago, she was prescribed a prescription cough suppressant. For reasons we still don't fully understand, it interacted with her epilepsy medication. She had a grand mal seizure and has been comatose ever since."

The sudden revelation drove the air from John's lungs.

"The prognosis?" John asked.

"Not good. She's on an experimental medication that keeps her from slipping into a vegetative state."

"Wow. Experimental? Sounds…expensive," John said.

"You could say that. Experimental drugs are beyond the purview of Medicaid. It's all self-funded. Eight thousand a month just to keep her from slipping away. Not to cure her mind you. Just to maintain the status quo. There's no guarantee she won't someday lose her brain function permanently."

"But is there hope she'll *ever* recover?"

"Sure there's hope. That's what the medication buys us," Buddy said, his voice cracking.

His face was long and his haunted eyes were studying the floor at John's feet.

"It gives her a chance. However small that might be," Buddy said.

"Buddy, I had no idea. I'm so sorry."

"I can only imagine what you think of me by now. A walking contradiction right? Studies the Bible, yet consumed by the almighty dollar. Never takes his eye off the bottom line."

Shame burgeoned in John's chest as the details rolled forth.

"No Buddy, I judged you unfairly. I…had no right to. I'm truly sorry."

"You didn't think it was Lester's idea to build that enormous chapel, did you?"

"Given the scandal, yeah, actually I did."

"Lester *was* greedy, but he lacked a business sense. When the medical bills started to arrive, I could see that my half of the revenue wasn't enough. So, after some arm-twisting, Lester agreed to the larger venue. We'd maxed out the chapel downtown years ago, so the timing seemed perfect. But Lester didn't have a clue. I mean, he knew about Beatrice, but not about the costs of keeping her alive. With the larger venue, we doubled our revenue. It all looked sustainable, right up until…we lost Lester."

"So, the new chapel was all about your wife?"

"That's right. It was all about raising the revenue for the medication. And, as long as you keep working your Sabbath day miracles, I can actually afford to keep my wife alive."

"Oh," John said, his disgust with himself beginning to grow.

The discussion John wanted to have suddenly seemed terribly inappropriate. Not just inappropriate, but rife with consequences he wasn't prepared to deal with.

"I apologize I left so quickly after church," Buddy continued. "I wanted to congratulate you on another outstanding sermon. Just, I got this text from Dr. Ignacio. It sounded urgent."

"Some sort of development with your wife?"

"They had detected a drop in her brain activity. Turned out to be isolated. Nothing serious. Not yet anyway."

"I feel very awkward having come here. This could have waited."

"No worries John. What's on your mind?"

John shifted his weight nervously. "Really Buddy, it can wait. I'm encroaching on personal time and I feel horrible. We can talk later. It was nothing anyway."

"You sure?"

"Absolutely. This isn't anything that needs to be hashed out today. A different day perhaps."

"You got it. Once again, you knocked it out of the park today. Mayfield loves you."

"Thanks."

John walked out of the room with the weight of Buddy's plight crushing down on him. The enigma of Buddy Holler had finally been solved. The truth was nothing he could have ever imagined. It was infinitely worse.

CHAPTER 21

Ethan raised his gaze to the nearly empty chapel and felt a claw of dread wrench at his gut. Without exception, the scattered faces he saw staring back at him were in his chapel for the very first time. The congregants who had occupied those very same seats a week earlier had simply, well, disappeared. Had it not been for the countless hours he'd spent knocking doors this past week, he might *be* staring at an empty chapel. He looked down at the sermon he held clutched in his hands and felt a chord of panic pluck somewhere inside him. He was about to find out if Brother John's blueprint for a successful sermon was enough to pull his ministry back from the brink.

He shot a nervous glance at his wife who sat off to his left, balancing Ian on her knee. The stony expression on her face did little to calm his rattled nerves. He did need to win over this latest wave of proselytes, but this was nothing compared to his most pressing task—punching through the wall of skepticism that had come between him and Jenny. Ever since she had learned of their unraveling finances, she'd waxed stubborn and cynical. If he had any prayer of convincing her of the viability of his ministry, it would have to begin at the pulpit. Ethan mustered what little courage he had left, peered out at the congregation and began to speak.

"It's my pleasure to welcome so many fresh faces to the worship services here at the Community Church of Christ. We will begin today's program by singing a congregational hymn found on page 189 of your hymnals."

Ethan turned to the CD player sitting on a small table behind him, punched a button, and heard the opening strains of "How Great Thou Art" waft out over the congregation. The dozen or so people scattered throughout the chapel scrambled for their hymnals and joined in the hymn. After a scattered, uneven rendition, Ethan offered a brief prayer of convocation, then raised his head. What he saw looking back at him did little to vanquish his mounting dread. The congregation looked impatient and testy. Maybe it was the mostly empty chapel, maybe it was the conspicuous absence of a pianist or chorister. Regardless, if he had any prayer of seeing these folks seven days from now, he'd have to deliver a humdinger of a sermon. Ethan glanced down at the pulpit, said a silent prayer, and began to speak.

"A few months ago I ran into an old friend who loves to climb mountains. This guy's idea of a good time is to find the most dangerous mountain around and try to reach its summit. His most recent climb, he told me, was to the top of Mount McKinley, the highest peak in North America.

"One morning, the schedule called for him to arise at 3 a.m., slip his legs into frozen pants, jam his feet into frozen shoes and, by the light of his headlamp, pickaxe his way up a dark and slippery slope for eight straight hours.

"This type of experience, as I would come to find out, is not unusual for my friend. As he related another half dozen experiences just like it, one thing became clear: my friend is unfazed by the prospect of dying a premature death. Curious, I asked him how many times in his climbing career he'd actually cheated death. To my amazement, he told me that he'd come face to face with death on at least ten different occasions.

"Fascinated and perhaps a bit terrified, I asked him how much longer he thought he could go on before the statistical realities of mountain climbing caught up with him. What he said surprised me: he'd already decided to stop climbing. When I asked why, he explained that over the course of the last twelve months, six of his friends had died in six separate climbing accidents. Had he been on any one of those trips, he would likely have died.

"The moral of my friend's story, I concluded, was that if you expose yourself to enough dangerous risks over a long enough period of time, the likelihood of death rises dramatically. In fact, we have all read about famous climbers at the top of their field who eventually died because of circumstances they simply couldn't anticipate. In some cases it was an avalanche, in some cases they fell into a hidden fissure, and in most cases, they just didn't see it coming. In short, it isn't the mountain that kills these climbers. It's the consistent exposure to very high levels of risk over long periods of time.

"Brothers and sisters, our spiritual journey here on earth is likewise fraught with peril. At times we like to loiter in dangerous places. It can be exhilarating to walk down forbidden paths. But these types of activities are not without their spiritual consequences. When we disregard God's commandments, we unwittingly set ourselves on a course that can lead to spiritual destruction. And, in many cases, it's just a matter of time."

For the next 20 minutes, Ethan shared additional stories and experiences that built upon the theme of safeguarding virtue. After each new story, he followed with a passage from the Bible that supported his theme. When he closed his sermon at 11:35, he looked out at the silent, scant congregation, trying to gauge their reaction. As his eyes darted from face to face, he felt the ball of dread reprise itself. Their faces were blank slates, empty of emotion. Ethan had no idea what was going through their minds, but he feared the worst.

As a flower of shame began to burgeon within him, he shifted his gaze from the congregation to his wife, hoping for a reaffirming look. But she was giving nothing away. Her lips were pressed into a line, her arms locked tightly about Ian. Not good. Not good at all. He had needed to win over his congregation *and* his wife. He had the sinking feeling that he'd failed to do both.

As his doubts continued to swirl, he grabbed his sermon, and stuffed it hastily into his jacket pocket. Then he grabbed his Bible, tucked it under his arm, and began charging down the aisle towards the back of the chapel. Halfway to the back, a man stepped into his path. He wore wranglers, cowboy boots and a plaid shirt, open at the chest. His face was tan and sported a couple days of facial hair. To his left stood his wife, a slender and attractive woman with dark brown hair that fell freely at her shoulders. She wore a yellow dress with a pink floral pattern. To her left stood their two children, probably about twelve and eight.

"You know, I took a chance on you Pastor," the man began in a quiet, gruff voice. His eyes squinted as he spoke.

Ethan felt a tongue of acid rise from his stomach and begin lapping at the back of his throat.

"And you didn't disappoint," he said after a long pause. "I'm glad I came. You keep this up, and I'll see to it this chapel gets filled."

Ethan's eyes sprung wide like saucers. His mouth moved, but words were slow to come.

"I…I don't believe I caught your name, Mr…" Ethan said extending his hand reflexively.

"Dinsmore. Jim Dinsmore," the man said, pumping Ethan's hand.

"We'd…be….honored," Ethan said trying to force a smile through the numbness that was spreading through his body.

Jim gave an almost imperceptible nod of his head, grabbed his wife's hand and then made for the back of the chapel, his two children trailing silently in their wake.

Before he could process what had just happened, Ethan felt someone brush up next to him. He turned to see Jenny looking up at him, a faint smile on her lips.

"I have just one question for you," she said.

"What's that?" Ethan said, his nerves dancing in his stomach.

"Where have you been hiding *that* for the last 12 months?" she said, her mouth spreading into a full blown smile.

"Uh, nowhere. All I did was exactly what Brother John asked."

"Ethan, it was phenomenal. I am so proud of you," she said wrapping her free arm tightly around his back and pressing her cheek against his shoulder.

"You just gave this ministry a new lease on life," she said, pulling back and meeting his gaze. "I mean, did you hear what that man said? If you keep this up, he's going to start spreading the word."

A thin smile began to pull at the corners of Ethan's mouth, but then the mathematical realities of their finances hit him like a fist to the midsection. The smile quickly faded.

"Yeah, well he better do it soon," Ethan said, "because we're running out of time."

Chapter 22

"So how was your sermon?" Sarah chirped merrily as she walked through the front door, wrapped her arms around her husband's waist and planted a tender kiss on his lips. The children filed past them, loosening neckties and kicking off Sunday shoes. Only the twins stayed behind.

"Big turnout. Really big turnout. Even bigger than last week. The congregation just keeps outdoing itself." John was trying to maintain an energy level that matched Sarah's, but he was failing miserably.

"Wow. Good thing you're cashing it in. About time you gave some of these other churches a fighting chance."

His mouth rose in a lame smile, but he said nothing.

"What's going on sweetheart? I know that expression. It means you're hiding something from me. You should be ecstatic. Today is the first day of the rest of our lives. We've found our home. We're spreading roots. We should be breaking out the Martinelli's. What's going on in that head of yours?"

Sarah tried to meet John's gaze, but he averted his glance. She slackened her grip on his waist.

"What aren't you telling me John? I know this John, and he makes me nervous. What happened today that you don't want me to know about?"

"It was just a thing with Buddy, that's all."

"What do you mean a thing with Buddy? You told him right? You told him you're quitting didn't you?"

John broke free of Sarah's grip and turned away from her. He walked a few paces and raised his hand to his brow, wondering how to begin.

"You know, this is turning out to be a little more complex than I thought it would be."

"Complex? There's nothing complex about it. We now own a house, and your continued preaching is no longer a risk our family can afford to take. Cut and dried. Anything but complex, actually."

"I get all of that. But there are mitigating circumstances that I failed to anticipate. Things you don't even know about. Things not even I knew about. Until today."

"Mitigating circumstances?" she said her voice rising in anger. "This is very easy to do. You pick up the phone, you call Buddy, and you tell him that your preaching days are over. Here, let me give you a hand."

She walked over to the cordless phone, grabbed it and punched a button. After a few seconds she spoke.

"Yes, operator? Can you give me the number for Living Christ Ministries?"

John hurried over to her and ripped the phone out of her hand, his eyes flashing anger.

"It's not that easy," he said forcefully. "If you'll hear me out for a change, you'll see what I mean."

"John, there is nothing you can tell me right now that will convince me that your preaching in that wretched church is the right thing for this family."

Her face twisted with anguish as tears spilled over her eyelids and ran down her cheeks.

"Sarah…"

"I'm through with this," she cried.

She walked over to the hall table and grabbed her car keys in an angry flurry of motion. She stuffed the keys into her pocket and then grabbed a twin in each arm. She swung the door open, and then turned to face John, tears clinging to her jawline.

"You're leading this family over a cliff John. I can no longer stand idly by and watch you do it. I'll be back for the others later."

"Where are you going?"

"I don't know. But you need some time to think about what's really important to you."

With that, she spun on her heels, marched through the door and down the walkway. John just stood there, rooted to the ground, unable to move a muscle. A thousand tiny needles pricked his skin as anger and remorse swirled within him. The fragile truce had unraveled in dramatic fashion.

"I'm not leaving Dad," came a voice from over his shoulder.

He turned his head and saw Jacob standing behind him. He'd heard everything.

"You haven't ruined *my* life. At least not yet."

CHAPTER 23

Sarah felt a gurgle of acid roil in her gut as she led her children up onto the porch and gave the door a hard rap. After a few tense moments she heard the patter of footsteps and saw the door swing open.

"Sister Peterson?" the man said, his eyes wide with surprise.

"I'm sorry Bishop Nelson, I know it's late. I...should have called first."

"Nonsense, nonsense. Please, come in," he said waving them inside.

With a twin in each arm, Sarah stepped through the doorway and onto the tiled floor of the Bishop's foyer. She was followed through the door by David, Rachel, Hannah, and Jane.

"Sarah?" came a voice from the end of a long hallway. Sarah turned to see the Bishop's wife walking towards her, her brow knit with concern.

"Hi Janice," Sarah said, trying to mask the emotion in her voice.

Sarah's eyes were puffy and bloodshot, her face long and haggard. She tried to force a smile, but her mouth curled quickly into a frown. It took all of her willpower to restrain the wall of tears that once again threatened to break loose. Seeing the raw emotion on Sarah's face, Janice turned her eyes upon the children.

"Who likes toys and games?" Janice said in her most enthusiastic tone.

At the mere mention of toys, Jane's eyes turned into silver dollars, and her hand shot up into the air. Rachel and David both nodded their heads gamely.

"Alright then, follow me," she said cocking her thumb towards the door through which she had just emerged. With that, the four oldest fell into line behind Janice and filed down the hallway. To Sarah's relief, both twins began grunting and pointing after the other children. She set them gently on the floor and they both scurried down the hall, disappearing through the door at the end of it.

As the room lapsed into silence, the Bishop turned towards Sarah, smiled gravely and motioned towards the living room. Sarah walked dazedly over to the sofa and collapsed onto it, while the Bishop took the armchair opposite her. His eyes were warm and kind but they reflected the gravity that was typical of these unannounced visits.

"Where's John?" the Bishop began.

Sarah bit her lip as if to restrain the tears but they came all the same. She blotted at her eyes with her sleeve, and then smiled as if to brush it all aside.

"Where do I begin?" she said, shaking her head wistfully, her face lined with pain.

"Why don't you tell me why you're here," the Bishop said softly.

Sarah gave another tortured smile, sniffed back more tears, and began. "Are you familiar with Living Christ Ministries on the east side of Mayfield?"

"Sure, I know the one. It's run by Buddy Holler and Lester Le Haye. Only I understand we lost Lester not too long ago."

"Yes, very unexpected. Well, not long after Lester's death, Buddy… asked John to preach to his congregation."

"What?" the Bishop said, his eyebrows flying upward, unsure if he had heard her right.

"That's right. But that's not the worst of it. They liked his sermon so much they decided to have him back. He's been preaching there for the last three weeks."

"Uh, let me get this straight," the Bishop said, his eyes wide with shock. "Your husband has been preaching sermons at Living Christ Ministries? My word, there must be 1,200 congregants there. That's nearly a third of the town."

"Even more by now."

"More?"

Sarah nodded her head. "Every week, the congregation gets a little bigger."

"And they don't know he's a Mormon?"

"No, no one has a clue."

"Oh boy," the Bishop said, collapsing backwards in his chair, his hands squeezing at either side of his face like a vice.

"Why Sister Peterson?" the Bishop finally gasped. "Why would he do such a thing?"

Sarah gave a quick summary of the events of the last month including John's initial encounter with Buddy after the breakdown, Buddy's fruitless search for a substitute preacher, and finally both of John's alleged revelations.

"So, what do *you* make of all this?" the Bishop asked, emerging from his daze.

More tears welled in her eyes but she wiped them away.

"I've been against it from the start. This was supposed to be a fresh start for us Bishop. We're supposed to be spreading roots. Now…it's like our life has turned into one big, ticking time bomb."

The Bishop began studying his hands as his mouth fell into a frown. In another moment he raised his troubled gaze.

"Sister Peterson, what do you know about the history of the Church in Mayfield?"

Sarah stiffened, eyeing the Bishop warily.

"Not a thing," she said ominously. "Why?"

"Look, I know this isn't what you want to hear right now but, given the circumstances, I think you should know. There's a reason you're the only Mormon family in Mayfield."

A chill raced up Sarah's spine as she braced for whatever bombshell the Bishop was getting ready to drop.

"About ten years ago, the Church sent a pair of missionaries to Mayfield. Small, friendly town—seemed ripe for missionary work. The missionaries worked hard and made great progress for about a month. They had a whole slew of investigators, even had a few baptismal dates on the docket."

"What happened?" Sarah said, bating her breath.

"One by one the investigators started falling away. They stopped returning calls. Wouldn't come to the door when the missionaries stopped by. In the arc of seven days, someone stopped those missionaries cold in their tracks."

"Who? Why?" Sarah asked, her voice a mixture of curiosity and dread.

"Nobody knows. But whoever it was, they couldn't stand the idea of the Mormon Church making inroads in Mayfield. I mean we're talking a ruthless, mean-spirited campaign that was meant to send a clear message: the Mormon Church is not welcome. Anyway, when things got too hostile, they shipped those missionaries right out of town. Town hasn't had missionaries since."

Sarah's head was now shaking back and forth in horrified disbelief.

The Bishop continued: "I only tell you this Sarah because, if past is prologue, things are going to get pretty nasty when your secret gets out. And your secret *will* get out. You know that don't you?"

Sarah bit her lower lip as another wave of anguish swept over her.

"I don't know," the Bishop continued. "Maybe it isn't too late. I suppose if he quit today, then laid low for a couple months, it could all blow over. But with every new sermon he preaches, the dangers compound. Isn't there any way to get through to him?"

Sarah stifled another sob, took a minute to gather herself, and then trained her bloodshot eyes on the Bishop.

"I'm afraid that bus left the station a long time ago. I've talked, I've pleaded, I've cried. And now, I refuse to sit idly by while his reckless preaching endangers my family. He needs some time on his own to figure out what's really important to him."

The Bishop favored her with another frown, but seemed determined to hear her out.

"Which leads to my reason for coming." Another pause, followed by more dabbing at her eyes with her shirt sleeve. "He's made it clear he isn't going to stop preaching. Not anytime soon anyway. In the meantime, the children and I need someplace to go while we wait out this insanity."

A furrow dug across the Bishop's brow as he processed her request. After another long pause he spoke.

"You know this can only be a temporary solution, right?"

"Of course," Sarah said.

"Well, there's always Sister Bigelow. She lives in a great big house on the north side of town. She's been widowed going on three years now. She could sure use the company. I suppose I could make a call."

"I'd really appreciate it," Sarah said, sighing with relief.

"Before I make the call though, I need to press one final point. If you can't get through to your husband, and soon, things *will* get worse… much worse. There's someone in that town that hates our church with a passion. And the longer your husband preaches, the more disastrous the day of reckoning. And trust me when I say it Sister Peterson…there will be a day of reckoning."

Chapter 24

A house without a family was hardly a home. Maybe it was a dream to be realized piecemeal. At least that's what John hoped. It had consumed most of his evenings that week but, with Jacob's help, they had finally transferred the contents of their apartment into their new home. It was Saturday night around 10 p.m. John sat in his recliner, surveying his living room, stung by the reality that his dream of a new home was only partially fulfilled.

"Still no word from Mom?" Jacob said, stepping into the room, his voice heavy with concern.

"Not a word," John said, making no effort to conceal his disappointment. "Her cellphone's been off all week. Goes right to voicemail."

"Where could she be?"

"It's got to be someone in the ward. A home teacher, a visiting teacher, someone she knows."

He suddenly had an idea. John fished his smartphone out of his pocket. He quickly scanned through his personal contacts, and then punched a button. The phone rang a few times and then picked up.

"Hello."

"Bishop Nelson?"

"Speaking," came the voice on the other end.

"Hello Bishop, this is John Peterson."

"Hello Brother Peterson," the Bishop said evenly.

"I apologize for calling so late." John paused, collecting his thoughts. "Listen, I don't quite know how to say this but...I can't seem to track down my family. I was hoping you knew something."

There was silence on the other end of the line. After a few seconds the Bishop spoke.

"Yes John, I know where your family is."

John let out a sigh of relief. "Thank goodness," he said. "If you can just give me the address, I'll head right over."

More silence. Finally the Bishop spoke.

"Look John. I can't legally conceal their whereabouts, but I have to tell you, I think Sarah's going to need a little more time."

"Understood."

"By the way, as long as I have you on the line, I should tell you I have serious concerns about what you're doing over there at Living Christ Ministries. It's rife with unintended consequences. If you don't bow out now, this thing could really blow up on you. The blowback looming for you and your family could be devastating. Like I told your wife, there's a reason you're the only Mormon family in that town."

This little revelation made John pause, but not for long.

"Just the address Bishop."

Another pause and a deep breath.

"She's at Sister Bigelow's house. 418 Oxford Street. Just remember, she's in a very delicate state. Has been all week. She needs time. You might want to take a little time yourself. You know, reevaluate the wisdom of your present course."

"I'll take it under advisement," John said curtly. "I appreciate the information."

"No problem. And John, we really would like to see you in church one of these days."

"Yeah, well we're working on it."

As John hung up the phone, a tiny glint of hope burgeoned in his chest. Now that he knew her whereabouts, he could begin to make his case. He'd test the waters with a phone call.

As he pulled the ward directory up on his smartphone, he heard a knock at the door. A tingle of excitement sprouted within him. It had to be Sarah. A week of separation had simply been too much to bear. A smile raised his cheeks as he raced to the front door, unlocked it, and threw it open. The smile slowly disappeared when he saw the uniformed figure standing before him.

"Mr. Peterson?"

"Good evening officer. Uh, what seems to be the problem?"

"Sorry to drop by so late, but there's been an incident with some members of your congregation."

"My congregation?"

John began to correct the officer but thought better of it.

"What do you mean incident?"

"Some of your boys jimmied the lock over at the country club and stole some golf carts."

"Oh no," John said, his face screwing up with worry.

"Yeah, went on a little joyride. One's sitting in a public fountain downtown, another's in a lake not far from here."

"Drinking?"

"Oh yeah, breathalyzers were off the charts."

"Who officer? What are the names?"

"Scottie Williams, Mike McCrcedy, Justin Thibadeau, and Carter Markham. All football players and all members of your congregation. We've got 'em locked up downtown."

"Has anyone told Coach Connelly yet?"

"No, their mothers specifically requested that I contact you first. They don't want to deal with the coach right now."

"Contact me?" John said, surprised. "I hardly know those boys. Paul Connelly would be the right guy to talk to."

"Like I said, they're not ready to deal with Paul right now. They have their reasons."

"Uh…ok. Well, I appreciate you coming by officer. I'll see what I can do."

The officer turned to go and John closed the door. When he turned around, Jacob was standing there waiting for him.

"What's going on Dad?" he said, a touch of worry in his voice.

"A few of your teammates got into trouble downtown. Went on a little golf cart joyride. Didn't end well. They wanted me to know."

"Because everyone thinks you're their pastor, right?"

"Uh, yeah. That's right. How'd you know?"

"That's no secret Dad. There's a reason I'm the most popular kid on the team right now, and it's not just because I'm the starting quarterback."

"Oh?" John said, his eyes spreading wide.

"Oh yeah. I'm the son of the rock star preacher at the local mega church. All the good will they have for you seems to be trickling down to me. For better or for worse Dad, you're the most popular guy in town."

"Rock star preacher? I'm a guest preacher, Jacob. I'm week to week, only until they find a fulltime replacement."

"Look, perception is reality. They see you behind the pulpit every week, and that's how they perceive it. For all intents and purposes, you *are* their pastor."

John bristled at the inference. A public perception that he was the pastor at Living Christ Ministries could mean only one thing: he was that much further from getting Sarah and the kids back.

"Can we talk about this later?" John asked, slightly annoyed. "Right now, I have to pay a visit to Coach Connelly. And if what I fear is true, it's not going to go well. Not well at all."

CHAPTER 25

Paul Connelly let out a groan as he threw back the covers. He rolled out of bed and stumbled into the hallway. The light on his front porch was on, and he could see shadows dancing against the wall through the window above the door.

Paul stopped at the door, wiped the sleep from his eyes, and then pulled it open.

"John Peterson?" he said, his face balling up in disbelief.

"We finally meet," John said, mustering a thin smile, and extending his hand.

Paul grabbed it, and shook it tentatively.

"Come in, come in," Paul said, motioning for John to enter. He quickly snapped on the lights in his living room and directed John to an overstuffed chair. Paul settled onto the couch opposite him.

Paul was still recovering from his shock as he peered across the table at the lay preacher extraordinaire and the father of his prized quarterback.

"Well if I don't have the pleasure of finally meeting Brother John, face to face."

John's face didn't register the warmth it usually projected on Sundays. For some reason he was all business.

"Yes, Coach, it's good to finally meet you. My son's told me a lot about you."

"All good I hope."

John managed a weak smile. "Listen, I'm going to cut to the chase here. I wish I were here under more favorable circumstances. Some of your boys are in jail downtown: Markham, Williams, Thibadeau, and McCreedy."

Paul's world suddenly telescoped, as he collapsed backwards against the sofa.

"Uh, what do you mean? Like arrested?"

"That's right Coach. Drinking, joyrides on stolen golf carts, nothing good. They were arrested earlier tonight."

Paul stared at the ceiling, his heart thudding in his chest, as he tried to process the implications.

"And how exactly did you come by this information Mr. Peterson?" he said, lowering his eyes to John.

"An officer came by my house about half an hour ago and gave me the word."

Paul's body stiffened, his face tightening.

"Now that's interesting. Why would an officer be passing by your home with this particular news?" Paul asked, his eyebrows pinching together.

"When their mothers were notified, they asked that I be notified as well."

Paul's arms folded tightly across his chest.

"And you've come to share this news why, may I ask?"

"Because, I wanted you to be the first to know."

"But I'm not the first to know *Brother* John," Paul said, with mock derision. "*You* were the first to know."

"Look Paul, first or second, I don't think it really matters. What's important is that four boys that are members of your football team are looking at the inside of a jail cell right now. That has implications for you, and it has implications for your team. I wanted to let you know so that you could stay ahead of the news and put the right spin on it."

"You know, I find this all very disturbing," Paul sniffed. "You roll into town a month ago, and before anyone knows it, you're running the show at the largest church in town. Then, a few of my boys have a brush with the law, and *you're* the one they notify? Don't you find that just a *little* strange Mr. Peterson?"

John met Paul's icy gaze without flinching.

"Look Coach. I came here as a favor to you. From a public relation's standpoint, I thought that you would like to stay on top of this. Your reputation as a disciplinarian is what brought you here. If you let this thing spiral out of control, people are going to start wondering if you're still on your game."

"That's ridiculous Peterson."

"Look, this isn't the first I've heard of it. Scottie Williams' mom stopped by the other night. She had concerns even then. She's not the only one. Others have called. The fear is that, somehow…you've taken your eye off the ball."

"I can't believe what I'm hearing," Paul said, his nails sinking into his palms. "How dare you have the audacity to march into my house, and tell *me* how to do *my* job. How about you Peterson? How about we turn the microscope on you, huh? You know, I'm starting to realize how little I actually know about you."

Paul could see the blood running out of John's face.

"Yeah, that's right," Paul continued. "You waltz into town, and the next thing any of us know, you've got this town wrapped around your little finger. You know, if this town needs to worry about something, I think it's you. What do we really know about *you?*"

John suddenly rose from his chair, his face flushing red, his lip curled back in contempt.

"I can show myself out," he growled. He walked over to the door, threw it open and slammed it behind him.

Paul leaped from the sofa and stormed into the kitchen. He stopped at the refrigerator and ripped a post-it note off.

"I should have done this a long time ago," he muttered to himself. He looked at his watch. It was late, but it would be an hour earlier in Oregon. He punched the numbers and waited.

"You have reached the office of Coach Ralph Johnson," came the voice on the other end. "I am unable to take your call. Please leave a message and I will return your call as soon as I am able." Then came the beep.

Paul cleared his throat and began to speak.

"Hello Coach, this is Paul Connelly, head coach of the Mayfield Mustangs. I was fortunate enough to win the Jacob Peterson sweepstakes. He's settled into our system and is working out quite nicely. I just wanted to bend your ear for a moment and get a sense for the type of offense you ran and how you think Jacob can best flourish. Reach me at 555-254-1619. Anytime. Thanks Coach."

Paul hung up the phone, hot perspiration clinging to his brow. There was something about John Peterson that made Paul very uneasy. First his meteoric rise to the most consequential pulpit in town. Now he was usurping the moral authority Paul had spent four years trying to burnish. He wasn't just going to stand by as his life slowly unraveled. It was time he went on the offensive. He'd begin by solving the mystery of John Peterson.

CHAPTER 26

O n Sunday morning, John pulled his rental car out of his driveway and began the five minute drive to Living Christ Ministries. As he drove, a maelstrom of thoughts bandied about in his head. He was still torn about Sarah. He now knew where she and the children were, but didn't know what to do about it. If she really wanted to talk to him, wouldn't she have returned his calls by now? And then there was that tense exchange with Paul Connelly. His parting words had echoed through his mind into the early hours of the morning.

As he drew closer to the church, his thoughts were suddenly diverted by the spectacle that was unfolding almost 200 yards from the turnoff to Living Christ Ministries. A line of cars had parked on both shoulders of the road, stretching off into the distance. Confused, he looked down at his watch. It was Sunday morning, 8:30 a.m. No, it was the right day and he had the right time. But who were all these people? He continued forward, numb and glassy eyed, gaping at the families as they trudged along the shoulders, pressing towards the chapel. He drove past the entrance to the church and settled into a spot nearly 200 yards further down the road. As he got out of the car he could scarcely make out the outline of the chapel through the dense thicket of trees. Estimating he had about a quarter mile to cover, he set out at a brisk pace.

After five minutes of huffing in the stifling August heat, he finally reached the enormous stony façade at the church's main entrance. When he stepped into the coolness of the cavernous foyer, his body went limp. The doors to the assembly hall had been propped open and hundreds of folding chairs now filled the foyer. Large speakers had been positioned on stands on either side of the room, connected to a vast network of cables that ran the length of both walls and snaked into the chapel.

John circled around the chairs, already brimming with congregants, and turned into the hall that led to Buddy's office. Midway down the hall he stopped and peered into the administrator's office. Buddy was standing behind his desk, staring at his cellphone. His face drooped with sadness and his shoulders were rounded. When Buddy looked up, John saw a forlornness in his eyes that stabbed at his heart.

"What's wrong?" John asked. "Have you seen the cars out there? This may be our finest hour yet."

Buddy managed a deferential smile. "Congratulations," he said softly. "You keep outdoing yourself."

"Buddy, this is great news! You should be dancing in the aisles. Why so down in the mouth?"

Buddy's gaze dropped to his hands. "Sorry John. I'm happy, I'm very happy. I don't know how to thank you enough."

"It's Beatrice, isn't it?"

Buddy nodded his head slowly.

"Any news?"

"Just got another text. They'd hoped this newest combination of drugs would accelerate brain activity. But, she didn't respond at all. Not one little bit. They're afraid that if there isn't any improvement soon, she'll start to regress. These drugs can only buy her so much time."

John nodded his head morosely.

"Just so you know, my friend, I'm here to help. I'm committed to seeing this thing through. I'm here for the long haul. I just wish I'd known earlier."

"I can't tell you how much that means to me John. And I apologize for keeping you in the dark. There aren't many people that know what you know. Never been my habit to solicit sympathy."

"I understand."

Buddy mustered a wisp of a smile.

"How about you my friend?" Buddy countered. "You keeping on top of things at home?"

John's countenance fell, the light disappearing from his eyes.

"Uh, we've seen better days on the home front. But nothing a little fasting and prayer can't overcome."

• • •

Anger and confusion had hammered away at Paul's fragile psyche, making for a restless night. Something about John Peterson just didn't feel right. After his unannounced visit and alarming news, he'd been in no mood to go to church. He'd instead spent the entire morning, prostrate on his sofa, brooding over the recent revelations. Four of his boys arrested. What was worse, the parents of *his* players had confided in John Peterson, not in him. Somehow, Peterson had wormed his way into the community's pecking order. His rise was somehow…too meteoric. He was arrogating too much influence far too quickly.

For years Paul had worked tirelessly to break the proud spirits of his players, only to build them back up into young men of character beyond reproach. Now, a few had suffered setbacks, and it wasn't Paul they had alerted. It was John Peterson. This little fact had burrowed under Paul's skin and begun to fester. There was too much praise. Too much rock star adulation. And what was most shocking, the town of Mayfield didn't know the first thing about the man they had placed on that pedestal. And neither did Paul Connelly. But that was about to change.

Paul bounced around the house for a few hours, a restless, pent up energy building within him. He'd googled John Peterson weeks ago, but it had produced nothing of value. But there was *someone* who had to know *something* about John Peterson. Of this he was sure.

At around 2 p.m., the phone rang. Paul sprang from his chair, and sprinted over to the phone. He grabbed it from its cradle, caught his breath, and then pressed the button.

"Paul Connelly," he said.

"Hi Paul, this is Ralph Johnson returning your call."

"Well hello there Coach," Paul said, assuming his friendliest demeanor. "I appreciate you returning my call so promptly."

"No problem at all. So *you* won the Jacob Peterson sweepstakes? Special kid. Never seen anything like him."

"No question about it. Unbelievable talent. We count ourselves very fortunate."

For the next 15 minutes they immersed themselves in the minutia of the West Coast Offense, passing formations, quarterback drops, and receiver routes. When the conversation finally reached a lull, Paul made his play.

"Say Coach, I hope you don't mind me asking but, just as an aside, what can you tell me about John Peterson?"

"Ah yes, John Peterson. I was wondering if you were going to get around to that."

"Oh?" Paul said, surprised. "Why do you say that?"

"Just a hunch. He seems to make ripples wherever he goes."

Paul's eyes narrowed. "What do you mean by that Coach?"

"Well, his Italian program was a pure stroke of genius. There really is no reason it shouldn't have been renewed. Kids just loved it. He just about turned this high school into Little Italy."

"Ok...," Paul said warily.

"Yeah, the reason that family keeps bouncing around isn't because the man isn't employable."

"Then what is it?" Paul asked.

"If you ask me, it's all his talk of religion."

Paul felt his pulse quicken.

"Religion?" Paul asked.

"When he brings his religion into the public forum, it just doesn't end well. It starts out harmless enough, I guess, but it always ends in disaster. After what happened, the school board just couldn't see clear to renew his contract. Same story in all the other towns."

"So, you're telling me that his religion, his preaching, has been his undoing everywhere he's been?"

"Did a little digging myself when he came to town. Been a pattern for years. I hoped, for obvious reasons, that our town would be different. But, in the end, it was the same old thing. He was just a little too zealous, I'm afraid."

"Well Coach, I'd be lying if I said he hasn't been making a spectacle of himself in our town. He's been an enormous distraction since the moment he got here."

"Yeah, well, same guy, different town. Just remember Paul, you can't begrudge his religious propensities too much. After all, they're the real reason you have Jacob Peterson."

"I understand."

"You have to remember, these Mormons are natural proselytizers. It's in their blood. It's what they do. It's just part of the package. You kind of have to take it or leave it."

Paul's breath caught in his throat. For a seemingly interminable moment, he stood there in his kitchen, unable to utter a word.

"You still there, Coach?" Ralph said when the prolonged silence had grown awkward.

"Uh yeah, still here Coach. Listen, I appreciate the return phone call. I'll check back if I have any other questions."

"My pleasure. Call back anytime."

The identity of John Peterson's church came crashing down on Paul like a wheelbarrow full of bricks. The answer to the question "Who is John Peterson?" was more terrifying than he could have ever imagined. John Peterson was not, in fact, a Christian as he had led so many to believe over the course of the last four weeks. John Peterson was a *Mormon*.

But the true identity of John's religion was only one facet of Paul's revulsion. He had sat in the congregation for three consecutive weeks while John's heresy spewed forth from the pulpit. Yet Paul had failed to detect it. Certainly he had been disturbed by the speed and ease with which Peterson had usurped control of the congregation. But this could simply be chalked up to Buddy's inability or, unwillingness to find suitable alternatives. What vexed Paul to no end was his own failure to detect the Mormon themes embedded deep within John's sermons. Surely they were there. Let anyone talk for long enough and their words eventually betray them. It had been Paul's self-appointed duty to monitor the message. That was his whole purpose for attending Living Christ Ministries. The souls of his players, his de facto family, had been placed in peril. And it had happened on his watch.

Maybe Paul *had* taken his eye off the ball. As he collapsed onto the couch, he began to retrace the last four weeks of practice. What had he done differently from seasons past? Where had he deviated?

As he closed his eyes, he found himself carried backward in time. It was the first day of practice. He was watching a tall, wiry quarterback fire a tightly wound spiral 65 yards down the field. Now he was addressing the mysterious new addition to his practice field.

"Who are you son, and what are you doing on my practice field?" the conversation had gone.

"Jacob Peterson. I'm sorry I'm late," the boy had replied.

And then Paul remembered the wave of euphoria that had nearly overcome him. There could be no disciplining *this* boy for being late. He was the answer to all his prayers. He was the key to his season. He needed to be treated with kid gloves, not made to run hills.

Then he saw Donavan Dooley's dropped pass and a dozen other infractions, all overlooked. He'd simply let it slide. In fact, there'd been only one instance of hills all season. It had been Trevor Bickle. But why? Of course, the cheap, blind side hit on Peterson.

And that's when all of the isolated memories coalesced into one glaring, but undeniable truth. Jacob Peterson had been the catalyst behind all of his moral lapses on the practice field. He had been intoxicated by the prospect of a conference championship, and it had colored his judgment, toppling the pillars of moral fortitude that kept his world from crumbling around him.

As the shame filled Paul's breast, he was rocked by another revelation. He thought back to the series of events that had culminated with the arrival of the Peterson family in Mayfield. He recalled his Google search and then his lobbying efforts before Principal Skinner. He could justify his actions a hundred different ways, but in its most distilled form, what he had done was tantamount to recruiting. He had resorted to the same tactics that had tainted the careers of both Frank Bellamy and Chan Yarber, two coaches he despised. He cursed himself for falling into this snare.

All at once, an ironclad resolve began to gather in Paul's bosom. He *had* drifted from his spiritual moorings, but it wasn't too late to change course. He could still regain the trust of his boys' parents. He could still regain his moral standing in the eyes of the community. There *was* still time.

He sprang from the couch, threw open his front door, and strode out into the light of day. He closed his eyes, inhaling the warm summer afternoon air, feeling his body come alive with determination. He *had* failed. He *had* taken his eye off the ball. But, there was something he could do to atone for his sins. There was something he could do to set his world aright. He would begin by exposing John Peterson.

CHAPTER 27

"Hello Mr. Holler."

Buddy Holler looked up from his desk and saw Paul Connelly standing in the doorway of his office. He wore a cryptic expression that Buddy found very unsettling.

"Coach Connelly," he said motioning towards the chair opposite him. "Please, have a seat."

Paul walked slowly towards Buddy's desk.

"I don't mind standing," he said ominously. "I won't be long."

"Fair enough."

"I'm not going to mince words here Holler. I'm concerned about the direction of this ministry. I'm concerned about the spiritual wellbeing of this congregation."

"Uh, how do you mean Paul?" Buddy asked, his eyes squinting in confusion.

"The Sunday after Lester's death, you promised us a rotation of guest preachers. You scared everyone away with the first one, and then, to my great dismay, you decided to put all your chips on black. One guest preacher the rest of the way. Your actions are disturbingly out of step with your rhetoric."

Buddy gave Paul a narrow, inquisitive look.

"Well, Lester's loss, as you know, was devastating. Put us in a really tight spot. But the Lord, in His infinite goodness, saw fit to send us Brother John. And, as you can tell, we've managed to bounce back."

Paul's eyes grew dark and cold, his lip receding into a snarl.

"Yeah…about this Brother John…since we're on the subject. What exactly *do* you know about Brother John? I mean, surely you did your due diligence before giving him free reign over this congregation, right?"

Buddy was beginning to bristle at Paul's line of questioning. His mouth drooped into a frown as he regarded Paul standing above him.

"Well, I know that he's lay clergy in his own congregation, he's a good family man, a good Christian and he's preaching at my congregation at great personal sacrifice."

"Yeah, about his congregation. Which one did you say it was?"

Buddy frowned again, looking into his lap as he searched his memory for any mention of a name.

"You know Paul, I don't know if I have an exact name for you, but I do know they meet in the next county over. Where is this going, may I ask?"

Suddenly Paul slammed his hands down violently upon Buddy's desk creating a loud smack. He towered over Buddy, his eyes red with rage.

"I'll tell you where this is going," Paul said, his voice rising several decibels. "You don't know the first thing about John Peterson. Because if you did, you'd know that he's a Mormon. You've had a Mormon preaching to your congregation for the last four weeks Mr. Holler. Do you have any idea what you've done?"

Buddy's face went slack, a prickly heat rising within him. Too stunned to say anything, he just sat there.

"Well, do you?" Paul repeated, this time more forcefully.

The room grew thick with tension as Buddy met Paul's angry gaze in silence. Finally Buddy responded.

"Ok Paul, I'll tell you exactly what I've done. I've put a man at that pulpit who has single-handedly pulled us back from the brink of financial ruin. Further, we're beginning to reach folks that Lester could never reach. You can't deny this Paul. You've heard him preach. He's got the tongue of fire. Mormon or not, Brother John's the best thing that's ever happened to this congregation."

Paul's face twitched with anger. He leaned even closer to Buddy, their faces now only a foot apart.

"He's a *Mormon*," Paul bellowed. "He's trying…to convert…your congregation. Don't you get it?"

Buddy began shaking his head. "No, no Paul, you've got him all wrong. He isn't trying to convert anyone. *I* asked him to preach because I was at the end of my rope. He agreed to preach only reluctantly. He's been trying to wiggle out of this thing from the moment I asked."

Paul let out a dark chuckle. "Oh, these Mormons *are* devious aren't they? The thing you have to know about Mormons, Holler, is that they're *proselytizers*. There isn't a Mormon alive that wouldn't jump at the chance to preach in front of your congregation. He may have shown resistance initially, but that's all part of the game. He sucked you in Holler. He's played you for a fool."

"Look, I don't know the first thing about Mormons, but I can assure you, it has never been Brother John's intention to convert this congregation. Every single week it's all I can do to persuade him to preach another sermon."

Paul huffed impatiently. "I just got off the phone with Ralph Johnson. Do you know who Ralph Johnson is Mr. Holler?"

Buddy shook his head.

"Ralph Johnson is the head coach at Thousand Oaks High School. He was Jacob Peterson's football coach last year. He told me everything I needed to know about John Peterson. Did you know that this is John Peterson's third town in three years? You know why that is?"

"No, no I don't."

"They've been run out of town everywhere they've been."

"Kind of like what you're trying to do now right now?"

Anger flashed in Paul's eyes. "Don't try to twist this around Holler. They had to leave because of John's aggressive proselyting. What he's doing here is an exercise in mass conversion. Same as he's done in other towns. He works his way into a position of prominence, lulls in an unsuspecting public, and starts to spew his evil doctrine. Of course, aggressive proselyting is off-putting to the school board, so they simply don't renew his contract."

"Paul, I think you've got the wrong guy. Brother John doesn't have an aggressive bone in his body. From day one, the last thing he's wanted to do was talk to me about religion. He's rendering Christian service in our moment of dire need. He's as good a Christian as I know."

Paul pulled his hands down over his face as he let out a groan of frustration.

"Christian? Trust me Holler, there isn't a Christian bone in that man's body. And as long as you continue operating under that illusion, you put your congregation's salvation in peril. In fact, as a member of your congregation, and not an inconsequential one I might add, I demand that you publicly disavow John Peterson forthwith."

Crimson waves fanned out across Buddy's cheeks as the anger bubbled within him.

"How dare you. How dare you have the…effrontery to tell me how to run my congregation. Get out of my office Paul. This conversation's over."

In a torrent of anger Paul slammed his fist down on Buddy's desk, his dark eyes seething within their sockets.

"If you don't act on this, I'll see to it myself that John Peterson never preaches another sermon. Not here, not anywhere."

"Get out of my sight. John Peterson will continue to preach to this congregation whether you like it or not."

With bulging eyes and trembling limbs, Paul whirled about and stormed out of Buddy's office, slamming the door behind him. Buddy remained in his chair, his pulse pounding, sweat streaming down his temples. Admittedly, Buddy knew very little about the Mormon religion. But, if what John Peterson was preaching from the pulpit each Sunday was, in fact, Mormonism, then it was single-handedly saving his church.

CHAPTER 28

By the time Paul reached his car, he had already seized upon a brilliant idea. It was grim and calculating, but it was nonetheless brilliant. Paul fished his cellphone out of the cup holder between his seats, took a deep breath, and began punching numbers.

"Jasper Bickle," came the voice at the other end.

"Jasper. It's Paul Connelly calling. Do you have a second?"

"What do you want Connelly?" he said coolly.

Paul winced at the icy reception. Ever since relegating Jasper's son to backup quarterback, relations between them had grown tenuous. Nevertheless, Paul persisted.

"Jasper, I'll cut right to the chase. I'm calling you first because you are both a member in good standing of Living Christ Ministries and the president of the school board. I'm afraid I have some disturbing news."

"This better be important Connelly. After what you did to my boy, I don't know that I have a lot to say to you. Other than the word is you're starting to lose your handle on your team. Fancy new quarterback rolls into town and all of the sudden you've got the world by the tail."

Paul felt another burst of guilt. He'd forgotten how fast news travels in a small town.

"Jasper, I'll be the first to tell you I've taken my eye off the ball these last few weeks. But I want to make it right. And I think I've come up with a solution with which you'll be pleased."

"Paul, I can't conceive of anything you could do or say right now that could possibly bring about that result."

"Bear with me on this. Listen, there's been some major developments over at Living Christ Ministries. It affects my team, it affects the church, and I'm pretty sure it affects your son. You're going to want to hear me out on this."

There was a silence on the other end of the phone. Finally Jasper spoke. "Alright, I'm listening."

"I don't think we should talk about this over the phone."

"Just tell me now Connelly. I don't have time for this."

"Trust me Jasper, you're going to want to hear this in person."

There was another pause on the other end.

"Alright Connelly, this better be good."

"Meet you at my office in, say, 20 minutes?"

"Fine. I'm on my way."

• • •

"Thanks for coming so quickly. Please take a seat," Paul said, motioning to the only other chair in the tiny office.

Responding only with a nod, Jasper settled his enormous frame onto the rickety metal chair that groaned in protest.

"Alright Connelly. What's this all about?"

"Well, as you know, Jacob Peterson's father has been guest preaching over at Living Christ Ministries these last four weeks."

"Yeah," Jasper said. "What of it?"

"Well, given that he now has the town, including many of the players on my team, eating out of his hand, I thought it might be important to know something, anything about this guy's past."

"What's wrong Connelly, you feeling threatened? You losing your monopoly on moral authority in this town?"

Paul bit his tongue. Jasper was clearly jaded by his son's demotion.

"No Jasper, that's not it at all. Now that he's the de facto pastor of the largest congregation in town, it just seemed prudent to do some research. So, I decided to make a call."

"And that produced what?" Jasper said impatiently.

"It produced a not inconsequential detail about John Peterson's religion. He is not...as advertised."

"Meaning?"

"Meaning, he isn't even Christian."

Jasper grunted contemptuously. "Come on Connelly, you're up in the night. If there's one thing that's clear about John Peterson, it's that he's Christian. Haven't you listened to any of his sermons?"

"Every last one of them. And here's the problem. His sermons do have every appearance of being Christian. But John Peterson himself is *not* a Christian. Jasper, John Peterson is a Mormon, and I can prove it."

"Mormon?" Jasper said, practically choking on the word. "John Peterson is a *Mormon?*"

"I'm afraid so. I had my doubts about him from the start, but I didn't act on them until yesterday. I decided to call Jacob Peterson's last high school coach. Got the return call about an hour ago."

Jasper was now shaking his head and huffing in disgust.

"This needs to be dealt with Connelly, and it needs to be dealt with yesterday. You hear me Connelly? Yesterday."

Paul was beginning to warm to Jasper's anger. For some reason, the Mormon thing had really set him off. Much more than Paul had expected. He was turning into the perfect ally in his efforts to silence John Peterson.

"And that's exactly why we're here," Paul responded. "I've got a plan, but in order to pull it off, I'm going to need your help."

"I'm listening," Jasper breathed.

"As you know, John Peterson's son is my starting quarterback. And if John Peterson's a Mormon, then his son, by extension, is also a Mormon. And if his son is any bit as dishonest and conniving as his father, he could never be an effective leader in my huddle. I've made mistakes this season, but starting my season with John Peterson's son as my quarterback won't be one of them."

"Go on," Jasper said, clearly intrigued.

"Now Jasper, if I move your son back to starting quarterback, there is a chance that our team won't be as competitive as we are right now."

"That remains to be seen if you ask me."

"Look Jasper. Jacob Peterson is a blue chip quarterback. Last season alone, he had 35 touchdown passes against 3 interceptions. He's the real deal."

"What's your point?"

"My point is, if I make your son my starting quarterback, I'm going to need some insulation against any blowback from the community. You know, in the event we were to… sustain some losses along the way."

"I get it Connelly. What do you want me to do?"

"Well, first of all, I need you to make sure the school board gives me some leeway. My job is hanging by a thread as it is. Benching my star quarterback is not exactly going to strengthen my position."

"Go on."

"If the community can be made aware of John Peterson's religion and his intentions, my actions in benching his son will be seen as more… acceptable."

"I think I get the picture Connelly. So, what's the next step?"

"Well, as you have pointed out, my standing in the community has taken a hit. They don't like me as a coach, and I'm rapidly losing sway as a moral authority. You, on the other hand, are a respected member of the community. You have clout, especially among the membership at Living Christ Ministries. This will be stronger coming from you. I need you to see if you can't round up four or five of the most prominent members of the congregation. People you trust implicitly."

"Shouldn't be too hard," he said.

"We'll meet back here tonight at 8 o'clock. I've already got a plan in place."

"Consider it done."

• • •

As Jasper pushed open the locker room door and made for his car, the bitter memories came roaring back. It was 25 years ago. He was a floundering student at a small liberal arts college on the other side of the state. It was early fall, and he found himself in the library scanning through rows of books on a bookshelf. Suddenly, he saw a flash of movement in his periphery. As he turned to his right, he felt his breath catch in his chest. She was the most exquisite creature he'd ever seen. His eyes fell to the tag on her shirt. It read Susan Christensen, Assistant Librarian.

To the surprise of all his professors, Jasper took a sudden and keen interest in all things academic. He didn't have a chance with an assistant librarian he told himself, unless he could demonstrate some proficiency in literature. He spent hours at the library with his nose in his books, occasionally wandering over to her desk, a thoughtful question about the Dewey Decimal System always at the ready.

For the first few weeks, he'd been unable to crack her granite exterior. But he was undeterred. In time, his bookish ways and his omnipresence chipped away at her stony wall of indifference. Eventually, she relented to a first date.

In the early stages of their courtship Jasper was surprised to learn that Susan was a devout Mormon. This was an inconvenience for Jasper, but not a deal breaker.

After five months of dating, Jasper laid plans to make Susan his wife. He got a small loan from his old man and bought a half-carat diamond from the local jeweler. He planned a romantic dinner after which he'd drop to his knee and propose.

At 6:30 p.m. on the appointed evening, Jasper took the steps to her apartment two at a time, a cheerful whistle on his lips, a nervous excitement building in his chest. Everything was going to be perfect.

When Susan opened the door, she had a nervous half-smile on her lips. When she stepped away from the door, Jasper saw two figures seated on the couch in the living room behind her. They were young men, no older than 19 or 20. They rose enthusiastically from the couch, smiles spanning their fresh faces. Their hair was perfectly cropped and they wore impeccably white, short-sleeved shirts with ties and black name tags.

"Jasper, I'd like to introduce you to Elder Sorensen and Elder Whitten," Susan said.

Confused, Jasper extended a limp hand to the young men, and turned quickly back to Susan.

"Uh, what's going on here? Who are these guys?" Jasper asked, his words short and measured.

Susan bit her lip nervously, her eyes shifting quickly to the missionaries and then back to Jasper.

"Jasper, these are missionaries. I invited them over because…I thought you might be interested in learning more about my church."

Jasper felt his heart sink into his chest. He wasn't interested in her bizarre religion. He'd heard the stories. He knew about Joseph Smith and the gold plates. He wanted to marry Susan, but it was *in spite* of her religion. He massaged the little suede box in his jacket pocket nervously. The timing of this little ambush couldn't have been worse.

"Learn more about your church?" Jasper said, with a look that said "Don't do this to me now, not tonight of all nights."

The missionaries began shifting uncomfortably in the middle of the living room as they observed the exchange. Susan turned to the missionaries, and flashed them an awkward look.

"I'm terribly sorry Elders. Would you mind giving me and Jasper a minute alone?"

"No problem Sister Christensen. We'll be right outside," one of them said.

The men stepped outside and closed the door behind them. Susan turned to face Jasper.

"What, did you think I would never bring it up? You know my church is everything to me."

"Of course your church is everything to you. But it's your church, not mine. Susan, I'm interested in you, not in becoming a Mormon."

Susan's face fell as Jasper's pronouncement rung in her ears. Sensing her disappointment, Jasper stepped towards her, grabbing her by the arms.

"Look, I've never had any problem with you being a Mormon. I think you should be the best Mormon you can possibly be. But why can't I love you without being a Mormon? Susan, I would have you for my wife."

He took the box out of his jacket pocket and handed it to her. She opened it with a snap. When she raised her head, her face was long, her eyes moist with tears.

"Jasper, I'm so, so sorry. If I knew that's how you really felt, I would have never let it come this far."

"But Susan, you know I would never keep you or….or our children from going to the Mormon Church. You can go every day and twice on Sundays if you like. But me? Why ask this of me?"

Susan was shaking her head as the tears streamed down her cheeks. Jasper could feel a full-fledged panic take hold of him.

"I'm so sorry Jasper," she said between sniffles. "This could never be." She closed the box and handed it back to him.

A surreal numbness washed over Jasper. This couldn't possibly be happening. Not to him. Not now. Not after all they'd been through.

"So, just like that then? After five months together? We should just throw it all away?"

"I'm so sorry Jasper," she said, reaching an arm towards him.

But he brushed it away. An ember of fury had ignited somewhere inside him.

"No, *I'm* sorry. I'm sorry I ever laid eyes on you. I should have known there was something about you Mormons that I just couldn't trust."

CHAPTER 29

Paul looked out over the semicircle of men that had gathered in the boys' locker room. The odor of sweaty pads and grass stained jerseys hung thick in the air. Some of the men wore solemn looks. Others had their arms folded tightly against their chests, a subconscious reaction to the news that had brought them together.

"Gentlemen," Paul began. "I'd like to thank each of you for sacrificing family time on the Sabbath in order to address what we can all agree is a grave crisis. You have been enlisted tonight to help put a stop to John Peterson. As you all know by now, John Peterson is not at all who he says he is. He is a Mormon. What's worse, he's spent the last four weeks waging a campaign of stealth conversion against our congregation. In doing so he has put our salvation and that of our families in peril."

Heads nodded up and down in solemn approbation of Paul's opening remarks.

"Lest anyone in the room fail to appreciate the gravity of the situation, let me put it another way. A non-Christian, masquerading as a Christian has, through deception of the worst kind, infiltrated our church's ministry and seduced us with heretical doctrines. Who are the victims? As of last Sunday, nearly half the town."

They all wore expressions of men who had just been told they had six months to live. Paul could sense his message was striking just the right chord.

"Earlier this evening, I confronted Buddy Holler with incontrovertible evidence of Mr. Peterson's religion. To his discredit and to my great disappointment, he did not act on this information. Mr. Holler is aware of John Peterson's deception but refuses to disavow him. Money is rolling into the coffers, and attendance is at an all-time high.

"Given Mr. Holler's obvious financial motivations, we will have to resort to other more proactive means of silencing John Peterson. Now, I don't assume that what you know about Mormons is the same as what I know about Mormons. So, for starters, what *do* you know about the Mormon threat?"

Eyes narrowed in concentration as the men searched their collective memories for any incriminating facts about Mormonism.

"Like you said," came a voice from Paul's left, "we know without question that they are not Christians. Of that we can be sure." It was Steve Cattrell, AP History teacher at Mayfield High.

"That's exactly right," Paul said. "And that alone would be enough to justify the course of action I suggest we pursue. But it doesn't end there."

Clay McGill raised a tentative hand. He was the owner of a local trucking company and part of a devout core of congregants at Living Christ Ministries.

"Go ahead Clay," Paul said.

"Well, there's the other book of scripture. The blasphemous one. They call it the Book of Mormon. Now, I'm no biblical scholar, but isn't there some verse in there that warns against adding or taking away from the Bible?"

"That's exactly right Clay, Revelation 22:18," Paul said. "If any man shall add unto these things, God shall add unto him the plagues that are written in this book."

The eyebrows in the room shot upwards in surprise at the ease with which Paul recalled the scripture.

"Sorry, former preacher," Paul said with a faint smile. "Force of habit."

"Of course, there's the whole polygamy fiasco."

Paul turned his head in the direction of the voice. It was Kip Welbach. He taught Math at the high school.

"Why anyone would want more than one wife…," Kip muttered under his breath, giving his head a sad little shake.

Chuckles resonated throughout the room.

"Anything else?" Paul asked, his eyes scanning the men before him.

"Well, you can't talk about Mormons without bringing up Joseph Smith," Jasper sneered. "All that foolish talk of angels and gold plates."

"Second Corinthians 11: 13-14," Paul responded quickly. "For such are false apostles, deceitful workers, transforming themselves into the apostles of Christ. And no marvel; for Satan himself is transformed into an angel of light."

The five men looked at each other with wide eyes, dumbfounded at the breadth of Paul's knowledge.

"Well brethren, it sounds like I don't need to impress upon you the seriousness of what it means to have a Mormon in our midst. So, if there's no objection, I will proceed with the details of the plan."

With that, Paul began passing out clipboards with scratch paper and pens. In a few moments, the five men had their pens poised, and their eyes trained on the coach.

"First order of business," Paul began. "I hold in my hand," he said, raising a sheaf of paper in the air, "the list of emails to every single member of Living Christ Ministries. Fifteen hundred in all. Given Jasper's strong standing in both the community and the congregation, an email will be sent from his account. The email will inform the congregation that John Peterson is a Mormon. Further, the email will explain that from day one, he has been intent upon the conversion of the congregation. To ensure that the message gets opened and not discarded, I will simply put the following question in the subject line: 'Is John Peterson a Mormon?' Any objections?"

Heads in the room were bobbing up and down in agreement as their hands scribbled feverishly across their clipboards.

"Now, for some of our fellow congregants, being a Mormon will have little or no significance. So, we're going to have to make our case. I'll include in that email the most incriminating aspects of the Mormon faith, i.e., they're not Christians, extracanonical scripture, et cetera. At the end of the email, of course, I will invite them to boycott this Sunday's meeting, and every meeting thereafter, so long as John Peterson is the one preaching the sermons."

The eyes in the room widened, heads nodding their approval.

"Now, there will be a few outliers who simply won't pay us any heed. This goes without saying. John Peterson has been blessed with certain oratorical gifts. Of that, there is no question. And so long as there are those among us who can be swayed by his rhetoric, regardless of its doctrinal fallacies, there will be resistance. To that end, I propose an addendum be placed at the end of the email, by which we can ascertain the naysayers among us. It might go something like this: 'If you think we're acting rashly or in any way not in keeping with gospel tenets, simply explain your perspective by way of a return email.' Conversely, if they concur with our perspective, they can likewise respond accordingly.

"By so doing," Paul continued, "we will ferret out the members of our congregation who need a little more individualized attention. A little more *coaxing* if you will."

Enthusiastic smiles spanned their faces as they realized the genius of Paul's plan.

"Once I have a list of the dissenters, then we'll divide and conquer. The six of us will begin a campaign to address their concerns, one by one, over the telephone. Sometimes a warm voice can help persuade and cajole better than an email. For most people, a phone call from a respected member of the congregation will suffice. For those who are a little more stubborn, we'll have to make personal visits.

"Remember, gentlemen, the clock is ticking. Our efforts must be comprehensive and they must be devastating. We are to leave no stone unturned, no family untouched. Our goal is absolute repudiation of this man's ministry. A wolf has entered in among us, intent upon the destruction of our families, and our way of life. He must be neutralized and, if necessary, run out of town."

"Any questions?" Paul said with a tone of finality.

A grave silence filled the room as his words hung in the air.

"Good. Jasper, I'll forward the email to you in about 30 minutes. You copy and paste it into your own email and send it out tonight. Stay glued to your computers. By tomorrow afternoon, the list of families you will need to contact personally will be in your email inbox. And remember, what we're doing *is* the will of our Lord and Savior Jesus Christ."

As the men filed past Paul and out of the locker room, Jasper Bickle hung behind.

"I have to admit Connelly. That's a heck of a plan. This'll go a long way towards ensuring that fraud never sets another foot in our chapel. Or any other Mormon for that matter."

"That's the goal," Paul said. "Complete and utter marginalization."

"Well Connelly, I have to say, I'm feeling a lot better about you already. You showed good leadership here tonight. I'll be sure to spread the word," he said with a wink. "Your coaching prospects have never looked so good."

CHAPTER 30

Sarah had yet to respond to any of the messages John had left on her cellphone. But now that John knew her whereabouts and had a direct number, he could finally plead his case. John's heart thumped wildly in his chest as he lifted the phone from its cradle and began punching numbers. After a few rings it picked up.

"Hello."

"Hi, Sister Bigelow. This is John Peterson. I was hoping to speak to my wife."

"Um...will you hold please?" came the hesitant voice from the other end.

While John bated his breath, he could hear the faint exchange of voices in the background. John strained to make out the words but could not. As time passed, he began to grow nervous. After a seemingly interminable delay, Sister Bigelow finally came back.

"I'm sorry Brother Peterson, she's unavailable."

"What do you mean she's unavailable?" John asked in obvious frustration. "I could hear you guys talking in the background."

"Look Brother Peterson," she said, her voice lowering to a whisper. "Between you and me, the longer you preach at that church the harder this is going to be."

"Sister Bigelow, it's not that cut and dried. There are mitigating circumstances."

"I'm just calling it like I see it," she said in hushed tones. "Gotta go. Goodbye Brother Peterson."

"But Sister…"

She had already hung up.

John collapsed onto the sofa, his world growing bleaker by the minute. His thoughts drifted back to the first revelation he'd received over a month ago. Since heeding the call, his life had done nothing but spiral out of control. He hadn't seen his children in days and his wife had cut off all channels of communication. *Some reward for obedience*, he thought.

Just then, John heard a knock at the door. John pushed himself up from the sofa and stumbled over to the entryway. He rubbed is hands over his face, composed himself, and then pulled the door open. It was Buddy Holler. Lines of anguish creased his brow, sadness swimming in his eyes.

"Buddy?" John said, a touch of dread in his voice. "Please, come in."

"Thank you Brother John," he said, stepping through the doorway.

"So, this is it. The new house, make yourself at home," John said, pointing towards the sofa.

Buddy looked around deferentially as if giving the house a brief appraisal.

"Thanks John, but I won't be long." There was something unmistakably grim about Buddy's demeanor. John felt a nervous energy tingling in his limbs.

"Um, ok," John said.

"I'm not going to waste a lot of your time here tonight John. I just need you to level with me. Someone just came into my office claiming you're a member of the Mormon Church. All I want is the truth."

John felt the blood begin to drain from his body. *Not now. Please God, tell me it's not happening now*, he thought.

John looked into Buddy's haunted eyes. "Yes Buddy. I am a Mormon."

"Now John, I don't care about your denomination so long as it's Christian. This same person swears up one side and down the other that Mormons are *not* Christians. Further, he claims that any Mormon pretending to be Christian is selling a bill of goods. So John, I'm going to ask this once and only once. Do you believe in Jesus Christ?"

"Have you not heard a single word I've preached from that pulpit these last four weeks?"

"I know what I heard," Buddy snapped. "Just answer the question. Are you a Christian?"

John could sense that Buddy was in no mood for nuanced explanations.

"Yes Buddy, of course I am. I mean, the name of our church is 'The Church of Jesus Christ of Latter-Day Saints'. What more do you need to know?"

"So you are affirming your Christianity 100%? No equivocation?"

"Buddy, as sure as I stand before you now, Jesus Christ is my personal savior. I am irretrievably and incontrovertibly Christian."

Buddy's eyes narrowed.

"So why am I hearing these things John? What do they know about you that I don't?"

"First of all, who's telling you these things?"

Buddy took a deep breath. "It's Paul Connelly. He says these past four weeks you've been engaging in a stealth crusade to convert my congregation to Mormonism. All your talk of Christianity is just that, talk. Says you're a wolf in sheep's clothing."

"Buddy, think about what you know about me. I've given you resistance from day one. You had to drag me to that pulpit kicking and screaming. Do you really think I'm trying to convert your congregation to Mormonism?"

Buddy paused and then shook his head.

"He was just...so...*angry*. It's been a while since I've seen anyone that worked up. In fact, he said if you didn't stop preaching forthwith, he'd have to take matters into his own hands."

John felt another wave of panic crash down upon him.

"Tell me you agreed with him," John said frantically. "Tell me you canceled my sermon for Sunday."

"Cancel your sermon? You know I can't do that John. The implications are unthinkable."

"No, the implications of *not* canceling are unthinkable. You've got to call him Buddy," John said, digging frantically into his pocket to retrieve his smartphone.

"I *can* call, but calling won't undo this," Buddy said, pulling a folded piece of paper out his breast pocket and handing it to John.

John unfolded the paper and began to read. As his eyes scanned, a look of pure terror spread over his face. When he was done, the paper fell from his hands and cascaded to the ground. John fell to his knees and buried his face in his hands.

"I got copied on that email about half an hour ago. It originated from Jasper Bickle's email account, but let there be no doubt—Paul Connelly is behind this."

John looked up, a crazed look in his eyes.

"Who got this email Buddy? Who was on the distribution list?"

"Every member of our congregation."

John let out a groan that sprang from the very depths of his soul.

"Buddy, do you have any idea what this means for me and my family? Any clue at all?"

Buddy stood there in silence, his eyes haunted, his face lined with pain.

John could feel a surreal numbness creeping through his body as he staggered to his feet and pulled open the door.

"Just leave Buddy. It's all over."

Buddy gave John one last plaintive look, paused, and then disappeared through the door. John closed the door, collapsed against it, and then slid onto the floor.

"They found out, didn't they?" came a voice from somewhere above him.

John looked up and saw Jacob standing there. He nodded his head slowly.

"Yeah...they found out."

Jacob's hands flew up to his face, masking the terror that was spreading across it.

"You were supposed to stay on top of this Dad," Jacob groaned.

"It was nothing I did Jake. Nothing I said."

"Then how did they find out?"

"You don't want to know."

"Who was it Dad?" Jacob asked, a hard edge of anger in his voice.

John looked up at his son, lines of regret crisscrossing his face.

"It was your coach. It was Paul Connelly."

"Well that's just *perfect*," Jacob said, throwing his hands in the air. "There goes my life. Thanks Dad. Really, thanks for everything." He whirled around and stormed down the hallway. Somewhere in the house John heard an angry door slam.

John pulled himself to his knees, crawled over to the phone, pulled it out of the cradle and hit redial. The phone rang a few times before it picked up.

"Hello."

"Sister Bigelow, it's Brother Peterson," he said, his voice barely audible.

"Brother Peterson, I thought I told you…"

"I know you did," he said in a flash of irritation. "Look, I have a message for my wife, if you could be so kind as to pass it along."

"Um…ok. That would be fine."

"Let her know that the secret is out. The whole town knows that we're Mormons. She and the children should prepare accordingly."

CHAPTER 31

Jacob lay in in his bed, sleep eluding him, a number of apocalyptic, doomsday scenarios running through his head. For nearly four hours he'd lain there, brooding over the horrifying implications of his dad's miscalculations.

Things had finally started to look up for Jacob. He was now solidly entrenched in the starting quarterback role. And, notwithstanding Trevor Bickle's efforts to maim him, the team had rallied around him. His offensive line had proven serviceable, and with Donavan Dooley as his sure-handed target, the path to a conference championship never seemed so clear.

And then there was Ashley Hudson. He hadn't seen her since that magical moment in the ice cream parlor, but that warm, prolonged handshake and flirtatious banter left no doubt as to her intentions. With the school year upon them, they would rekindle the flame that had ignited three weeks earlier.

But his dad's latest blunder had changed everything. Jacob had looked forward to the first day of school with relish, especially given the extracurricular activity in the ice cream parlor. Suddenly, school was the last place he wanted to be. His father was quite possibly the most hated man in town. That had implications for Jacob's life that he couldn't even begin to fathom.

• • •

"Jake, I want to give you a little preview of what you might be dealing with today," John said as they pulled onto the main drag.

"What's the point? My life's a disaster. Nothing you can say will bring me any more clarity on that fact," Jacob responded.

John considered this for a moment. "Jacob, your life is not a disaster. It's simply going to be different. A little more challenging."

"Yeah, no kidding. Just like the last two towns?"

John paused before responding.

"No Jake. It's not going to be just like the last two towns. It will probably…be worse."

Jacob threw his dad a quick look of irritation. As he did, he saw the gravity on his father's face.

"Worse? How could it possibly…"

"Look, there are going to be rumors floating around school that I've been trying to convert the entire congregation over at Living Christ Ministries."

"But it's all a lie," Jacob protested.

"Well, you and I know that, but no one else does. And because of that, people will treat you differently. Maybe even say some nasty things. And they won't do it just because you're a Mormon. They'll do it because you're my son."

Jacob huffed his displeasure.

"Dad, I thought you said you were guided in this decision. How could you have let this get away from you? Haven't you ever heard of the law of unintended consequences? This is a going to be a major, major trauma in my life. I can't believe I actually thought this town was going to work out for us."

John bit his tongue, buying time as Jacob's anger diffused throughout the car.

"I know Jake. I can't tell you how sorry I am. This was not my intention when we first got here. But, the answers I received were real. They didn't make sense at the time. They make even less sense now, but I can't deny what I felt. Why our world has spun off its axis is anyone's guess. My only point here is that you need to have some sort of plan when the persecution starts."

"Plan? What are you talking about?" Jacob said coldly.

"Jacob, there are to be no reprisals. We turn the other cheek. We serve, we make contributions to the community, but under no circumstances are there to be reprisals. I can tell you firsthand what happens when you try to meet this stuff head on. Got it?

"Yeah, whatever Dad," Jacob grumbled.

John pulled the car up to the school's front entrance and came to a stop.

"Here we are. Be strong, and remember who you are. I'll check on you a little later. I've got a little time during fifth period."

"Don't bother," Jacob snapped. "You've already done enough."

Jacob pushed the door open, stepped out of the car, and slammed the door behind him. He lumbered up to the front door of the school and, with great trepidation, yanked it open. He looked inside and saw an ocean of students swirling through the hallways. As he stepped through the door, he cast his eyes to the floor, and began trudging down the hallway.

After an agonizingly long walk, he arrived at the locker whose number matched the slip of paper in his hand. He spun the combination lock around and then gave it a quick tug. He pulled the door open, and buried his head inside, anxious for a reprieve from the incriminating stares his trip down the hall had doubtless engendered.

In another two minutes the bell rang mercifully. He waited another 30 seconds, just for good measure, then turned to leave. As he closed his locker with a clank, he suddenly heard a voice from down the hall.

"Jacob, Jacob, Jacob. What is *up* my man!?"

He turned his head in the direction of the voice. It was Donavan Dooley, his star receiver, and right about now, a sight for sore eyes. Donavan had an easy, carefree way about him that Jacob found magnetic. Jacob's sagging spirits began to lift as he saw his receiver approach.

When Donavan reached him, they exchanged a series of choreographed dance moves and handshakes that culminated in a chest bump. They had orchestrated this little end zone dance the third week in practice when it became evident that their new found chemistry would result in an historic number of touchdowns. By now it was clean, crisp, and ready to be unveiled on Friday night.

"Donavan my man. I almost didn't recognize you without your facemask. I mean, for obvious reasons, I prefer to not see your face, but I guess the helmet does have to come off eventually."

"Well, you know, with looks like these, I'm better off actually leaving the facemask on. Keeps the ladies from swarming me in the hallways. I'd prefer to make it to class, you know, unimpeded."

"I feel you brother. It's all about making it to class on time."

Donavan's arm curled around Jacob's shoulder as they walked down the hallway.

"So what do you think, is Mayfield's new star quarterback ready for his big unveiling on Friday night?"

"Only as ready as his star wide receiver."

Donavan's face lit up.

"You know I'm ready my brother. You keep throwing the rock, and these sticky hands will gobble it right up. I'm like the black hole. It goes in, but it never comes out. It's what I call the Peterson-Dooley downtown connection. Leaving the station in approximately five days."

Jacob laughed at his affable receiver. In a matter of seconds, his mounting fears had begun to melt away. Maybe his dad *was* overreacting. Even if this proved to be a reboot of their last two towns, it was always his dad who bore the brunt of it, not him. Jacob kicked himself for getting sucked into his dad's gloomy prognostications.

"Come on man, we're already late. Who's your homeroom teacher?" Donavan asked.

Jacob scrutinized the paper in his hand.

"Mr. Singer?"

"Sweet, me too. Follow me."

They strolled into the classroom just as Mr. Singer was beginning to take roll. As they entered the classroom, Jacob heard an explosion of noise from the back of the room.

"Hoo, hoo, hoo, hoo, hoo."

Five football players had congregated in the back row and were now waving their arms in a motion reminiscent of Arsenio Hall.

"Ja-cob, Ja-cob, Ja-cob," they chanted in mock adoration.

A broad grin crept across his face as he walked to the back of the room and exchanged high fives with each of his teammates.

He looked around for a seat and found one between Chad Cogan and Donavan. Jacob laughed and shook his head as he considered his dad's over-hyped warnings. If his first few minutes in class were any indication, today was going to go just fine. Just fine indeed.

He exchanged some brief banter with his teammates until it was clear they were interrupting the roll call. Jacob gave a friendly shush to his cohorts and then turned towards the front.

"Michael Goodwin," Mr. Singer said, scanning the room.

"Here," said a boy near the front of the class.

"Katherine Hawthorne."

Another hand shot up.

"Ashley Hudson."

Jacob felt a molten dagger plunge deep into his chest. He quickly began scanning the room for any sign of her. There, off to the right, towards the front of the class, he saw her. He could practically hear the angelic voices as a pillar of light descended upon her. She was even more radiant than he remembered.

"I'm here," she said, raising her hand.

Within seconds, the memories from the ice cream parlor came roaring back. Her intoxicating blue eyes and flawless ivory complexion had combined to take his breath away. The same conflagration reprised itself in his chest, only this time with more intensity. He smiled as he suddenly remembered that *he* was the school's starting quarterback. Didn't that fact alone carry unspeakable weight with the opposite sex?

"What you staring at Romeo?" came a voice in his ear.

Jacob turned to see Donavan leaning closely and smiling.

"Nothing man, nothing," he insisted.

"You're staring at Ashley Hudson, aren't you?"

"Ashley who?" he said, feigning cluelessness.

Donavan nodded his head in the direction of Ashley.

"Oh her? Wasn't staring. Just looking. Why do you ask?"

"Look man, you're new in school, so it's only fair I give you advanced warning. That is *the* Ashley Hudson. Sought by many, procured by none. Yes, she's gorgeous, but she's also untouchable."

"What do you mean untouchable?" Jacob asked, his eyebrows bunching together.

"She doesn't date. At least not football players, anyway."

Now why would that be? Jacob wondered to himself, his eyes fixed on Ashley like lasers.

"It's a matter of public record that she won't give a football player the time of day. Even if you *are* the star quarterback, Romeo."

"What's wrong with being a football player?" Jacob said, suddenly curious.

"Check this. Last year, Trevor Bickle thought he had the inside track, just because *he* was the starting quarterback. Crashed and burned man. Saw it myself. Not a pretty sight. This high school is littered with the corpses of football players who *thought* they had a chance with Ashley Hudson."

"Weird," was all that Jacob could manage. But he wasn't worried. His thoughts kept drifting back to their encounter a few weeks earlier. There had been an undeniable connection. He had felt it. Had it not been for his parents, they might still be holding hands, even now.

"Well, my friend," Jacob said, a playful look creeping across his face, "all that's about to change. Take some notes. As soon as the bell rings, you're going to see the master in action."

"Consider yourself warned Romeo. It doesn't matter that you're the starting quarterback. It doesn't matter that you're tall, dark and handsome. By now," he said, his eyes darting to their teammates on either side of them, "she knows you're a football player. Case closed. You're wasting your time."

Jacob kept smiling, betraying the fact that he knew something that Donavan didn't.

"Watch and learn," he said. "Watch and learn."

When the bell finally rang, the students sprang from their seats, and began a mad rush towards the classroom door. A wall of students now stood between Jacob and Ashley, and she was about to spill out into the hallway. Seeing this, Jacob began picking his way through the crowd, Donavan nipping at his heels.

By the time they had made it through the door of the classroom, Ashley was already a good 20 paces down the hall. Between the distance and the crowded hallway, Jacob suddenly wondered if he could reach her in time. At any second, she could dart into a classroom or, worse, disappear into the girls' room.

To his relief, he saw her stop at a locker and begin to twirl a combination lock. He slackened his pace, his nerves a live wire, his heart thundering in his chest. He walked debonairly up to her locker, Donavan in close pursuit.

"Well hello there," Jacob said, with all the smolder of which he was capable.

She turned her head towards him. "Oh…Jacob," she said, pausing awkwardly. "Um, hi."

Her words were vacant and cold, her face empty of emotion. All at once, Jacob felt his heart tumble into his stomach. In just four words, Ashley had succeeded in erecting an impenetrable wall of ice between them.

Jacob racked his brain for some pithy line that could somehow melt the frozen façade behind which she now stood, but he drew only blanks.

"So…how…have you been?" he offered lamely. Wow, was that honestly the best he could do?

"I've been fine," she said abruptly.

All the visions of fiery romance that had danced around in his head for the last three weeks now seemed incredibly absurd. Yet, he had an audience in Donavan. He had to at least… try.

"Listen, I'm sure you're incredibly busy, but I was wondering if one of these nights we could…"

The look of contempt Ashley flashed was enough to stop Jacob cold in his tracks.

"Look, Jacob, I think I can see where you're headed with this. As a matter of policy, I don't date football players. Surely your friend made that perfectly clear."

Donavan smiled awkwardly.

"Uh, yeah, it was clear," Jacob managed. "Crystal clear."

"Great. Well, thanks for stopping by," she said, making no attempt to conceal her irritation.

"Uh, sure. No problem."

He turned and trudged dazedly down the hallway, stunned at this sudden reversal of fortune. Jacob couldn't figure it out. It was as if that moment in the ice cream parlor had simply never taken place. If it weren't for the fact that she'd addressed him by his first name, he'd have sworn they'd never even met. He saw Donavan out of the corner of his eye trying to suppress an "I told you so" grin.

The deal breaker according to Donavan and now Ashley, was an oblong shaped ball made of leather and string. He could see persecution and ostracism for religion. People had been doing that for 6,000 years. But football? In this strange, bizarro town, being a football player had suddenly gone from being an asset to a liability.

• • •

By the end of sixth period, Jacob's preoccupation with blowback over his religion had become a distant memory. It had been replaced by the consuming anguish he felt over Ashley's heartless rejection. Amid all the confusion and pain, he tried to turn his thoughts to football. At least he still had that. He was still the starting quarterback, and the promise of glory on the gridiron still lay ahead of him. With this optimistic thought buoying his spirits, he hopped down the stairs and stepped into the hallway that led to the boys' locker room. As he stepped up to the double doors, he could hear the raucous sound of his teammates' voices issuing through the crack. Suddenly anxious, he pulled the door open and stepped inside. At the end of a row of lockers, he saw a large crowd of football players standing before the bulletin board, making no effort to change out of their street clothes.

Jacob stepped gingerly towards the crowd of players, his heart pounding in his chest like a jackhammer. As Jacob approached, heads turned, and voices descended into silence. The group slowly gave way, giving Jacob an unencumbered path to the bulletin board.

With the taste of acid burning in his throat, Jacob stepped up to the board. He fixed his eyes on the bold print at the top of the page. It was a revised depth chart. Jacob's heart went from a hammer to a wild flutter, his palms now damp with sweat. He scanned down the page, his eyes darting from position to position. Near the bottom of the page, in ink so fresh he could smell it, was the realization of his most horrific nightmare. Written in bold, stark letters he read: Quarterback #1: Trevor Bickle. Quarterback #2: *Jacob Peterson.*

CHAPTER 32

Suddenly, every breath Jacob took felt like it could be his last. As he stood there surrounded by his teammates, his dad's dire warnings came roaring back. Then, all at once, he saw a terrifying vision gather in his mind. He was standing on the sideline, clipboard in hand, uniform free of the green and brown stains to which he had grown so accustomed. The incubus was suddenly shattered by a booming voice coming from his right.

"Alright, cut the loitering. I need everyone dressed and on the field in 15 minutes, or we've got hills after practice."

It was Paul Connelly.

With that solemn pronouncement the group disbanded, scurrying this way and that in an attempt to meet the imposed deadline.

"Peterson," Paul bellowed. "In my office, now."

Jacob took a deep breath, willing his legs into motion. Like an inmate to the gallows, he began trudging towards the open door of his coach's office. Dazed and reeling, he stepped up to the door.

"You've seen the depth chart by now, I imagine," Paul began.

"Yeah…I saw it," Jacob mumbled, barely audible.

"Well then, I owe you an explanation. Jacob, you've got a lot of gifts. There's no two ways about it. You can flat out throw the football. But on the other hand, being a quarterback is more than just being able to throw the ball. You have to be able to command the respect of those in your huddle. Your teammates need to have the confidence that your character is above reproach. They have to know that they can rely on you when the game is on the line. And frankly, after learning more about you and your dad, I've started to have serious questions."

"What does my dad have to do with me?" Jacob said, feeling his shock morph into anger.

"Quiet Peterson. I'm not here to discuss this with you. I'm here to inform you. I run a Christian locker room, take it or leave it. Now, to be on this football team, you can be any religion at all. I don't discriminate. But one thing I will not tolerate is deliberate deception in an attempt to convert a congregation."

"No one was trying to convert anyone," Jacob protested.

"Better watch your tone Peterson. You're already on thin ice. The bottom line is this: your dad lied about his religion for four straight weeks. If I hadn't done some checking around, he'd *still* be spouting lies from that pulpit. As far as I'm concerned, you were complicit in that deception."

"My dad's no liar and neither am I," Jacob said, his voice rising.

"Look, it really is sad. You showed a lot of potential. And to think where we could have gone with you as our quarterback," Paul said, giving his head a sad little shake.

"Are we done here?" Jacob snapped.

"No, there's one more thing. If you choose to stay on this team, you'll lead the scout team in practice. In games, you'll back up Bickle. That may not be a role you're accustomed to so, I'd understand if you chose to quit. There'd be no shame in it. However, if you decide you would like to perform in that capacity, I expect you to be out there and fully dressed in 15 minutes. If I don't see you by then, I'll know what you decided."

Jacob had wheeled about and stormed out the door midway through his coach's last sentence. He wouldn't need 15 minutes to decide. He'd already made his decision: his playing days in Mayfield were over. His dad *had* shown some questionable judgment, but of one thing Jacob was sure: his dad was no liar. And neither was he.

He stormed towards the locker room door riding a wave of anger. Once through the door, he turned and kicked it shut, a loud, clanking sound resounding across the marble hallways. He continued his march down the empty corridor, a cloud of rage roiling in his wake. He had no idea where he was going, only that he had to get as far away from his coach as possible. His nostrils flared and his jugular throbbed as the hatred invaded him like a disease.

He'd made it halfway across the school when he suddenly stopped. What was he doing? Only exactly what his coach had *hoped* he would do. He replayed the conversation in his mind. There could be no doubt of it now. His coach was practically pushing him out of the locker room. He was purging him from the team in the same way he had purged his dad from Living Christ Ministries. By quitting now, Jacob was playing right into his scheme. Jacob's eyes fired with indignation.

He spun around, and charged back towards the locker room. Once inside, he collapsed on the bench in front of his locker, opened it up, and began to take out his pads. Not only would he show up at practice today, but he would be the last one to leave. He *would* defy his coach, but he wouldn't do it with words.

$$\bullet \bullet \bullet$$

With seconds to spare, Jacob jogged onto the field, and took his place in line with the rest of his teammates in their pre-practice stretching routine. As Jacob fell onto the grass, he looked up and saw his coach pacing in front of his players. As he turned and walked back in Jacob's direction, their eyes met. Jacob saw a disapproving scowl spread across his face. Jacob averted his glance, another wave of contempt exploding within him.

After a few more minutes of stretching, Paul blew his whistle and began barking orders.

"Alright men," he began. "As you know, our opener's in five days. How we practice today *will* set the tone for how we play Friday night. I want no lollygagging. I want to see assignments fulfilled with crispness and perfection. I have no problem rearranging my depth charts at a moment's notice. You should all know that by now."

So *that's* what this was all about? Restore order to your locker room by bringing the hammer down on the Mormon kid? Bring your "A" game or you'll end up like Peterson? His coach's twisted plan was beginning to come into focus.

The coach continued: "I want to see the starters on defense huddled around me. I want to see the second team offense with Coach Brooks. Bickle? Where are you Bickle?"

"Here Coach," Trevor said, raising his hand.

"Bickle, I still want to see you at outside linebacker. I'll need you on offense and defense this year."

A cocky smile spread across Trevor's face as he pulled his helmet into place and sprinted over to the defensive huddle.

"We will be going live gentlemen. You will be practicing under game conditions this week. You practice like you play. I want to see precision and discipline," Paul yelled, clapping his hands together.

Pursuant to the terms of their agreement, Jacob jogged over to the huddle that had gathered opposite the starting defense. He was met there by Coach Brooks, a towering man with an expansive girth.

"Alright boys," he began. "Remember, we're going live, so hold your blocks until the play is over. Now, as you may remember, New Haven runs a spread offense. This first play we're going to show was their bread and butter all last year. If this were our offense, we'd call it a 121 spread, x go, y flag, z drag. Got it?"

Jacob turned to his teammates and repeated the play. At Jacob's command, the second string offense broke their huddle, lumbered up to the line and assumed their three point stances. Jacob followed behind them, surveying the defensive scheme that lay before him, his head swiveling from side to side.

"Hut, hut," he barked.

The ball slapped Jacob's hands, and he took a quick five step drop, his eyes scanning downfield. No sooner had he planted his back foot than he saw large shadows converging upon him from every direction. At the last second, he tucked the ball away and braced for the impact. He was hit by defenders from every side in a bone crunching collision, then pile driven into the unforgiving turf.

Gasping for air, Jacob looked up at his assailants, his face a mask of pain and confusion. He tried to pull air into his lungs, but couldn't. Through squinted eyes, he could vaguely make out the identity of his closest assailant. It was Trevor Bickle.

"What do you think of *that* Mormon boy?" he sneered from behind his facemask.

One by one, the defenders pushed themselves off of the pile. As Trevor pushed himself up he let the full brunt of his weight crush down on Jacob's chest one final time.

Gasping for breath, Jacob crawled to his knees, paused for a moment, then rose to his feet. He limped back to the huddle, eyeing his offensive linemen warily.

"Alright gentlemen, tighten it up," Coach Brooks said calmly. "This time I want you to give me a 929 spread, x slant, tight end double squeeze."

Jacob paused, buying himself some time, then relayed the play to his teammates. As he limped up to center, his ribs ached, his whole body screaming in protest. He scanned the defensive formation, taking especial note of Trevor's location. Their eyes locked. A devious smile shone through Trevor's facemask.

Jacob took a final, labored breath, and then yelled, "hut!"

The ball slapped his hands and he dropped back into the pocket, his head on a swivel. Then suddenly, from his blind side, he felt himself uprooted, launched violently into the air, and once again driven mercilessly into the ground.

"Good read Bickle," Paul shouted, clapping his hands. "Excellent read."

"Why don't you quit before bones start snapping," Trevor sneered as he rolled off of Jacob. "We can keep doing this all day long."

Jacob stared back, his eyes brimming with contempt, but said nothing. Amid all the tendrils of pain, another feeling emerged. It was pure, unadulterated loathing, first for his coach, then for his teammate.

Trevor climbed to his feet and jogged back to his huddle, earning high fives from a few of his teammates.

"Well done Bickle. Textbook. You see that guys?" Paul said, turning to the rest of the defensive huddle. "Not only was that a textbook stunt through the A-gap, but the tackling form was impeccable. That's the kind of tackling that earns you playing time gentlemen."

By this time, Jacob had managed to roll over onto his stomach. He slowly pushed himself to his knees, every nerve in agony. He could quit.

He *should* quit. But then Coach Connelly would win. He would be giving him exactly what he wanted.

Once on his feet, he stumbled back to the huddle, eying his teammates warily.

"I think I get it now," Jacob said, his eyes darting from facemask to facemask. "Roll over on your blocks so they can plaster the Mormon kid all over the field. Is that it?"

Their eyes darted all about, refusing to meet his incensed gaze.

"Maybe if they hit me hard enough, I'll just quit. You think that's how this is going to go down? If you do, you have no idea who I am. Same play on two."

The huddle broke and Jacob strode up to center, an almost imperceptible swagger in his steps. He surveyed the defense, noting especially the positioning of the linebackers.

He began barking signals and then, after a brief pause, yelled "hut-hut." Jacob grabbed the ball and took a five step drop. He brought the ball to his ear, as if to throw, but at the last second tucked it beneath his arm and began charging towards the line of scrimmage. Trevor and the other outside linebacker were charging towards the pocket, but when they got there, Jacob was gone. Jacob had spotted a small seam between two linemen and was bursting towards it. He slid through a narrow hole in the line and past the linebackers who had been caught out of position. With the corners and safeties stuck in man to man defense, Jacob suddenly found himself in the secondary. He continued to accelerate, charging towards the end zone, still 40 yards away. The secondary attempted to give pursuit, but by the time they had arrested their momentum, Jacob was only 20 yards from the end zone. Jacob took one look back and, finding himself alone, slowed from a sprint to a jog, and then to a stroll.

He walked across the goal line and turned to face the defense. They were rooted to the ground, hands on their hips, staring at him in a mixture of surprise and disgust. The play had not gone at all like they expected.

As he jogged back through the tangle of players, his eyes fell upon Trevor. His lips had receded into a snarl, the contempt wafting off him like a foul odor. Jacob took the ball and flipped it in his direction. Trevor snatched it out of the air with disgust.

"Pesky little ball," Jacob said. "So hard to keep track of sometimes."

CHAPTER 33

John's first day as an avowed member of the Mormon Church in Mayfield had gone exactly as he thought it would. Just as he'd predicted, the news of his purported crime had spread like wildfire. Teachers in the hallways looked at him askance while students in his classroom favored him with icy stares and snide remarks. When the school day drew mercifully to a close, John grabbed his briefcase, and bolted down the hallway, through a side door and into the parking lot. As he folded himself into his rental car, he felt the tension slowly seep out of his body. Though his first day in the lion's den had been anxious and awkward, it had passed without major incident.

His journey home took him along the usual route. As he turned onto Tower Road, a familiar sight sprang into view. He had driven past it twice a day for each of the last two weeks, and it had never failed to pique his curiosity. The house itself was quaint and friendly looking, but it was hedged about by a half acre of property that was unkempt and wildly overgrown. The grass hadn't been cut in weeks, and marauding weeds had overtaken the flowerbeds. It almost looked as if the owner of the house had simply…well…died.

As he drove past the house this time, however, his eyes were drawn towards one additional detail. There in the front yard, straining over a lawnmower, was the bent figure of an old woman, yanking fruitlessly on a ripcord.

What's she doing? John thought to himself. *She's going to kill herself.*

As John continued down the street, marveling at the women's courage, the words he had once spoken to his family resounded in his mind.

"In our new town," he remembered saying, "we will not preach the gospel with *words*. However," he had said with an unwavering resolve, "we will never tire of preaching the gospel through our *actions*."

As John reflected on this counsel, his foot reflexively hit the brake. He pulled to the side of the road, idling the car as he turned this thought over in his mind. Then, all at once, he pulled his car into a U-turn, and came to a stop in front of the shaggy, weed-infested yard.

At the sound of John's approach, the old lady looked up from her mower, thankful for a respite from her futile escapade.

"Hello there," John said, stepping out of his car and up onto the sidewalk.

Exhausted from her losing battle with the lawnmower, she proffered only a wan smile and a wave of the hand.

"What seems to be the problem here?" John asked, a friendly smile spanning his face.

"Darn thing won't start," she said between breaths.

"You know you really shouldn't be trying to tackle this thing on your own," he said, his eyes scanning the yard. "Looks pretty daunting if you ask me."

"I know, I know. This is Rufus's territory. He could always, somehow, bend this dastardly machine to his will."

"Rufus being your husband?" John asked.

"That's right," she nodded.

"And where is Rufus?" John inquired.

Her face grew heavy and sad, her eyes distant.

"Passed on," she said softly. "I lost him, oh, coming on two months now."

John did a quick survey of the yard and confirmed that there was at least two months of overgrowth before them. The puzzle was coming into focus.

"I'm very sorry for your loss Mrs…"

"Huxley, Vivian Huxley."

"Ok Mrs. Huxley…"

"Please, my dear…call me Vivian."

"Ok Vivian. Even if you could get this thing to start, trying to cut grass this dense will be tough going. In fact, I'd advise against it."

Vivian's brow furrowed as the reality of her plight settled over her.

"That so?" she said, in a tone of surrender.

"No question about it. But, listen, I know a thing or two about yard work. Would you be opposed to me lending a hand?"

"Oh no," she said, waving her hand. "I wouldn't want to impose!"

"No imposition at all. If you don't mind waiting until Saturday morning, I'll get this whole yard whipped into shape. I may even enlist a friend…that is, if it's ok by you."

Vivian's face lit up, then broke into a smile.

"Won't you come in out of this heat Mr…"

"Peterson. John Peterson. But you can call me John."

"Well ok, Johnny. Won't you please come in? I've got some sweet iced tea steeping in the fridge."

"A cold glass of water would be perfect," John said as they walked slowly up the concrete walk.

Once inside, she led him to a round table inside a small, quaint kitchen. He surveyed the fifties style fridge and range as she poured water into his glass and tea into her own. John had the eerie sensation of being caught in a time warp.

"It really is so nice of you to offer to help. It's been…hard…since I lost Rufus. Had it not been for my ladies, I don't know what I'd do."

"Your ladies?" John asked.

"That's right, my ladies. But for them, who knows where I'd be."

"How do you mean?" John asked.

"Well, they're my support system. We get together every Wednesday. We play bridge, we talk, we…gossip." This last confession caused her face to screw up in a grin.

"But, don't let me bother you with those details," she said.

Something in her story, however, had sparked John's curiosity.

"Tell me more about your ladies," he said, leaning forward in his chair.

The light returned to her eyes as she began to speak.

"Oh, there's about eight or nine of us I reckon. Our group was larger, back when all our husbands were alive. Then they started to go, one by one. Mostly the husbands at first, but then the ladies started to go too. Rufus was the lone male hold out. When he passed a few months back, it left just us ladies."

Once again, that distant look crept into her face.

"You don't mind me asking about this, do you Vivian?" John asked.

"Oh no, not at all," she said, waving her hand at him. "Nothing to hide."

John looked down at the table, thoughtful, his fingers cradling his chin. After a few seconds he raised his glance.

"Listen Vivian, how many of these other ladies are dealing with what you're dealing with?"

"Dealing with...?" she asked, confused.

"Yeah, you know, big yards with lawns, houses that need to be maintained, maybe a bit lonely?"

A note of awareness spread across her face.

"Well, one of our ladies has a grandson who's always Johnny on the spot. But, by and large, most of us are on our own. You know, trying to make do."

John sat at the table, hanging quietly on Vivian's words, nodding his head. Then he spoke.

"I really don't want to impose, but what are the chances...," John said, his voice trailing off.

"Go on Johnny," Vivian said, shooing her fingers as if to coax the words out of him.

John smiled then continued.

"What are the chances I could meet these ladies of yours?"

"*Extremely* high I'd say," she said, batting her eye lashes softly. "A young, dashing man like you? Why, they'd like nothing better!"

"Alright, alright," John said, blushing. "Why don't we try this then? I'll come back on Saturday morning, 9 o'clock sharp. I'll take a look at taming this yard of yours. Then, you convene your ladies around 11 o'clock for a game of bridge. That way we all get acquainted."

"When I describe who's coming," she said coquettishly, "why, it's as good as done."

"Vivian, it was a pleasure to make your acquaintance," John said, rising from his chair, arm extended.

"Oh, believe me Johnny," Vivian replied, gripping his hand tightly, "the pleasure was *all* mine."

CHAPTER 34

Each step towards the locker room sent tendrils of pain shooting through Jacob's body. After ten minutes, he had worked his way past the water coolers and up to the parking lot that abutted the practice field. As he curled around the fence and onto the sidewalk that led to the locker room, he saw a pair of headlights snap on. An engine turned over, and then roared to life. Jacob's hand drew reflexively to his face, shielding his eyes from the bright beams. As he did, he became aware of the car's occupant. It was Donavan Dooley. Donavan held Jacob's gaze for a split second before looking over his right shoulder and backing out of his spot.

A hollow feeling gathered in the pit of Jacob's stomach. Donavan had driven Jacob home nearly every day since the start of practice a month earlier. Their rides home were spent scheming against their opponents, contriving trick plays and, forging a fast friendship.

Wow, that didn't take long, Jacob thought. *Donavan the fair weather friend.*

Jacob's teammates had always been the one group to which he could always cling, regardless of his dad's religious battles. Not now. Not in Mayfield. Not after his dad's latest fiasco.

He willed his legs once again into motion, resuming his excruciating death march towards the locker room. By the time he limped through the locker room door, the last of his teammates had long since gone. His solitude seemed to echo off the walls of the locker room, resounding back upon him, intensifying his sadness.

As he collapsed onto the bench in front of his locker, he heard a faint rustling sound coming from the direction of the equipment room. He poked his head around his locker and saw a beam of light splashed against the locker room floor.

Good ole Doc, Jacob mused. *Always burning the midnight oil.*

Jacob slowly unlaced his cleats and threw them noisily into his locker, caked on mud flying in every direction.

"You're here kind of late aren't you Peterson?" came a raspy voice from his left.

Jacob jerked his head up and saw Doc's frail figure standing next to him, that heavy sadness in his eyes. Jacob offered a shaky smile, trying to mask the dull throb he was feeling in his ribs.

"Yeah, well, tough practice," Jacob said, the smile disappearing from his face.

The lines in Doc's face deepened as he looked Jacob over.

"You know, Jake…," Doc said, shaking his head in disgust, "I couldn't be more ashamed of this town than I am right now."

"What?" Jacob asked, his eyes widening.

"Well, take your father for example. As good a man as I know. Yet by what you hear, you'd think he were Old Scratch himself."

"I'd rather not talk about my father," Jacob said bitterly.

"Well, I'm no expert on father-son relationships," Doc replied softly, "but I *am* a pretty good measure of character."

Jacob said nothing but continued to glower in silence.

"For all his frailties as a father, don't ever doubt that man's goodness. You understand me, son?"

Jacob lifted his head, met Doc's unwavering eyes, and then nodded his head reluctantly.

"So, what makes you so different Doc?" Jacob said, after a moment of silence. "Why aren't you falling in line with the rest of them?"

Doc's eyes grew distant.

"A long time ago I resolved to judge my fellow man by his deeds, not by rumor or innuendo."

"You do realize I'm not real high on my dad right now, don't you?" Jacob said.

"I do," he said, his old, tired eyes glowing with intensity. "But don't give up on your dad, and don't you dare give up on this team."

"I don't know Doc," Jacob said, lifting his arm, surveying the nicks and scrapes. "I don't know how much longer I can keep this up."

• • •

Jacob hobbled out of the locker room and out to the curb. He scanned the parking lot, looking for a car, a face, anyone he could recognize. Except for a few lonely cars, the lot was now empty. His heart tumbled into his gut. The trek home under normal circumstances was walkable. But today he was in no condition to pull it off. The crippling pain in his left leg alone was a deal breaker. He frowned as he contemplated what he was about to do. He stuffed his hand reluctantly into his pocket and grabbed his cellphone. He hesitated, then began dialing his father's number.

"You looking for a ride?" came a high, squeaky voice from behind him.

Jacob whirled around and saw standing before him Arnie Liebowitz. Arnie was the team kicker. Well, back up kicker. On a good day. He stood five foot four, and weighed all of 135 pounds, soaking wet. He wore his hair in a buzz cut and had thick glasses that slid repeatedly off his nose. Jacob pressed end and stuffed the phone back in his pocket.

"Yeah, why?" Jacob replied. "You got wheels?"

"I *do* have wheels. Nothing *you'd* really want to be seen in, but they'll get you home."

Jacob scanned the parking lot one last time as if to assure himself that this was, in fact, his only option. He took a deep, reluctant breath.

"Uh, yeah...I'd appreciate it," Jacob said, flashing a halfhearted smile.

"No problem man. Anything for the great Jacob Peterson."

"Huh?" Jacob said, following Arnie towards his circa 1985 Reliant K Car.

"Hop in," Arnie said, motioning to the passenger side.

Jacob yanked at the door and it opened with a creak. He tossed his backpack into the backseat and then slid into shotgun position.

"Did you just call me the 'great' Jacob Peterson?" Jacob asked.

Arnie stuck his key in the ignition and, to Jacob's surprise, it fired to life.

"Look," Arnie said as he backed his car out of his spot. "Everyone knows you're the real deal. I've watched you in practice. I've even researched you online. You were a preseason All-American. You could lead this team to the promised land with a broken throwing arm. Everybody knows that."

"Not everybody," Jacob said briskly.

"Who do you mean, Coach Connelly?"

"Bingo."

Arnie gave Jacob an appraising stare.

"You *do* know what's going on there, don't you?"

"Of course I know what's going on. He's pegged my dad all wrong, and now he's taking it out on me. That, *and* he's a bigot."

"Really?" Arnie said, his eyebrows rising in surprise. "Do you *really* think that's what's going on?"

"I know that's what's going on. The man told me himself."

Arnie began to chuckle.

"Boy, sometimes I get the feeling that I'm the only one in this town that really gets it. My powers of perception surprise even me sometimes."

"Alright, alright, before you break your arm patting yourself on the back, you mind telling me exactly what *you* think is going on?"

"Look, it's like this. Paul Connelly is on the way out. His job is hanging by a thread. Everybody knows it. He's kept it this long because of his track record as a disciplinarian. When you came along Jake, something happened. He stopped disciplining, he loosened his grip. It's like he thought you were the answer to all his problems. So, as they say, he took his eye off the ball."

"Alright, but that's nothing I didn't already know."

"I'm not done yet. This is where it gets interesting. When all of this extracurricular stuff started going down, you know, Markham, Thibadeau, and the others, the community started to worry. It was like the Mayfield 8 was happening all over again."

"Ok, I'm with you," Jacob said.

"So, Connelly had to find some way to reassert himself, you know, remind them of why they hired him in the first place."

"Okay," Jacob said, his eyes beginning to narrow.

"So that's where you come into play. This whole Mormon surprise presented him with the perfect opportunity to climb back on solid ground. If he can be seen as the ever-vigilant guardian of the public's welfare, well…maybe that buys him some time."

"Yeah, but without me at quarterback, he'll start losing games, no different than last year. He'll be out of there either way."

"True, but this time it's different. And this is speculation on my part, but I think I have a pretty good bead on it. You know, of course, who Trevor Bickle's dad is, don't you?"

"Yeah, president of the school board."

"Exactly. Jasper Bickle holds Connelly's job in the palm of his hands. Keep that guy happy, and Connelly keeps his job."

Jacob's eyes seethed with anger.

"You're telling me Coach Connelly made a deal with the school board?"

"Not the school board," Arnie corrected. "With the president of the school board. The father of the only other quarterback on the team."

"So, he could lose every single game, but so long as his players stay out of jail, and Trevor is his quarterback, then he lives to coach another day?"

"Basically."

"Well that's just *perfect*. You trying to cheer me up here?"

"Nope. Just telling you what I know."

"And how, may I ask, do you know all this stuff?"

He flashed Jacob a roguish smile.

"Well, beyond my own acute powers of perception…I do have other well-connected sources."

"Oh yeah? Like who?"

"Every Thursday I do yard work at my grandma's house. The old woman's wired. Belongs to some group she calls 'the ladies.' It's gossip central. Helps her keep her finger on the pulse of the town. Every once in a while she passes something along."

Before Jacob could delve any further, the car came to a stop. Jacob turned to Arnie in shock.

"You know where I live?" Jacob exclaimed.

Arnie looked sheepish as he stared back at Jacob. "Yeah, I guess I do."

"You know that's really kind of creepy, don't you?"

"What do you mean?" Arnie said, a hurt look coming across his face.

Sensing Arnie's umbrage, Jacob backed off a little.

"I just meant, you know a lot of stuff about me. Where I live, last year's stats, this little pickle I've gotten myself into. Why are you so invested in me?"

"Well, I think invested is a bit strong. I just make it my business to know things. As you may have noticed, I'm not the most popular kid in school. I'm not charismatic or athletic, and I don't have many friends. I can't be in the crowd, so I've settled on being in the know."

Jacob squirmed in his seat.

"So," Arnie continued, "I watch things unfold, I consult my sources, and I zero in on the stuff that interests me. Store it all right up here," he said, tapping his forefinger on his temple.

"Yeah, well, you just caught me off guard. Didn't think my life right now was really all that interesting."

"You're kidding, right? Your life's like a soap opera right now. Biggest scandal to hit this school in a long time. Sucked me right in."

"Yeah," Jacob said, "like I was saying, pretty creepy."

"Look," Arnie protested. "You gotta get off this creepy thing. I know stuff that I think can help you. And in return, maybe you can help me."

Jacob squirmed once again, leery of where this was headed.

"And how *exactly* do you think I can help you?" Jacob muttered, bracing for the response.

"I'll have to think about it. For starters, why don't we continue this conversation tomorrow. Meet me for lunch in the cafeteria...right around noon?"

Jacob hesitated. His social life was already in free fall. Was lunch with Arnie Liebowitz really what he needed right now? But then he thought about what Arnie knew. That could definitely come in handy.

"Alright Arnie. I'll see you at lunch tomorrow."

Arnie's face broke into a smile. "You won't be sorry Mr. Backup quarterback."

"That's right, pour salt in the wound," Jacob said, stepping out of the car and closing the door.

"My bad," Arnie said, in a flagrant attempt to sound cool. "By the way," he continued, "don't give up on Ashley. I still think there's hope there."

As soon as the words slipped out of Arnie's mouth, his foot slammed down on the accelerator and the car lurched away from the curb.

"What?" Jacob gasped as the car drove out of sight. "How does he know all this stuff?"

Whether Jacob liked it or not, it looked like he'd just made a new friend. He turned from the curb and began limping his way up the steps. After what seemed like an eternity, he collapsed against the front door, his lungs straining for air. Summoning his last bit of strength, he heaved himself against the door and tumbled into the foyer.

Jacob turned and saw his dad seated on a recliner in the living room, an Italian textbook cradled in his lap.

"What happened to *you?*" John exclaimed, his eyes darting from Jacob's arms, to his legs, and then back to his face.

"Trust me Dad, you don't want to know. Not that you can do anything about it anyway."

"No, *really*, I'd like to know. What happened?"

Jacob limped over to the sofa and collapsed onto it. He moaned as he searched for the one position that didn't send bolts of pain streaking through his ribcage.

"My life is over Dad. Everything that was worth living for is now gone. Football, any shot at a social life. It's all gone."

"Football, gone? What do you mean? They disbanded the team? Over that golf cart thing? Ludicrous."

"No Dad. It's even worse. You are now looking at the starting quarterback…on the Mayfield Mustang practice squad. I'm a scout team quarterback."

"What? He *benched* you?" John said, his jaw jutting indignantly. "How…is that possible?"

"It's easy Dad. You're a Mormon. Your religion is spawned of Satan. And I'm your son. Case closed."

Warring emotions spread across John's face like a rotating kaleidoscope. He could feel his heart pounding in his chest, an angry heat rising within him. *Don't give into it,* he said to himself. *For Jacob's sake, don't give into it.*

"Ok fine. So you've been benched. Nothing that can't be overcome. But why do you look like you've just been fed through a wood chipper. I mean, even scout team quarterbacks have the little red jersey."

Jacob let out a cackle of feigned laughter.

"Good one Dad. Look, when the coach no longer wants you on his team, the little red jersey tends to lose its value. And, when the only thing protecting you from the first string defense is the worst, lousy bunch of blockers you've ever seen, then this is what you get. Wood chips."

John felt the flame of anger reprise itself, but he squelched it. He'd seen where it had gotten him in the past.

"Well, without you, they're done. They're finished. What are they going to do, throw that Bickle kid in there? That's career suicide for Connelly and he knows it."

"Maybe, maybe not."

"Huh?" John said.

"For Coach Connelly, it's not about winning games anymore. It's mostly about rehabilitating his reputation. This last brush with the law took place on his watch. By turning you and me into the villains, and then ostracizing us in every possible way, then maybe, just maybe, he regains the public trust. And if they happen to win a few games along the way, it's icing on the cake."

John stared at his son in disbelief.

"I'm going to fix this Jacob. I *can* fix this."

"You're not going to fix anything Dad. You've done enough already," Jacob said as he rolled away from his dad, his hands tucked tightly against his ribs.

"I just need you to stay out of my life," he groaned. "Can you manage that for once?"

CHAPTER 35

Early Monday evening, Paul Connelly began to survey the vast cache of email responses that had been forwarded to him from Jasper Bickle. By midnight, he had worked his way through all of them discovering, to his delight, that nearly 90% of the respondents had approved of their strategy to contain John Peterson.

His first task was to separate the responses into two folders on his hard drive. The first folder consisted of those who had agreed to the boycott of Living Christ Ministries. Most had commended Paul for the dispatch with which he had identified and quarantined the threat. This brought Paul no small level of satisfaction.

The second folder consisted of a smaller group of outliers that would require further persuading. Paul printed these emails out and, armed with a pink highlighter, began to parse out the more objectionable ones.

"So, he's a Mormon? Big deal. It's not like Mormons aren't Christians. Or haven't you been listening in church? What are we now, the Grand Inquisition?"

"Mormons…aren't they the ones with those great family-centered commercials? Are we really opposed to that type of message? Isn't that what this town needs right about now?"

"I don't know Coach. I like everything about John Peterson. If this guy's a Mormon, then maybe it's time we all learned a little more about Mormonism. Boycott church on Sunday? I don't think so. If anything, we need more of John Peterson."

Paul chafed at such ignorance. How could they fail to appreciate the gravity of John Peterson's crimes? The email had been clear. The ruse had been on for nearly a month. They were all victims. The sooner John Peterson was banished from the congregation, the sooner they could pick themselves up, dust themselves off, and get on with their lives. Oh yes, these stubborn renegades would require some special attention indeed.

Within this second folder, Paul created six subfolders for each member of the committee. The emails in question were then divided equally among each member. He then opened up his email browser, attached the second folder to the body of the email and began to type:

"My brothers in Christ," he began.

"Our initial wave of emails has met with little resistance. It seems that most of our membership appreciates the seriousness of the breach, the dangers of Mormonism, and the necessity of a boycott on Sunday. For most, it is evident that Mormonism needs to be rooted out at every possible turn.

"I was saddened, but not surprised, by a small group of holdouts that will require a little more of our attention. Judging from their responses, the lines between Mormonism and mainstream Christianity have somehow been blurred. It is our job to clearly delineate the differences, and firmly define the two basic camps: Christians and Mormons. Mormons, especially those masquerading as Christians, present a fundamental threat to the congregation and need to be systematically ostracized and marginalized. We are to show no equivocation in this regard.

"To that end, I have attached a list of the primary offenders, as well as the most recent church phone directory. As previously agreed, we are to call the families in question and persuade them of the folly of their position. Impress upon them the true nature of Mormonism as well as the importance of the boycott on Sunday.

"I hope to have this portion of our outreach program completed by tomorrow night. Please email me with your results."

"Warmly,"

"Your brother in Christ, Paul Connelly"

Paul hit the send button, leaned back in his chair, and basked in the satisfaction that the first phase of his plan had been executed. Stage one had yielded impressive results. The stragglers in the congregation *were* a cause for concern. But few if any would escape the vast sweep of stage two. By Sunday, the entire congregation would be turned against John Peterson. More importantly they'd come to know the Mormon Church for what it really was. And then, maybe then, this town would remember why they'd hired Paul Connelly in the first place.

CHAPTER 36

Jacob stared into the dark recesses of his locker, contemplating the new depths to which his life had sunk. His football career had been snuffed out, literally overnight. The only reason he kept playing was that he hadn't yet managed to break every bone in his body. Given time, however, that too was possible. Then, to make matters worse, his best friend had kicked him to the curb right along with the rest of the team.

A junior year that was once filled with promise and glory was now sputtering on the cusp of irrelevance. His only lifeline had come from the likes of Arnie Liebowitz. And Jacob still wasn't convinced this was a lifeline. For all he knew, Arnie could turn out to be an anvil. The guy who had lived his own life of irrelevance wasn't exactly the solution to Jacob's problems. Jacob's benighted existence was growing darker by the hour.

"Hello there," came a voice from behind him, pulling him back to reality.

Jacob whirled around. He suddenly felt his breath catch in his chest. Standing before him, in all her glorious majesty, was Ashley Hudson.

"Huh?" was all Jacob could manage.

"I said hello there," she said, smiling, then biting her lip.

"Oh…hey, how's it going?" Jacob said, trying to strike a nonchalant tone. Inwardly, he was kicking himself. His first response sounded anything but cool. But then again, what was *she* doing here?

Ashley stared at the ground, her foot kicking nervously at the floor beneath her.

"Listen, I think we got off on the wrong foot the other day," she ventured timidly. "I was rude. I'd like to…start over."

Jacob's body went stiff as the shock waves rolled over him. After five seconds of stupefied silence, Jacob finally gathered his wits.

"Listen Ashley, like you said, I'm a football player," Jacob said, looking down at the bandage on his elbow. Plus, it's *really* not a good time for me. Wouldn't it be better if we just…"

"Look," she said, cutting him off, "I know that's been my policy in the past, and for good reason. But, there are some mitigating circumstances that have caused me to…reconsider."

Wow, mitigating circumstances? Jacob thought. *She's smart and beautiful?*

"Mitigating circumstances?" Jacob asked.

"Yeah, that's right. Circumstances have changed, at least from my perspective. You *are* a football player, but I sense you're not the usual brand."

Jacob regarded her bleakly.

"You noticed too, huh? I'm afraid my *brand* is exactly why this could never work out. Trust me Ashley, you don't want any part of this *brand*."

"What are you talking about Jacob?"

"Listen, every time I step onto the football field, my own teammates try to kill me. All of my friends have dropped me like…like I'm a leper, or something. I've got exactly one friend. His name is Arnie Liebowitz. I doubt you've heard of him. Not really on anyone's radar. So, I'm probably not the guy you want to be hanging out with right about now."

"Don't you get it Jake? That's *exactly* what makes you interesting. When I heard they were trying to smear you all over the football field, my little antennae went up. I mean, if *football players* are trying to kill you, how bad could you be?"

"Thanks a lot," Jacob said, shooting her a dour look.

"Look," she said, brushing the comment aside, "you have my attention. I'm here. I want to learn more."

She was biting her lip again, waiting for his response.

Jacob was about to fire back an especially witty rejoinder when he saw a shadow encroach in the corner of his eye. He looked to his right and saw a group of football players lumbering towards them. It was Trevor Bickle flanked by a few of the perpetrators from yesterday's massacre. As they drew closer, Jacob saw Trevor's eyes narrow. Then came the sneer.

"Well if it isn't the Mormon boy," he laughed, turning to his teammates. "Got any gold plates in that locker Peterson?"

Jacob's arms folded up to his chest, his lips tightening in contempt.

"What's wrong Peterson? You aren't going to cry are you? Why don't you just go home to your mommy. Or should I say mommies? How many mommies did you say you have? Three, four? Boy, it's got to be a real riot in your house."

Jacob heard the other players snigger in response. He turned back to Ashley, his face red with anger.

"Look Ashley, the last thing you need right now is to be seen with me," he said under his breath.

Jacob saw the hurt register on her face, but he brushed it aside.

"I gotta go. I'll see you around," he said, slamming his locker shut, and breaking down the hallway.

"Run home to your mommies," he heard one last time as he tore down the hall, followed by more laughter.

• • •

"Nice job bonehead."

"What do you mean?" Jacob said, setting his tray of food on the table next to Arnie.

"I understand that Ashley Hudson approached *you* and said she wants to get to know *you* better."

Jacob began shaking his head in confusion.

"And you know this how?" he said, his tone a mixture of curiosity and stupefaction.

"Never mind that," Arnie said with a wave of the hand.

"That's right. I forgot. Mr. Wallflower sees everything."

"I do see everything, which is exactly why you need me. I'll keep reminding you of that. Anyway, back to Ashley."

"What about her?" Jacob said, his face pinched with pain.

Arnie blew air out of his mouth impatiently.

"The whole football team's been after her for the last two years, Trevor Bickle leading the charge. One by one, they all get systematically rejected. Then she decides to make an exception to her personal anti-football player policy just for you, and you say no? You *are* a bonehead."

"Look, being seen with me right now is just not good public policy. Not for Ashley, not for anyone. Why get dragged down into this mess when life for her could otherwise be quite rosy?"

"Listen, numbskull, do you have any idea why she doesn't date football players?"

"I've got the gist of it. Football players in this school have a habit of breaking the law."

"Sure Einstein, but that's only part of the story. Remember that incident a few years back involving the Mayfield 8?"

"Sure, I've heard about it."

"Players stealing a school bus, donuts on opponents' fields, taking out a Quick Stop?"

"Right."

"Well, there was a lone cheerleader that took the brunt of that crash."

"Yeah, I heard."

"Well, that lone cheerleader just happened to be Ashley Hudson's older sister. She spent weeks in the hospital. Collapsed lung, compound fractures, you name it."

Jacob's mouth gaped open.

"That's right numbskull. It's nice to have all the information, huh? Anyway, Ashley was in the eighth grade at the time. After the nightmare of her sister's recovery, she vowed she'd never have anything to do with football players. No exceptions. Period. And to the great chagrin of nearly every player on the team, she's stuck to her guns. Even *after* the arrival of Paul Connelly."

Jacob's eyebrows bunched together as he analyzed the implications of Arnie's revelation.

"So you see Jake, the fact that she's willing to make an exception for a football player for the first time ever is, in a word, astounding. And for you to spurn her like you did is…well…the height of stupidity."

"Look Arnie, I'm not just any football player. I'm the least liked, most persecuted, most likely to not survive another practice, scout team quarterback. If she knew any of that, she'd rethink this little exception of hers."

"But that's *exactly* why she likes you. It's like you're the great *anti-football* player. If they're trying to kill you, then you must be the embodiment of all that is good."

"You think?" Jacob said, his eyes narrowing with skepticism.

Arnie expelled air in another burst of frustration.

"Boy are you lucky I'm your friend. Because I don't think you'd piece this stuff together otherwise. Frankly, I'm amazed you've lasted this long without me."

Jacob leaned back in his chair, the wheels in his mind spinning into motion. He stared off into space, his eyes squinting as he processed Arnie's statements. After a minute he returned his gaze to Arnie.

"Arnie, you make some good points. But at the end of the day, it changes nothing. As long as Connelly, the Bickles, and the rest of the team have me in their bull's eye, then being linked to me is going to be nothing short of a nightmare. I won't subject her, or anyone else to that. I'm tainted goods, man. Frankly, I'm surprised you even want to be seen with me," Jacob said, turning and looking over each shoulder.

"Are you serious? There isn't a guy in this school that wouldn't trade shoes with you in a heartbeat, even *with* all the persecution. Ashley Hudson is the real deal, man, and you're dropping the ball in every possible way."

CHAPTER 37

It was late and Ethan hadn't been expecting any visitors. He swiveled his chair, turning his full body towards the door as the footsteps grew louder. Within seconds, a tall figure emerged from the darkness of the foyer and into the light of his office. Ethan's face lit up with excitement.

"Brother John? What are you doing here?" he said, rising to shake the hand of his unexpected visitor.

John wore a beleaguered look, but through it all, Ethan could sense John was genuinely happy to see him.

"You know, just checking in. Wanted to see how things have been progressing."

Ethan smiled and leaned back in his chair.

"John, the Lord *is* blessing us. Attendance is up. Offerings are starting to rise. Slowly, but they *are* starting to roll in. We are by no means out of the woods, but I'm starting to hope again."

"That's great news Ethan," John beamed.

"Couldn't have done it without you, Brother John. I owe you *big* time."

"Well, the timing couldn't be more perfect," John said smiling, "because I could sure use *your* help."

"Sure thing. What'd you have in mind?"

"Well, I've come across an opportunity that I think just might be right up your alley."

"I'm all ears," he said with unrestrained ebullience.

John briefly recounted his meeting with Vivian Huxley and what he had learned about the ladies.

"I don't know Ethan, I just think there's a service opportunity here for you, me, maybe even your congregation. Weaving these types of activities into your ministry could be just the thing to push you over the top."

"I agree," Ethan said enthusiastically. "Tell me what we need to do."

"Well, I've arranged for Vivian to hold a bridge party with the ladies on Saturday morning at 11 a.m. If you and I could get there by 9, that'll give us two hours to subdue her yard. When the ladies show up at 11, they'll take note of our handiwork and the stage will be set."

"Count me in," Ethan said energetically.

"Perfect, I'll meet you there, say 5 minutes to 9?"

"I'll be there with bells on," Ethan quipped.

As John turned to leave, he stopped and then paused.

"Oh, and one other thing," he said. "I appreciate your understanding over this whole Mormon thing, I really do."

The smile disappeared from Ethan's face.

"Uh, how do you mean John?"

"You know, what happened over at Living Christ Ministries. I appreciate your understanding. It's been a really rough week, and I appreciate you not piling on."

"Uh, *Mormon thing*? What am I missing here John?"

Suddenly the blood drained from John's face.

"You mean…you haven't heard?" John asked, ashen faced.

"Haven't heard what?" Ethan said, his face clouding in confusion.

John stood there looking at Ethan for what seemed like an eternity. Ethan felt his heart flatten against his stomach.

"Ethan, I'm a Mormon," John said.

A shadow fell over Ethan's face as his arms drew up to his chest.

"No, no John. You can't be. I've heard your sermons. If what you preach is what you believe, you *can't* be a Mormon. You've *got* to be a Christian."

"Ethan, Mormons *are* Christians. The reason my sermons sound Christian is because I believe in Jesus Christ. I'm a Christian, Ethan."

"I see," Ethan said, straining at the news. "Might have been nice to know the little Mormon detail from the beginning."

"I couldn't tell you Ethan. At the time, I didn't have the luxury."

"What?" Ethan said, starting to look irritated.

"It's...complicated," John said helplessly.

Ethan suddenly looked down at his watch.

"Say, listen, I've still got some things I'm working on for Sunday. I better let you go."

"Um, ok. Well, I guess I'll just see you on Saturday."

"Yeah, about that," Ethan said. "Maybe some other time. With the all the momentum that's been building, I should probably be here. Have to take a rain check."

"Sure about that?" John said, his countenance falling.

"Yeah. Thanks again for stopping by."

• • •

Ethan heard John's footsteps slowly grow faint, and then he heard the front door open and close with a clank. He slumped deeper into his chair, his heart pounding in his chest, his nostrils flaring like a race horse. He brooded over the exchange for another 15 minutes before attempting to throw himself back into his sermon. If there was any antidote to the anger, the sense of betrayal he now felt, it was the pure, undefiled word of God.

But concentration wasn't coming easy. Anger and confusion continued to roil within him, muddling his thoughts, depriving him of focus. Mustering his last bit of resolve, he hit the space bar and saw his screen once again fire to life.

He began to read from the beginning, attempting to recapture the principal thread of the sermon. When he came to the first parable from Luke 10, he paused, his hand rising to his chin. Then he began to read: "And, behold, a certain lawyer stood up, and tempted him, saying, Master, what shall I do to inherit eternal life? He said unto him, What is written in the law? How readest thou? And he answering said, Thou shalt love the Lord thy God with all thy heart, and with all thy soul, and with all thy strength, and with all thy mind, and thy neighbor as thyself. And he said unto him, Thou hast answered right: this do, and thou shalt live. But he, willing to justify himself, said unto Jesus, And who is my neighbor? And Jesus answering said, A certain man went down from Jerusalem to Jericho, and fell among thieves, which stripped him of his raiment, and wounded him, and departed, leaving him half dead. And by chance there came down a certain priest that way: and when he saw him, he passed by on the side. And likewise a Levite, when he was at the place, came and looked on him, and passed by on the other side. But a certain Samaritan, as he journeyed, came where he was: and when he saw him, he had compassion on him. And went to him, and bound up his wounds, pouring in oil and wine, and set him on his own beast, and brought him to an inn, and took care of him. And on the morrow when he departed, he took out two pence, and gave them to the host, and said unto him, take care of him; and whatsoever thou spendest more, when I come again, I will repay thee. Which now of these three, thinkest thou, wast neighbor unto him that fell among the thieves? And he said, He that shewed mercy on him. Then said Jesus unto him, Go and do thou likewise."

After finishing the passage, Ethan sank back into his chair, lost in thought. He stared absently at the screen, the words of the parable resounding in his mind. Ethan had always been quick to fathom a scripture's meaning, yet when he read this parable, his mind clouded over.

He began to pick his way through his muddled thoughts, searching for meaning, anxious for illumination. Yet for a full ten minutes, he saw only fog and darkness.

"Which now of these," Jesus had said, "wast neighbor unto him…Go and do thou likewise."

As his eyes retraced these words, Ethan felt a sudden and overwhelming surge of shame. He replayed his exchange with John Peterson in his mind. Had he truly loved John Peterson in the same way the Samaritan had loved the man who had fallen among the thieves? He had certainly loved John when he had stood to gain from his expertise. When the shadow of John's celebrity eclipsed even that of Lester Le Haye, he had *everything* to gain by their association. But when John had revealed himself to be a Mormon, Ethan's love had waxed cold.

Ethan's stinging rebuke, devoid of love as it was, had been no different than the priest's refusal to render aid to the injured man. Even if John Peterson *were* a Mormon, it didn't absolve Ethan of his basic responsibilities as a Christian. His behavior had been woefully out of step with his religion.

Ethan winced in shame, the full impact of his hypocrisy pounding on his chest like an enormous hammer. His head fell into his palms, as the anguish engulfed him.

"What have I done?" he groaned into his hands. "What *have* I done?"

Chapter 38

By Thursday morning, their cumulative phone calling efforts had yielded impressive results. Of all the families in folder two who professed support for John Peterson, only six had held their ground. Among these, some had known Mormons in other towns, while others had simply been taken by the charisma of John Peterson. The pied piper had lured them in, and for now, there would be no breaking the spell, at least not over the phone.

To finish the job, Paul would set in motion the plan's final phase. He logged onto his email account, opened up a new message, and started to type.

"My brethren," he began.

"Efforts to quarantine John Peterson have met with little resistance. Through our collective efforts, we have received either written or verbal commitments from nearly all of our membership to boycott Living Christ Ministries until such time as John Peterson is no longer a threat to our congregation. To date, there are only six families whose intransigence warrants further action. Might I suggest that we divide these families along geographical lines:

The Jonathan Olsen family: Jim Mahoney

The Jerry Fowler family: Steve Cattrell

The Otto Barnes family: Kip Welbach
The Clarence Whitaker family: Clay McGill
The Randy Wooderson family: Jasper Bickle
The Nathan McLean family: Paul Connelly
"Remember, emails and phone calls have had little impact on these families. If we are to break through to them, we must engage them within the walls of their very own homes. It is not necessary that you apprise them of your coming.

"May I remind each of you that we are on the Lord's errand, to whose assistance we are entitled."

"Your brother in Christ, Paul Connelly"

• • •

At 7:30 p.m., Paul pulled to a stop in front of 279 Maple, home of the Nathan McLean family. Its windows emitted a warm glow that cut through the darkness of the fading twilight. His nerves buzzed wildly as he hopped out of his car and made the short walk up the concrete pathway.

Once at the door, he knocked lightly, waited, and then heard the patter of footsteps. The door swung open, and Nathan McLean filled the doorway.

"Coach Connelly?" he said, a look of surprise on his face. "Um, please, come in. Have a seat," he said, motioning towards the living room.

"Hon! We have a visitor," he yelled towards the kitchen. Paul took his place in an armchair, and Nathan the sofa.

In a few moments, Nathan's wife Emily emerged from the kitchen and sat next to her husband. Paul rose from his chair and extended his hand.

"Paul Connelly," he said warmly.

"Oh sure," she responded. "Football coach, right?"

"That's right," he said, the smile still propping up his cheeks.

"How can we help you?" Nathan asked as Paul settled back into his chair.

"I do apologize for dropping by unannounced. But the circumstances, I'm afraid, warrant it. Do you have a few minutes?"

They looked at each other, then back at the coach.

"Not a problem," Nathan said. "What's on your mind?"

"Well, I'm not sure if you're aware, but the person who has been preaching at Living Christ Ministries for the last four weeks, is not... how should I put this...as advertised."

"John Peterson?" Emily asked. "Yeah, we got the email and the phone call. How can we help you?"

Paul tried to read their stony faces but they were giving nothing away. This was going to be a lot harder than he thought.

"Well, for starters, I'd like to convey a little background on John Peterson."

Paul continued without waiting for their assent.

"We were told from the outset that John Peterson belonged to a Christian congregation in a neighboring county. We were not told the name of his congregation, only that he was a good, mainstream Christian. When we discovered that John Peterson was, in fact, a Mormon, it left many of us, well...troubled."

"Troubled?" Nathan said.

"That's right. Troubled. Given the lengths to which John Peterson went to conceal his religion, we believe him to be a threat to our congregation, our community and, frankly, our way of life."

Both of their arms were now folded against their chests, their lips pressed tightly together.

"Anyway, I've come here tonight to personally discourage you from any further attendance at Living Christ Ministries until such time as a suitable replacement can be found. Can I get your commitment that you'll join with the rest of the congregation in these efforts?"

Nathan unfolded his arms and then leaned towards Paul, his elbows on his knees.

"Look Coach," he began, "I've always had a lot of respect for you in what you're doing with those boys, on and off the field. There's no better man than you. Our community needs your leadership, and your commitment to moral rectitude. But this campaign you and your group have been waging against John Peterson, I guess...well...it's left *us* troubled."

Paul's eyes narrowed.

"Um, ok. So tell me where we're going wrong," Paul said, leaning towards them.

"Well, for starters," Nathan said, "we've known Mormons. There was a Mormon family that lived right next door to us in our last town. We watched their kids, they watched ours. Of all the neighbors we've ever had, we respected them the most. Now, I don't profess to know a lot about Mormon doctrine, but if the true measure of gospel living is the life that you lead, well, they were as good a Christians as we've ever known."

Paul took a deep breath as he saw the enormity of his task begin to grow.

"I do appreciate everything that you're saying," he said, his eyes moving from Nathan's face to Emily's, "but sometimes things are not always as they seem. A member of the Mormon Church, under the guise of Christianity and through the worst kind of deceit, worked his way into our good favor and, for nearly a month, carried out a stealth indoctrination of our congregation. Not exactly Christian behavior if you ask me."

Nathan was now shaking his head in protest.

"Isn't all this a little overblown? I mean, seriously, trying to convert the congregation? That's just not behavior consistent with the Mormons we've known. Quite the opposite actually."

"Nathan and Emily," Paul broke in, "it *can* sometimes be difficult to appreciate the danger of a threat unless we're acquainted with the details. Case in point. Did you know that Mormons believe in scripture other than the Bible? They claim that a man named Joseph Smith dug some gold plates out of a hillside and, by the power of God, translated it into another book of scripture."

Emily stood up, walked over to the bookshelf and took down a blue, hardback book with gold lettering on the front. She gave it to Paul as she sat back down next Nathan.

"This the one?" she asked.

"That's right," he said fanning through the pages. "The Book of Mormon. The single greatest evidence that Mormons are not Christians."

"Subtitle notwithstanding?" Emily objected. "Says there it's 'Another Testament of Jesus Christ'."

Paul nodded his head and then turned in the direction of the bookshelf. "Do you have a Bible on hand by chance?"

"Sure thing," Nathan said, rising from his chair. Within seconds he was back with a Bible in his hands.

"You mind finding a verse for me?" Paul asked.

"Um…ok," Nathan said, unsure where this was headed.

"Revelation 22:18. You mind reading that out loud?"

Nathan fanned through the pages, found his spot, and then began to read.

"For I testify unto every man that heareth the words of the prophecy of this book, If any man shall add unto these things, God shall add unto him the plagues that are written in this book:"

"Thank you," Paul said softly. "I would bring to your attention that chronologically, these are among the last verses ever written in the Bible. We must therefore concede that any scripture that professes to add to the Bible, the Book of Mormon included, by definition violates both the spirit and the letter of these verses. By accepting additional scripture, we render the Bible null and void. Can someone who *claims* to be Christian, openly declare the Bible null and void?"

Paul's words hung over the table as their faces took on grave expressions.

"I…guess I can see what you're saying," Nathan said, almost inaudibly.

"Furthermore," Paul continued, "did you know that Mormons believe that their church is the only true church on the face of the earth, and that every other church, by definition, is false and misguided? That includes Living Christ Ministries, Nathan and Emily. The very mission of their church is to bring us out of ignorance and into the redeeming light of Mormonism. That being said, what are we to make of a Mormon who intentionally conceals the name of his church while preaching to the largest congregation in town? Don't you think there's a reason he didn't disclose the name of his church?"

Nathan's tongue was slowly describing circles against the inside of his cheek.

"When you put it that way…I guess I can see your point," he conceded.

"Moreover," Paul said, hitting his stride, "did you also know that there are some Mormons who still engage in the practice of plural marriage, in spite of our country's strict prohibition against it?"

"No!" Emily gasped, her hand rising to her mouth in revulsion.

Nathan began shaking his head in disbelief.

"I guess appearances aren't always what they seem," Nathan said sheepishly.

"Look, I am in no way suggesting that these neighbors of yours weren't doing what they *thought* was right. Good people get led astray every day. I just think it's dangerous to suggest that having good intentions is the same as being Christian."

They both shifted uncomfortably in their seats, their eyes glued to their laps.

"We...we had no idea Coach," Nathan said.

Emily nodded her head in agreement. "None."

"Can I commit you both then, to join us in boycotting Living Christ Ministries until the John Peterson threat has been purged from the congregation?"

They looked quickly at each other, and then back at Paul. Without hesitation, they both said, "Yes."

"May the Lord bless you," Paul said with a smile.

CHAPTER 39

The first crush of angry phone calls had begun arriving early Monday morning, persisting unabated until late Wednesday evening. By midday Thursday, Buddy had arrived at a painful realization. John Peterson would not be preaching at Living Christ Ministries on Sunday. Not then, and not ever. By Friday morning Buddy had resolved to do the one thing he had promised himself he would never again do. He would renew his search for a stopgap within the Mayfield-based Christian ministries.

As this horrifying reality weaved cobwebs of gloom throughout his fragile psyche, another painful truth settled over him. Making inane supplications over the telephone to intransigent pastors would yield little in the way of results. If he had any hope of finding a substitute by Sunday, he would have to change tactics. He would have to make his case in person.

Buddy spent the greater part of Friday morning walking into the same pastors' offices making impromptu pleas for help. Though the packaging of the pleas was decidedly more personal, the responses were still the same. Making his requests in person only gave them a voice *and* a face towards which they could direct their testy responses.

After the fourth straight rejection, Buddy slid dejectedly behind his steering wheel, appraising the last name on the crumpled sheet of paper in his hand. There could be no question as to how this visit would go. More anger, more rejection, more upbraiding for the role his church had played in the decimation of the town's congregations.

Buddy drove for several minutes before the church's steeple rose into sight. He pulled into the parking lot, maneuvering his car into a spot in front of the church's administrative wing. He walked up to the glass door, pulled it open, and followed the signs pointing towards the pastor's office. After weaving his way through the hallways, Buddy came to an open office door. He stepped gingerly into the doorway and saw an enormous desk, upon which were strewn some loose papers and an assortment of books. Behind the desk sat Pastor Jimmy Barnes.

"Knock, knock," Buddy said, stepping through the doorway.

The pastor looked up from his book and squinted his eyes.

"Hope I'm not disturbing," Buddy said deferentially, his cheeks rising in a warm smile.

Pastor Barnes regarded him with an air of suspicion. "Mr. Holler," he said flatly. "I don't think I've spoken to you since that day I told you to never call me back."

Buddy tried to swallow the lump in his throat but couldn't.

"And here we are, only a month later, and you're standing in my office. This had better be good," the pastor said coolly.

Buddy shifted nervously, evaluating the logistics of a hasty exit. But his thoughts turned quickly to Beatrice, and then the ministry. He could leave, but then what? His situation was grim and the angry man seated before him was his last ray of hope.

"Well, Pastor Barnes, you may already suspect the reason for my coming, so I won't try to get cute with it. I'm in a tight spot for Sunday. We have yet to find a permanent replacement and frankly, I could use your help."

The pastor regarded him bleakly, his mouth turned in a disapproving frown.

"That right?" he said, his eyes returning to the book on the desk before him.

"There are a million different reasons why you should say no, and I wouldn't begrudge you any of them. But we're at the end of our rope here Pastor. From one Christian to another, I'm asking if you could…"

Buddy paused, and then took a gulp.

"…please favor us with a sermon on Sunday."

Buddy braced for the stinging rebuke. But the pastor only stared back at him, as if he were actually weighing the request. As the silence persisted, Buddy felt a small germ of hope spark within him.

"I do agree," the pastor began after an interminable pause, "that the spirit of Christian brotherhood has been sorely lacking in this community, especially among competing ministries."

Another pause. Through the deafening silence, Buddy could hear his heart hammering away in his chest. Beatrice, the ministry…they all came down to this.

"So, Mr. Holler, I will agree to preach to your congregation on Sunday. I can't say I'm tickled about the prospect of preaching to all my former congregants, but maybe it's time we put all the bad feelings behind us."

Buddy's mouth fell open, his brain scarcely able to process the pastor's response.

"Say again," Buddy said, stunned.

"I said, Mr. Holler, that I accept your invitation. While we are competitors, it couldn't hurt to introduce a spirit of mutual cooperation into our ministries. Are we not, after all, attempting to build up our Father's kingdom? Perhaps we would all be better served if we pursued that objective in a spirit of harmony and brotherly love. Anyway, what time did you say on Sunday? 9 a.m.?"

As the numbness suffused his body, Buddy could only stand there, a vacant expression on his face.

"9 a.m.?" the pastor repeated.

This time the words got through.

"Uh, 9 a.m. would be perfect," Buddy said, springing to life.

Buddy rushed over to the desk and grabbed the pastor's hand in both of his own and began to pump it enthusiastically.

"You're an example worthy of emulation," Buddy gushed. "A true Christian."

"Well, you know, who hasn't gone through a rough patch here and there? We clergy do need to stick together. After all, if we don't look after each other, who will?"

"Couldn't agree more," Buddy said, his spirits beginning to revive.

Jimmy Barnes flashed a warm smile.

"Meet you in your office at, say, 8:45?" he said.

"8:45 it is. I'll have them put your name on the marquee first thing. The good folks of Mayfield need plenty of advanced warning. This Sunday, the Lord's anointed will once again be in our midst."

CHAPTER 40

John stepped out of his car at 8:55 a.m. on Saturday morning and felt a claw of panic wrench at his gut. He hadn't thought it possible, but Vivian's yard appeared even wilder and more untamed than he had remembered. The grass, easily a foot long, was now spilling onto the sidewalk in torrents. The flower beds were so encumbered with weeds that its principal residents were now scarcely visibly.

How could he have been so delusional as to think he could tackle this job by himself? In two hours? He pulled his smartphone out of his pocket and turned it on. He quickly pulled up his home number and pressed call. Jacob was likely still in bed convalescing, but he badly needed reinforcements.

The phone rang twice before John pressed the end button. He'd forgotten. Jacob was a world away from him right now. Ever since their little secret had gotten out, Jacob had been pinning all of his woes on him. John turned to face the yard, the task looming before him like Mt. Everest.

With slumped shoulders, he began a slow shuffle up the walkway towards Vivian's door. He mounted the steps, pulled the screen door open, and rapped lightly on the wooden door. He heard some shuffling sounds, then saw the door swing open. Vivian looked out at him with a beaming smile. But when she saw that John was by himself, the smile began to fade.

"Oh me. I guess I thought there'd be more of you. Such a big job for you to do all by yourself Johnny."

As John opened his mouth to proffer some lame explanation, he heard the whirr of an engine approach from behind. He spun about and saw a Ford F-150 pulling a trailer come to rest in front of Vivian's house. In the trailer John saw multiple lawnmowers, rakes, blowers and all manner of landscaping equipment. The driver's door swung open and out hopped Ethan Reddick.

"Sorry I'm late!" he yelled as he scurried up the walk to join John at the door.

"Ethan Reddick," he said enthusiastically, grabbing Vivian's hand in both of his own.

"Ethan's the pastor over at the Community Church of Christ," John explained, confusion and relief competing for control of his face.

"Oh my," she said grabbing Ethan's hand, batting her eyes and looking at John. "You didn't tell me you were bringing someone that was just as handsome as you Johnny."

"We...aim to please," John said, feeling his cheeks flush.

"Well dear, you hit the mark on this one," she said, giggling to herself.

Both John and Ethan smiled this time.

"Anyway, we'll get to work here. You relax and take a load off. Hope to have everything done by bridge time at 11."

"Alright Johnny, if you say so," she said smiling, her eyes twinkling. She retreated back through the door, closing it behind her.

"Ethan, how in the world did you pull this off?" John said, motioning towards the truck and trailer.

"One of our new members owns a landscaping company. He agreed to part with it for the next couple of hours. In exchange I agreed to give him a tithing discount."

John laughed heartily, shaking his head in disbelief.

"By the way," Ethan said, "about the other day..."

John waved his hand at him, cutting him off.

"Water under the bridge my friend. Let's get to work. We've got some senior citizens to impress."

• • •

Over the next two hours, they mowed the grass, picked the flower beds clean of all offending weeds, trimmed the hedge and bagged the clippings. At 10:45, they stood on the sidewalk, marveling at the miraculous metamorphosis their actions had wrought. They were sweaty and grimy, and John's hay fever was acting up, but the gratification they felt in their breast seemed to override it all.

As the two men loaded the equipment back onto the trailer, the door to the house creaked open. Vivian stepped through the door and onto her porch. As she surveyed her yard, a hand sprang to her mouth, tears gathering at the rims of her eyes and then spilling over.

"Come," she gushed, walking towards them, her arms ready to swallow them in an embrace. The two men walked towards her, meeting her half way across the freshly cut lawn. She gathered them both in, pulling them close, tears of joy streaming down her cheeks.

"You're angels sent straight from heaven," she said between sniffles. "My two guardian angels."

• • •

As John, Ethan and Vivian sat at her modest kitchen table drinking lemonade and making small talk, they heard a rap at the door. Vivian looked up at the clock on the kitchen wall.

"That must be them," she said, waving her hands in the air, her excitement almost palpable. She sprang from the table, and shuffled out of the kitchen. From inside the kitchen, Ethan and John heard the door spring open and the happy exchange of salutations.

Over the course of the next ten minutes, seven more knocks sounded at the door and soon Vivian's living room was buzzing with all the energy of a gaggle of geese at feeding time.

After a few more minutes, the men heard Vivian clear her throat, as if to call the meeting to order.

"Thank you all for coming," she began. "Before cards start flying, I wanted to introduce two delightful young gentlemen whose acquaintance I have recently had the pleasure of making."

This was their cue. John and Ethan rose from the table and stepped into the living room, taking their place on either side of Vivian. Their appearance was met by a chorus of "oohs" and "aahs" followed by a series of unintelligible whispers exchanged between the women. Some primped their hair. A few batted their eyelashes. All trained their sights on the two men before them.

"You may have noticed something different about my yard when you pulled up today. Well, these are the dashing young men I have to thank for it."

More whispers, more movement and more bobbing of heads.

"Before the festivities start, I'd like to give my new friend Johnny a few moments."

With that, Vivian took a small step back, yielding the floor to John.

"Thank you Vivian," John said, taking a step towards the group of women. "My name is John Peterson, and this here is Ethan Reddick. We're here today because we'd like to lend a hand. Sometimes, when you're on your own, it's not always easy to get things done around the house. Is that a fair statement ladies?"

His query was met by a chorus of yeses, uh-huhs and more bobbing of heads.

"Losing a spouse can sometimes mean having to confront chores and tasks that are new and in some cases daunting. What are we talking about here? Ever had to mow your lawn, prune the hedge, or even fix a leaky faucet? It would be our distinct pleasure to unburden you of these tasks."

The palpable buzz in the room ratcheted up a notch.

"What do you charge?" came a raspy, dolorous voice from the back of the room.

"Not a dime Eleanor," Vivian interjected. "John and Ethan do this out of the goodness of their hearts. They do it because they're Christians."

This was met by another chorus of approval and more nodding of heads.

"Now Ethan here," John said pointing to his counterpart, "is the pastor over at the Community Church of Christ. Along with myself, Ethan and his congregation are prepared to assist you ladies in any way that we can. So, before this party gets started, we'd like to know how it is we can help."

John's question hung out over the room for about 15 seconds before the first hand shot up.

"I've got leaves in my gutters. That something you can swing?"

"Yes, in fact, gutters are squarely within our repertoire," John said.

Ethan fished a notebook out of his breast pocket and began to scribble.

"And your name ma'am?" Ethan asked.

"Dolores. Dolores Pritchard."

"Thank you Dolores. What else?" John asked, looking out at the rest of the women.

After another period of silence, shorter this time, another hand shot up.

"Name's Millie Clayborn. I've got the same problem as Vivian. Yard's just too big and these old legs just don't move like they used to. Doc says it's osteoarthritis."

"Very good. Well, as you can see," he said, nodding towards the window, "we definitely do yards."

With that, a few more hands shot up, the momentum in the room clearly starting to build.

Over the next ten minutes, John fielded 27 more requests from the roomful of ladies, as Ethan took fastidious notes.

When the requests finally subsided, John grabbed the notebook from Ethan and began to survey the list. For the first time in over a week, John felt a flicker of hope in his breast. He *had* been inspired when he stopped to help Vivian. This was *exactly* what he needed.

"Thank you very much ladies for your time," John concluded. "We'll get your addresses and phone numbers from Vivian and reach out to you within the next week or two. Sound like a plan?"

Then, to the utter surprise of both John and Ethan, the small group of women rose creakily to their feet and broke into spontaneous applause.

CHAPTER 41

Paul's eyes slowly blinked open. And then the memory of their brutal loss settled over him like a wet blanket. He groaned as his hands drew reflexively to his face, rubbing the sleep from his eyes. As he pulled himself upright, the nightmarish memory flooded into his mind. Trevor Bickle dropped back into the pocket, cocked his arm, and let loose a wobbly, errant pass. The ball drifted, almost in slow motion, down the field and into the awaiting arms of the free safety. It was a horrifying sequence that had played itself out four times over the course of the prior night's game.

The devastating loss would do little in the way of placating Stan Carraway. Stan's idle threats had hovered over him all summer, while visions of Chan Yarber danced about in his head. He had been warned to start the season with a bang. He had hoped to do it on the strength of his surprisingly ragtag defense. But with their anemic offense, it simply hadn't been enough. He desperately needed a quarterback. Without one, he was simply rebooting the woefully inadequate team from last year's two and eight season. Unless something changed, the losses would begin to pile up.

Paul's thoughts turned briefly to Jacob Peterson. *Jacob Peterson.* Paul allowed the luxury of Jacob Peterson to linger in his head for a few seconds before crowding it out. He had to remember why he'd been hired to begin with. This was not about winning at all costs. He'd seen where that had gotten the program in the past. Even Paul himself had been seduced by the siren call of winning football games, whatever the price. He felt a surge of shame as he reflected upon the weakness he had shown. Never again would Paul try to win football games at the expense of moral rectitude. Jacob Peterson's playing days were over.

Paul glanced over at the clock on his nightstand and felt a spark of panic. Films began in 15 minutes and he had yet to shower. Being the moral authority in town meant showing up on time to your own meetings. He threw back the covers, hopped out of bed and sprinted towards the shower.

After showering, shaving and dressing, Paul took another look at the clock. Five minutes to ten. He didn't have the luxury of walking today. He grabbed the keys off his dresser and bolted through the front door.

• • •

As Paul passed 5th Street, he saw the high school come into view. He checked his watch again. Two minutes to ten. He let out a sigh of relief. He was going to make it. The high school was now only 30 seconds away.

As he drew closer to the school, Paul's eyes were drawn in by a flurry of motion off to his right. He turned and saw two men attempting to subdue a yard that was wildly overgrown. The taller man pushed a lawn mower while the other snapped at the wayward branches of a bush with a pair of pruning shears. Paul recognized the house immediately. It was Vivian Huxley's. She'd finally hired someone to corral the dense thicket of weeds and grass that had taken up residence in her yard.

As Paul rolled past, he slowed to see if he could recognize the faces of these miracle workers. Paul zeroed in on the taller of the two. When the man's features finally came into focus, Paul felt his breath catch in his throat. Standing behind the lawnmower was none other than John Peterson. Paul's eyes darted quickly from John to his companion to see if he recognized him. He did not.

Paul felt a wave of acid rising in his throat as he struggled to make sense of what he had seen. Within seconds, he'd pieced it together.

Deprived of a pulpit, John Peterson was now taking his message directly to the public. He would begin with the old free service routine. He'd lure them in, gain their trust and, once they were ripe, he would reap the spoils. To Paul's horror, John Peterson was targeting the weakest, most vulnerable members of the community. He was proselytizing the widows.

• • •

Paul went through the motions during the film meeting, his mind a world away. The game last night *had* been a disaster, but what was unfolding in Vivian Huxley's front yard was even more cataclysmic. And Paul wasn't going to stand idly by just watching it unfold.

Five minutes after the meeting ended, Paul stepped up to Vivian's door and gave three loud raps. Paul heard footsteps then saw the door swing open.

"Coach Connelly?" came the surprised voice from behind the screen door.

"Good afternoon Vivian. I hope I'm not disturbing."

"Why, not at all. Please, come in."

Paul pulled the screen door open and stepped into the small foyer.

"Thank you Vivian. I won't be long."

"Take your time Coach. What's on your mind?"

"Oh, nothing really. I was just driving by your house earlier this morning and noticed some gentlemen working on your yard and…"

"Oh yes," she interrupted, her face lighting up like a Christmas tree. "That was Johnny…and Ethan. That's right, Ethan was his name. Such *fine* young men. So nice and helpful."

His face darkened as he surveyed her temperament.

"Why Coach, is there a problem?" she said, her brow pinching with concern.

"No, no of course not," Paul said, waving his hand at her. "Another quick question though, if you don't mind Vivian. And excuse me if it seems an unusual one. Did the topic of religion happen to come up while they were here?"

Vivian's finger drew up to her chin, her eyes drawing upward and to the left.

"Matter of fact it did come up," she said.

Paul's heart skipped a beat.

"Would you mind sharing what they said?" Paul said, trying to maintain his composure.

"Nothing preachy if that's what you mean. But John did mention that Ethan was the leader of some congregation."

"That right?" Paul replied, the acid in his stomach beginning to churn.

"Uh-huh. But you want to know the best part about it Coach?" she asked, the glow returning to her eyes.

She forged ahead without waiting for his response.

"After cleaning up my yard, they met with all my ladies. Offered the same services to them. You do know about my ladies don't you Coach?"

The force of Vivian's revelation drove the air from Paul's lungs. John's plan was even more devious than he had suspected. Vivian Huxley was just the first domino. They would gain her trust, foist their religion upon her, and then do the same with the rest of her address book. With Peterson's charisma, this was doubtless an achievable goal.

"Did they happen to mention the name of Ethan's congregation Vivian?" Paul asked, clinging to his last shred of composure, yet feeling it slip away.

She shook her head slowly as she stared off into space, picking through the cobwebs of her memory.

"Darn it if I can't remember the name. I tell you, more and more these days those little details escape me. If I do happen to remember, why I'll just give you a call."

Vivian's inability to remember, however, was inconsequential. Paul already knew the answer. Mormons always proselyted in twos. Some of their most devastating results were achieved by young Mormon missionaries, marching through neighborhoods, knocking on doors two by two. It fit the pattern perfectly.

"Fair enough Vivian. I apologize again for the intrusion."

"No trouble at all my dear. Stop back any time."

As Paul walked towards his car, he heard the old refrain echo through the chambers of his mind: *When the front door is locked, you go through the back door.* When John Peterson had arrived at Mayfield a little over a month ago, he had walked right through the front door. Now that the identity of his religion had been revealed, the front door had not just been locked, it had been barricaded. To Paul's horror, however, the back door of the community still hung wide open. And now, armed with reinforcements, John Peterson had begun his assault.

CHAPTER 42

"Thank you again, brethren, for arriving on such short notice. Normally, I wouldn't call you away from your families on a Saturday but the situation, I'm afraid, warrants it."

The five men stared back at Paul solemnly, awaiting his explanation for the emergency meeting.

"A few hours ago I observed John Peterson and the leader of his congregation performing yard work at the home of an elderly widow from our congregation. Their motivation, as I'm sure you're aware, is not to clean up the community, though that's sure to be a byproduct. Their primary objective, pure and simple, is to gain converts. Their goals haven't changed, brethren, only their tactics."

"Are you saying that we *still* haven't fixed the Mormon problem?" Jasper huffed.

"No, I'm afraid we haven't. Remember, a man that can work his way into the largest congregation in town is capable of anything. Banishing him from our congregation might have slowed him down, but it didn't stop him. He still has his sights set on conversion."

"Well we need to protect the town," Steve Cattrell said, his voice anxious.

"Sure," Paul said, "but how do you do it?"

"You do it the same way you'd protect it from a deadly disease. This town must be inoculated," Kip Welbach said, his tone hard and resolute.

"Inoculated?" Paul asked.

"That's right. If they know what's coming, they'll be protected against it," Kip said.

"You're suggesting we give them some sort of a warning? It's not like we can just send out a bunch of emails this time around. We're talking an entire town," Paul said.

Brows furrowed as Paul's statement tumbled about in their collective psyches. Soon their eyes converged on Jasper, who was leaning back in his chair, arms folded about his massive girth, a devious smile pulling at his mouth.

"I'll tell you exactly what we have to do," he said, his tone conveying the brilliance of his plan. "We *do* have to, in the words of Brother Welbach, warn the good folk of this town. But that's no easy task. The five of us alone could *maybe* hope to accomplish it in ten, twelve weeks' time. But by that time, the tentacles of Mormonism will be so deep, so entrenched, you might as well send this whole town down to hell. If we're going to act, we must do it quickly and decisively."

His mouth fell into a frown as he began shaking his head.

"If we're serious about neutralizing the threat," he said, "we've got to change our thinking. Think…bigger…more devastating."

"We're all ears Jasper," Paul said, prodding him on.

"There are five other fairly good size churches in our town in addition to our own," Jasper continued. "When you add their congregations to ours, we're talking 95% of the church going folk in this town. You get the ear of these pastors, convince them of the danger, then *they'll* do all your heavy lifting."

The men looked at each other, nodded their heads and murmured their approval.

"Jasper, are you suggesting that we make our case directly to the pastors?" Paul asked.

"That's exactly what I'm suggesting. These folks won't bat an eye if it's coming from a member of a *different* congregation. But, if they hear it over the pulpit in their very own church? Believe you me, that'll put the fear of God in those people. And if there's anything we need right now, it's the fear of God."

Paul's eyes darted from Jasper to the others.

"Are we agreed then?" Paul asked.

Heads moved up and down in silent approbation of Jasper's plan.

"Alright then. Just like last time, we'll divide and…"

A quick hand of protest shot out from Jasper's side, cutting Paul off midsentence.

"As I'm sure you are all keenly aware, my reputation in this town is not, how should I put it, inconsequential. Over the years, these fine pastors have come to…*value* my perspective. I'll do the talking this go 'round gentlemen. I know *exactly* what to say."

"What about the rest of us?" Kip asked, turning to Paul. "There's got to be something we can do in the meantime."

"Matter of fact there is," Paul said, a roguish smile creeping across his face.

"While Jasper's working his magic with the pastors, we're going to hit John Peterson broadside. Kip, Steve, I'm going to need *your* help on this one."

CHAPTER 43

Jimmy Barnes' name recognition along with a series of conciliatory emails had combined to settle the nerves of Buddy's congregation. Whatever had happened in Pastor Barnes' office on Friday morning was just the miracle Buddy needed.

At 9:00 a.m. on Sunday morning, Buddy peered out from behind the curtain and saw that the assembly hall was about three-quarters full. This fact alone convinced Buddy that things were finally beginning to break his way. Buddy smiled inwardly as he strode across the stage and settled in at the pulpit.

After a prayer, an opening hymn, and a brief introduction of Pastor Barnes, Buddy took his place behind the curtain stage left. After offering Buddy his heartfelt thanks for the opportunity of addressing his congregation, Pastor Barnes introduced the title of his sermon: "The Joys of the Consecrated Life". As the pastor's sermon got underway, Buddy could feel that familiar burning sensation flowering within him. Pastor Barnes, to Buddy's delight, was likewise blessed with the tongue of fire. And right now, the tongue of fire was just the thing his congregation needed.

From his position behind the curtain, Buddy scanned the vast assembly hall. He saw congregants sitting perfectly upright in their seats, attention rapt, heads nodding their approval. As the pastor's sermon built to a climax, Buddy heard a series of spontaneous Amens rise up over the congregation. A smile of hope spread across Buddy's face. This truly *was* a miracle.

But then, without any warning at all, the pastor's sermon took a terrible turn.

"In our congregation at Divine Providence," the pastor said, "we bring the joys of the consecrated life to a whole new level. To assist our newest members in this important goal, we offer a number of outstanding programs. Our fellowship committee, for example, is charged with welcoming and embracing our newest members. This committee holds weekly fellowship dinners, networking meetings, and even employment training. The clergy in our congregation is likewise heavily involved in the fellowship process. Beyond our Sunday sermons, we provide weekly opportunities for pastoral counseling, a Wednesday night Bible study, and a strong framework of spiritual shepherding. Such programs ensure that our new members have ample opportunity to partake of the consecrated life."

Buddy's eyes darted from the pulpit to the congregation as a wave of panic rushed over him. His congregants sat in their chairs, more enraptured than ever, soaking in every word. Buddy's panic soon morphed into terror.

Suddenly it all made sense. This had been no miracle. This had been a well-orchestrated plan to recruit Buddy's congregants. Jimmy Barnes had been given the opportunity to preach to the largest captive audience in three counties and had seized upon it. Buddy cursed himself for being so naïve. This scoundrel had been intent upon plundering Buddy's congregation from the moment the invitation had been extended. And judging by what Buddy was seeing, he was doing a first rate job of it.

Pastor Barnes concluded his sermon by inviting all in attendance to do whatever was necessary to achieve a consecrated life. He then closed in the name of Jesus, the congregation chiming in with an enthusiastic Amen.

The pastor then flashed an unctuous smile, gathered his notes, and then began walking in Buddy's direction.

"Quite the congregation you have here Mr. Holler. I enjoyed it immensely," he said, as he approached, his hand extended. When the pastor saw the look on Buddy's face, his hand fell limply to his side.

"What kind of stunt you trying to pull here Barnes?" Buddy said, his voice dripping with venom.

The pastor's forehead wrinkled, his face screwing up into a ball of confusion.

"Uh, how do you mean Mr. Holler?"

"You didn't come here in the spirit of *harmony* and *brotherly love*," Buddy said, his eyes gleaming with contempt. "This was a recruiting visit. Wow them with your sermon, sing the praises of your ministry and then practically invite them out to church. The only detail you left out was your address and starting time. Don't worry about that though, they can find all that on your website, right?" Buddy said.

The pastor's hands shot up defensively, a hurt expression on his face.

"I'm afraid I don't know what you're talking about Mr. Holler. I came here today to preach about the joys of the consecrated life. It's only natural that I would want to draw upon real programs and real experiences from my own congregation."

Buddy glared back at him, raw fury in his eyes.

"It's patently obvious why you came here today. You're not interested in looking out for other congregations. This was about looking after *your* congregation. You're a snake in the grass Barnes. Nothing but a snake in the grass."

Buddy's arm, shaking with anger, rose from his side and pointed towards the exit.

"Leave now before I have you thrown out," Buddy growled.

The confused, hurt look suddenly disappeared from the pastor's face.

"Ok Holler," he snarled. "If that's the way it's going to be, then we should just drop all pretenses. You've been plundering my congregation for years, so it's only time you got your just dues. Starting today, I'm putting the full court press on your congregation. I'll conduct three services a Sunday if I have to. I didn't want it to go down this way, but you've drawn the battle lines. Dig in Holler, because you've got a war on your hands."

CHAPTER 44

It had been two whole weeks since John had spoken to his wife. He'd left countless messages on her cellphone, but never to any avail. Now that Sunday was upon them, he had the first opportunity in over a month to attend his own congregation. Maybe, just maybe, this was his shot at reconciliation.

John stepped up to his dresser mirror and nuzzled his tie up to his collar. He pulled the collar down, centered the tie and gave himself one final, appraising glance. Satisfied, he padded out of his bedroom and into the kitchen. Jacob sat at the kitchen table working his way through a bowl of corn flakes.

"I've been meaning to ask you Jacob," John said in his best, by-the-way conversational tone. "What do you think we should do about church today?"

Jacob heard his father's voice, but his eyes remained fixated on the vitally important message inscribed on the back of the cereal box.

"I know what *I'm* doing about church, but I don't know what your plan is," he said with an air of cold indifference.

"Well that's just the thing. I'm not really sure. I mean, how do you think your mother would react if I were to…show up at church today?"

John held his breath as he waited for Jacob's response.

"Uh, not too good," Jacob said through a mouthful of corn flakes. "Judging by our conversation yesterday, definitely not a good idea. You gotta remember, when you do things to ruin *your* life, it ruins everyone else's lives too. You've lost a lot of credibility Dad. I'd keep my distance if I were you."

John felt a squeezing sensation around his heart, like the cinching of a belt.

"So where exactly am I supposed to go to church?" John asked, a defeated look on his face.

"Try the Potter City Ward. It's a few counties over, but if you leave now," he said glancing at the digital clock on the microwave, "you can still make it."

"But what about you? How are you going to get to church?" John protested.

"I've made my own arrangements," Jacob said in a tone that suggested that the conversation couldn't end soon enough.

Just then, they heard a honk from outside. Jacob leaped from the table, grabbed his scriptures, and bolted towards the door.

"Talk to you later," Jacob grumbled and ran out the door.

• • •

Arnie was sitting in his car, waiting for Jacob by the curb. He was dressed in a T-shirt and shorts, his left wrist draped limply over the steering wheel.

"I appreciate this Arnie. I really owe you one," Jacob said, pulling open the door and slipping into the passenger's seat.

"No problem," he said as the car lurched away from the curb. "That's what friends are for."

Jacob was still wrapping his brain around the whole notion that he and Arnie were now friends. Arnie was the last person who could resurrect Jacob's flagging social life.

"Nice duds by the way," Arnie said, his eyes darting from Jacob's shoes up to his tie.

Jacob looked down at his clothes, and gave Arnie a courtesy smile.

"Thanks, standard Mormon issue."

Arnie smiled and nodded his head. They drove in silence for the next 15 minutes, with Jacob breaking the silence only to provide directions.

Soon a chapel rose up before them. Following Jacob's instruction, Arnie turned into the parking lot and pulled to a stop in front of a set of double glass doors. Jacob unlatched his seatbelt and then turned to look at Arnie. He extended his hand over the console that separated them.

"I owe you one," Jacob said.

"Anything for a friend," Arnie replied.

Jacob smiled awkwardly. Arnie was taking this friendship thing way too seriously. Jacob turned to get out of the car before the mood got a little too weird. He closed the door behind him, and then leaned against the side of the car, his head poking down through the window.

"You know your way back?" he asked, a slight look of concern on his face.

"Come on Jake. You know nothing escapes my all-seeing eye. Of course I can find my way back."

"That's right, I almost forgot," Jacob said, chuckling warily. "You see everything. Thanks again," he said, rapping on the roof.

"Sure thing. Oh, and by the way," he said as Jacob turned towards the glass doors, "give my regards to Ashley."

"What?" Jacob said, briefly confused.

But Arnie said nothing. He had already begun to pull away.

"Arnie!" he yelled in exasperation, running after the car. "Tell me you didn't!"

But Arnie wasn't stopping. He flashed Jacob a quick wave, just as his car disappeared around the building.

Dread fanned out across Jacob's chest as he stepped towards the double glass doors. *Give my regards to Ashley?* Jacob had no idea what Arnie had been doing behind the scenes, but he feared the worst.

Jacob walked through the foyer and pulled up just outside the entrance to the chapel. He quickly scanned the congregation, his eyes tracing frantically up and down the pews. But there was no sign of Ashley. His pulse began to slow, and his breathing returned to a normal clip. *False alarm*, he thought to himself.

He took one step into the chapel, pausing briefly to consider the best route to his family's pew. And then he froze. He hadn't seen her at first. But nestled right between his mother and his sister Rachel sat Ashley.

Jacob steadied himself against the door jamb as he felt his legs give way beneath him. Pulling himself upright, he began a slow, plodding march towards his family's pew.

He slipped quietly into the empty spot next to his brother David as the first of a series of apocalyptic scenarios unfolded in his mind. Not only had Ashley Hudson shown up in church, she was sitting next to his mother. Impossibly, his life at school was about to get much worse. When the meeting came to a close, Jacob sprang out of his seat and speed walked to the back of the chapel. Ashley had already been seen with his family, so *some* damage had already been done. But if *he* could somehow avoid being seen with her, then he had plausible deniability on his side.

He ducked into the cultural hall and made towards the back door on the opposite side. He'd make his escape, then hang out in the men's bathroom until all the dust settled. But halfway to the door he heard a voice from behind. His heart sank. It was his mother.

"Jacob," Sarah called.

Jacob froze in his tracks, hesitated for a moment, and then slowly wheeled around. His mother was walking towards him with Ashley by her side. A hot flame kindled within him as the glorious vision settled over him.

Fight it off, he thought. *You have to fight it off.*

"You remember Ashley from the ice cream parlor, don't you Jacob?" Sarah said.

"Hello Jacob," Ashley said, her smile revealing a perfect row of pearly white teeth.

Jacob looked over each shoulder, as if fearful of eavesdroppers.

"What are you doing here?" he hissed under his breath.

"What do you mean, what am I doing here?" she said, the smile slowly disappearing from her face.

"I thought I told you. We can't be seen together. The timing couldn't be worse."

Jacob continued to cast furtive glances in every direction.

"What? You think I'm here just because of you?" she said, a look of irritation flashing across her face.

"Of course I think you're here because of me. You're sitting in the pew next to my mother for crying out loud," Jacob said, keeping his voice just above a whisper.

"Look, Bucko, I don't know what your problem is," Ashley said, her face flushing crimson. "I came here to learn more about your church. I noticed something different about your family that day in the ice cream parlor. When I found out you were a Mormon, I started to connect the dots. I just expected a little bit of a warmer reception, especially from you of all people."

"You're telling me Arnie didn't put you up to this?" Jacob said.

She paused, considering Jacob's accusation.

"So Arnie gave me a little prodding. But that doesn't mean my motivations for coming aren't pure. I came because I wanted to learn about your church. Is there a crime in that?"

"No crime at all," Jacob snapped. "Just an incredibly long list of unintended consequences."

"Come on," Sarah said, pulling Ashley by the elbow. "Let's go to Young Women's and let Mr. Grumpy here stew in his little cloud of gloom and doom."

"Show me the way," Ashley said, flashing Jacob one last look of irritation.

CHAPTER 45

E than could kick himself for being so foolish. Saturday morning had always been the most productive for missionary outreach, yet he had squandered it clipping hedges, and mowing lawns—activities that had little to do with saving his ministry. The paper in his hand provided ample evidence of his massive misappropriation of time. The sheet slipped from his fingers onto his desk as the numbness migrated from his chest to his extremities.

His face was haggard and his shoulders slumped as he trudged out of his office and into the tiny, poorly lit foyer. He paused at the door of the chapel, voided his face of emotion, then pulled it open.

When he peered into the room he saw, to his utter astonishment, that every chair was filled with congregants, rendering the tiny chapel almost unrecognizable. *Why were all these people in his chapel?* Eyes wide with wonderment, he began a slow, stunned walk down the center aisle.

All the heads in the room turned towards him, the low buzz in the room building to a rumble. Ethan managed a few nods of the head and a half smile before approaching the spindly wooden pulpit.

Now behind the pulpit, his eyes fell upon his wife who sat in the front row, Ian perched on her lap. She flashed a huge smile, her thumb shooting upwards in a gesture of encouragement that only he could see.

After 15 seconds of stupor, and an "It's now or never" look from his wife, Ethan opened his mouth.

• • •

When Ethan finished his sermon nearly 35 minutes later, he was shocked by what he saw. The hordes of people who had crammed into his tiny chapel were now regarding him with rapt, steadfast gazes. They sat in their chairs as if entranced. But for the gurgling of babies on the laps of their mothers, not a sound could be heard.

Perplexed by the congregation's bizarre response to his sermon, Ethan stepped away from the pulpit and made for his wife in the front row. Before he reached her, a man in his early thirties holding an infant stepped into his path.

"So they were right about you," he said, pumping Ethan's hand.

"How's that?" Ethan said.

"Everything my neighbor said about you is true."

"Thanks…I think," Ethan said cautiously.

"My neighbor's Jim," the man said, cocking his thumb towards the back of the chapel. "Jim Dinsmore. He told me about your sermons. Said I'd have to hear it to believe it. Well, I just wanted to tell you that you did *not* disappoint."

"Well…uh, I'm very happy to hear that," Ethan said, trying hard not to sound *too* surprised.

Over the course of the next 20 minutes Ethan worked his way around the room, shaking hands with each one of his new congregants. As he learned their names, and the referral source, the picture slowly came into focus. Time and time again, the new attendees cited the testimonials of the same congregant: Jim Dinsmore. Word of mouth from a single individual had finally propelled the Community Church of Christ to critical mass.

When the last of the congregants had disappeared through the door in the back of the chapel, Ethan found himself alone with Jenny and Ian. Jenny unleashed a scream of ecstasy as she threw her free arm around Ethan's neck, enfolding him in a tight embrace.

"You've done it, Ethan. You've really done it," she gushed, her forehead touching his, her hand caressing the back of his head.

As their heads slowly pulled apart, Jenny tried to meet Ethan's eyes, but he averted his glance. When he refused to meet her gaze, her smile slowly faded.

"What's wrong Ethan? Didn't you see what happened here today? God has finally answered our prayers."

"God didn't answer our prayers Jenny," Ethan said, his eyes dark and cold.

"What?" she gasped.

"All this," Ethan said, waving his hand around the chapel. "All this would have been great about two months ago. But now…now it's all too late."

"Ethan sweetheart, that's ludicrous. It isn't too late. You're hitting your stride. You're building momentum. This is exactly what we prayed for. This is God's hand."

"We needed *this* two months ago," Ethan said, sweeping his arm around the chapel. "A lot of good it does us now. We're out of money Jenny. We could have a congregation three times this size and it still wouldn't be enough to keep us afloat."

"But…the student loan," she sobbed. "It…it can buy us time until the offerings start to grow."

"Student loan?" Ethan said with a grim chuckle. He reached into his pocket and pulled out a piece of paper.

"The money's all dried up," Ethan said, pressing the paper into her hand. "Our day of reckoning is upon us." He turned and began walking towards the back of the chapel.

"But you said we had more time," she cried in anguish.

"It was a best guess," he said, pausing briefly as he looked back at her. "But I was wrong. We gave it our best shot. This is the end of the road."

CHAPTER 46

Paul's nerves buzzed with ambivalence as he navigated the well-worn path from the secretary's desk to the principal's office. Stan Carraway had assured him that the only thing that could keep Chan Yarber at bay was victories, early and often. Yet, he'd lost his first game in convincing fashion. Jasper Bickle, conversely, had assured him that the losses were inconsequential. Keep his son in at quarterback, maintain a semblance of order in the locker room and marginalize John Peterson. Do all that and the job was his to keep. He rapped lightly on the door, unsure of what awaited him on the other side.

"Come in," came the response.

Paul pushed the door open and stepped gingerly into the office. There behind his desk sat Principal Mike Skinner.

"Hey Paul," he said with a smile.

A smile, this was a good sign. Paul felt his tensed nerves begin to relax.

"Good morning Mike," Paul said.

"My secretary said you'd be dropping by. Said it sounded urgent. What's keeping you awake these days Paul?"

Paul's face turned serious as he considered where to begin.

"A lot I'm afraid. I appreciate you seeing me so soon."

Mike laid the riff of papers he had been examining down on his desk.

"Well, you've got a captive audience. Fire away."

Paul slid into the chair opposite the principal, his face pinched with concern.

"It's John Peterson," Paul began.

The expression on Mike's face didn't change. He seemed to be expecting it.

"Ah, yes. Our friend John Peterson. They get everything resolved over there at Living Christ Ministries?"

"Yeah, he'll never set foot in that chapel again."

"Ok. So where's the problem?" Mike said, cutting to the chase.

"Mike, Living Christ Ministries is safe. It's on lock down. It's the rest of the town I'm worried about."

"Why's that?" Mike said, his eyebrows rising.

"John Peterson is teaming with other Mormons to create a service organization that has begun targeting elderly widows. They show up, perform free yard work, and then slowly transition to religion."

"You sure about this?" Mike asked.

Paul went on to explain what he saw in Vivian's yard that day and the details of their subsequent conversation.

"I see," Mike said. "So how can *I* help?"

"Well, if John Peterson is bold enough to take Mormonism directly to the members of this community, what's to stop him from taking it to the students in his very own classroom?"

Mike frowned with skepticism.

"You really think he'd do that?"

"He's already done it Mike," Paul said. "This is exactly what he's done in every town he's ever lived in. It's how the guy operates. Do you really want to be looking back at this train wreck two months from now wondering what we *should* have done differently?"

"Yeah, but I can't just fire the guy because he's mowing some lady's yard."

Paul flashed an impatient smile.

"Look Mike. I'm not suggesting you up and fire the guy."

"Ok, so what then?"

"I think you should establish boundaries. You know, a zero tolerance policy vis-à-vis his proselytizing. I'm talking one strike and you're out."

"Go on," Mike said.

"Meet with him, delineate the boundaries, and if so much as the mention of Joseph Smith or The Book of Mormon falls from his lips, you send this guy packing."

Mike studied his hands for a few moments before raising his eyes to Paul.

"I don't know Paul. Sounds a little Orwellian to me."

"Maybe it does Mike. But you're going to have to trust me on this. You have to put this guy in a box. You give him any wiggle room at all, and you're going to get an earful from angry parents wondering why their children have been proselytized in school."

Mike gave Paul another frown.

"Talk to him Mike," Paul pushed. "Spell out the boundaries before things get out of hand."

Mike's hand tapped anxiously against his desk as he turned the thought over in his mind. Suddenly the tapping stopped and the frown melted away.

"Alright Paul," Mike said, looking at his watch. "I suppose it couldn't hurt. I'll call him in."

• • •

"John Peterson to Principal Skinner's office," came the dreary voice from the intercom above John's head. "John Peterson to the principal's office."

John looked up from the papers he was correcting and eyed the box warily.

"Great," he muttered to himself, as a fresh wave of anxiety washed over him.

As John walked slowly through the hallways towards the administrative offices, his thoughts began to race. *This couldn't be about Living Christ Ministries...or could it?* He paused just outside the door, girding himself up for whatever lay beyond it. He pushed the door open and stepped inside.

"Oh...hello," the secretary said, as if John had a third arm sprouting out of his chest.

John ignored the hostile reception.

"Hi there. I was told that Principal Skinner needed to see me."

She didn't respond. Instead, she picked up her phone, punched a button, and whispered furtively into the receiver. She then nodded, and returned the phone back to its cradle.

"You can head on back," she said, her eyes narrow with suspicion.

John walked past her and down the hall. The principal's door was already ajar so he poked his head through it.

"Principal Skinner?" he said, his face partially concealed by the door.

"Ah, Mr. Peterson. Come on in," he said waving his hand. "Have a seat."

John settled into one of the empty chairs opposite the principal.

"I trust your first few weeks have been pleasant ones?" he asked.

"Sure have," John said, hoping to start things off on the right foot.

The principal gave a smile, but it soon faded.

"Good…good. Listen, I know you're busy, so I'll cut right to it. There's been some concern among the faculty about…how should I put this?" he said stroking his chin. "Your propensity for proselytism."

John shifted uncomfortably in his chair.

"There's some fear, given your track record, that you could use your classroom as a pulpit," the principal continued.

John's air of diplomacy suddenly evaporated.

"Track record?" John said, springing bolt upright in his chair. "You're not talking about what happened at Living Christ Ministries are you?"

"Well, that, and all the trouble that seems to follow you just about everywhere you go."

John bit his tongue as a fresh wave of anger swept over him.

"I know about the other towns John. And really, I'd like to keep you around. But I can't do it if this turns into another repeat performance."

"You don't know the first thing about what happened in those towns," John snapped.

Mike's hands rose in front of him defensively.

"Look, there are always two sides to every story. No one knows that better than a high school principal. Given that reality, I'm willing to give you the benefit of the doubt."

These last words struck the right note. John could feel the tension slowly drain from his body.

"Look John, you strike me as an intelligent person. I'm impressed with your program. I *would* like to keep you around. But here's the deal.

I can only ignore my faculty's concerns for so long. You have *got* to keep the proselytizing in check. If I hear that you've been talking religion within the walls of this school, even in idle conversation, then that lends credence to everything else I've been hearing. And that, Mr. Peterson, would force my hand."

"No problem," John said curtly, rising quickly from his chair, anxious to end the conversation.

"I have your word that the subject of religion won't come up in your classroom or in idle conversation?"

"You have my word on it," John said crisply.

"Good. Because if I hear otherwise, the consequences will be swift and severe. It's a one strike policy John. This school is a tinderbox right now. You start stirring up controversy, and it's liable to explode. I can't have that in my school John. Do you understand?"

"Perfectly," John said, turning to leave.

"Thanks for stopping by," Mike said, as John disappeared through the door.

John walked back to his classroom, anger bubbling within him. This was Paul Connelly's doing, John was sure of it. He had been behind the Living Christ Ministries meltdown, and he had almost certainly arranged this little pearl of a meeting. He was forcing him into isolation, boxing him in at every turn. He was mustering his allies, one by one, in an attempt to impose what amounted to…a spiritual quarantine.

CHAPTER 47

What had started out as a fresh, clean slate had devolved into a debacle far worse than any of the other towns. There was only one positive thought that continued to tap at the back of John's mind. Not much more could possibly go wrong.

At the end of fourth period John sprang from his chair, anxious for lunch and a change of scenery. He followed the last of his students out of his classroom and shut the door behind him. He weaved his way between thickets of students and headed towards the teachers' lounge. He would pop in, grab his lunch from the refrigerator, and spend the balance of his lunch hour decompressing off campus.

He pulled the door to the teachers' lounge open, and saw five other teachers sitting at tables and armchairs dispersed throughout the lounge. As he stepped into the room, they all seemed to stiffen, eying him warily. John kept his eyes glued to the floor, and made for the refrigerator.

"Well if it isn't the most famous Mormon in town," came a voice from his left.

John turned in the direction of the voice. It was Steve Cattrell.

"Hi Steve," John said politely, anxious to avoid a confrontation. He pulled the refrigerator door open, ducked his head in, and began rummaging around for his lunch.

"Say, John," Steve continued, "mind if I ask you a few questions?"

"Uh, I suppose that depends on what you want to talk about," John said, his head still buried in the refrigerator.

"Well, for starters, how is it that the Mormon Church is the only true church on the face of the earth? I mean, where does that leave the rest of us? You know, I started to do the math on that and, do you realize that under your program, only .002 % of the world would be saved from the fire and brimstone of eternal damnation?"

John's head popped up from behind the door, a smile on his face.

"Sorry Steve, not going to take the bait," John said, still managing a diplomatic tone. "If you don't mind, I'll just take my lunch and leave."

Just then Kip Welbach moved his sturdy frame in front of the door.

"You don't care to comment on the overwhelming injustice of the Mormon God?" Steve asked, feigning incredulity.

"No Steve, I'm not interested in having this conversation with you. Now, if you don't mind, I'm going to take my lunch outside and I'm going to eat it," he said, taking two steps toward Kip.

"How about Joseph Smith then? I still can't get over this Book of Mormon thing. How he managed to dream that thing up I'll just never know. What was it John, all the whisky, or was he just plain delusional?"

John froze in place, and then wheeled slowly around to face Steve.

"It was neither," Kip chimed from behind John. "Don't you know it was all about the seer stone? Throw that little guy in a hat, see those funny little letters, and before you know it…presto…you've got yourself some scripture."

John gave Kip a contemptuous glare before turning back to Steve.

"That right John? That how it all went down?" Steve prodded.

"I can't believe I'm having this conversation," John said. "It's like I'm dealing with the bully in the school yard when I was in the third grade. That's the *third* grade Steve. And you Kip, are you seriously blocking the door?"

"Just need a few questions answered, that's all John," Steve said, coming to Kip's defense. "Strange how easy it was for you to preach your Mormonism over there at Living Christ Ministries. Now, all of the sudden, the cat's got your tongue. We just want to know exactly *how* Joseph Smith went about inventing the Book of Mormon. That's all."

Just then, something exploded within John's chest. Steve's questions were pushing all the right buttons. This last barb sent John over the edge.

"Have you ever written a book Steve?" John snapped.

"Matter of fact I have," he said, his arms rising to his hips.

"About how long did it take you if you don't mind me asking?"

"About a year and a half," he responded. His eyes narrowed as he wondered where John's line of questions was leading.

"How many revisions you make before sending it over to your publisher? Fifteen, sixteen?"

"Uh, sure. At least."

"What if your publisher told you that you didn't have 18 months to pull it off? You only had 59 days. Oh, and by the way, you won't have the benefit of reviewing what you'd written each time you started to write. Just pick up where you left off, day after day after day. What if your publisher then said that you needed to include in your book a detailed description of the ancient institutions among a civilization that lived two millennia ago? Easy you might think. Just head over to your local library. Only your local library can't help you. Those books haven't even been written yet. While you're at it, include an intimate description of the life of a family wandering in the Arabian desert, an ancient coronation rite, and ancient money systems. Your publisher will also be interested in hearing about the techniques of preserving and transmitting sacred texts as well as a sweeping description of the rise, prosperity and fall of an ancient civilization over the arc of two millennia. Oh yeah, and before you're done they're going to need you to invent over three hundred proper nouns to include people, cities and geographical landmarks.

"Then you've got to convince 11 of your closest associates to stake their reputations and livelihoods on the notion that you didn't actually write this thing, but that you found it in a hill and translated it by the power of God. Think you can pull that off Steve?"

The smile had disappeared from Steve's face. For a few seconds, he seemed tongue-tied.

"It's a fabrication Peterson, pure and simple," Steve finally responded. But John could detect a waver in his voice. The confident façade had begun to crack.

John chuckled as he began to hit his stride. Steve Cattrell was on *his* turf now.

"You know anything about the study of forged documents Steve?"

Steve didn't respond this time, regarding John nervously.

"It's been known for centuries that the easiest forgeries to detect are the lengthy, historical ones. Even a cursory examination will reveal their inconsistencies and fraudulence. You want to forge a document, you're much better off to keep it short and sweet. Any idea how long the Book of Mormon is Steve?"

"Why don't you tell me," Steve responded, a touch of panic in his voice.

"It's 240,000 words. If it's a clumsy fraud, then there are surely thousands of experts the world over capable of refuting its authenticity within the hour. Just remember Steve, whichever expert you find has to be prepared to subject his own methods to the exact same level of scrutiny. You ready to do that Steve? You think the old whisky theory's going to hold up?"

Steve's face had turned a dark shade of crimson as he began to realize he was in way over his head. John's answers had revealed a breadth of knowledge that he had failed to anticipate.

As Steve squirmed about in silence, John saw movement to his right. The door to the teachers' lounge swung open and in strode Paul Connelly, a haughty grin on his face.

"You don't need to bother answering that last question Steve. I believe Brother John here's given us everything that we need."

"What are you talking about Connelly?" John said, casting him a fierce look.

"The amazing thing about these intercoms," Paul said, motioning to the box on the wall above their heads, "is that they're all two-way. And the sound that they pick up is so crystal clear. Hardly any static at all. I have to tell you John, I really enjoyed this little give and take between you and Steve. Principal Skinner…not so much. But me? I thought it was just perfect."

Chapter 48

D read clamped down on Jacob's heart as he picked up his cellphone and began punching the keypad.

"Mom, it's me," he managed, his voice barely audible.

"Jacob? Is everything alright?" Sarah said, her voice filled with trepidation.

"No, Mom," Jacob said gravely. "Everything isn't alright."

"Another scout team ambush?" she said, a touch of anger sounding in her voice. "I have a mind to…"

"No, Mom," Jacob said cutting her off. "If only the news were that good."

"What then?" she asked, her voice now suffused with panic.

"It's Dad. He went and got himself fired," Jacob said, a hard edge of bitterness in his voice.

Jacob heard a gasp on the other end, followed by a muffled noise that sounded to him like sobbing. The tortured sounds continued unabated for the next 20 seconds.

"How…why?" she finally managed, still choking on her tears.

"Dad was called into the principal's office yesterday and advised that the faculty considered him a threat," Jacob began.

"A threat? A threat to do what?" Sarah said, her voice rising in anger.

"Use your imagination, I don't know. To preach the evils of Mormonism from the lectern. The usual tripe."

"They're afraid John's going to be preaching to his students?" Sarah said in disbelief.

"Students, teachers, whatever. It's all the same to them. Anyway, Skinner called him into the office and laid out a one strike policy. Told him if he so much as breathed a word of Mormonism within the walls of the school, he'd be out on his can. Well, within a couple of hours Dad was defending Joseph Smith and the Book of Mormon to a couple of teachers in the teachers' lounge."

"What?" she exclaimed. "But he promised us he wouldn't!"

"I know Mom. This was going to be a new town, a clean slate. Nothing but empty promises. I can't believe I thought this place was actually going to be different."

More silence on the other end of the line. Jacob continued.

"So, right after Dad finished going all Hugh Nibley on these guys, Coach Connelly charged into the room. He made some snide little comment about how the intercom system had two-way capability, and then marched out of the room. He and Skinner had been listening in on the other end the whole time. Dad was totally blindsided. You'd think he'd learn his lesson by now."

"Of all the dirty, Machiavellian things a man can do," Sarah cried. "Why does Paul Connelly hate our family so much?"

Furious, desperate sobs were now spilling out of Jacob's cellphone. She was clearly furious over his dad's actions. He shared in it. But at the mention of Paul Connelly, his mother had simply come unhinged.

"I won't take this any longer," she said, the anger cutting through the anguish. "I'm not going to stand by while that man sucks the life out of my family." And then there was a click.

• • •

"Do you have any idea who I am?" came a voice from Paul's left.

Paul turned his head and saw a blonde woman with haunted green eyes standing in his doorway. Surprised, he sprang up in his chair, then swiveled to face the woman.

"Uh, no ma'am, no I don't," he said, curiosity and panic battling within him.

"My name is Sarah Peterson. Maybe you know my husband John, my son Jacob?"

Panic vanquished his curiosity and began spreading through his chest. What was *she* doing in his office?

"Mrs. Peterson," he said, trying to remain calm. "How can I help you?"

"You can help me by explaining why you've single-handedly destroyed my family's life. That's how you can help me," she bellowed.

A droplet of sweat pealed down Paul's temple as he felt the full measure of the woman's wrath wash over him. Suddenly, there was nowhere to hide.

His hands rose before him, palms outward, as if to parry the onslaught.

"Look, Mrs. Peterson. I think perhaps all of this anger is a little misdirected here. Don't you think at least some of this ire should be directed at your husband?"

"No, actually, I don't. *You're* the one bent on destroying my family, not my husband."

Paul winced, stung by the forcefulness of her attack. He scrambled.

"Well, *he* was the one that tried to convert an entire congregation. I certainly had nothing to do with that."

Paul could tell this touched a nerve. Sarah's nostrils began to flare, fire burning in her eyes.

"Do you honestly think that that was what he was trying to do? How can you be so naïve and so presumptuous, all at the same time? My husband wasn't trying to convert your congregation. You concocted that whole mass conversion poppycock in that little pea sized brain of yours and then sold it to the public."

Paul's hands once again rose to his chest in a defensive posture.

"Now Mrs. Peterson, your husband *can* choose his actions, but he can't choose the consequences to his actions. When he made the decision to conceal the true identity of his religion, he chose to walk down a path that would invariably incite this town's ire. There are consequences, good and bad, to everything we do in life Mrs. Peterson. Surely with all the moving your family has had to do, you know that by now."

Angry lines broke out across Sarah's forehead, as her upper lip curled into a snarl.

"You know nothing about our family," she inveighed, "and nothing about what we've been through. How about I give *you* a little lesson about the consequences of actions? Do you even realize that my son was a preseason All-American? He could write his own ticket to any school in this country before he met you. How's a row of zeroes by his name after his junior year of high school going to work out for him? Huh? Kind of a deal breaker don't you think?"

Paul shrugged his shoulders and raised his palms towards the ceiling as if to emphasize his earlier point about consequences.

"Oh you are so high and mighty, such the moral authority in this town. Well try this on for size. My husband's now out of a job because of you. How do you think we're going to pay the mortgage on our new house? I can practically hear the bank calling me now. Nothing like a foreclosure for the old credit rating."

"Like I said, Mrs. Peterson…," Paul said, attempting to strike the same note on consequences. But in a burst of anger, she cut him off.

"So, let me see if I can summarize the impact you've had on our lives Mr. Role Model. Lost job? Check. Lost house? Check. Lost college scholarship? Check. Social alienation for all seven of my children? Check, check, check, check, check, check and check.

"The only real question that I haven't been able to answer is this: how do you manage to live with yourself? At some point the guilt has to start to wear you down. Unless of course you don't *have* a conscience."

A toxic feeling began to mushroom within Paul's chest. He knew his plan had been devastating, but he hadn't stopped to consider the personal impact of the devastation. He shifted uncomfortably as the verbal onslaught began to take its toll.

"I am so done with you," she said, striking one final blow. "When we leave this town, I will count it a singular blessing if I never have to lay eyes on you again."

• • •

Sarah wheeled about, and charged out of the office. She turned right and tore down the hallway towards the door through which she had entered. She leaned heavily against it and found, to her surprise, that it wouldn't budge. Had someone locked the door while she was in Paul's office? In a burst of frustration she whipped around and charged back in the other direction, searching desperately for a different door. She strode past Paul's office, turned the corner and nearly ran into a wall of boxes that had been stacked in the middle of the hallway, blocking her path.

"Why can't I just leave this dreadful place," Sarah cried, her head collapsing against her hands while the rest of her collapsed against the wall.

"Oh dear. Looks like I've really done it this time," came a quiet, raspy voice off to her left.

Sarah turned and saw a frail, elderly man standing in front of her. His face was lined with wrinkles, a touch of sadness encroaching on his eyes.

"Oh, I'm sorry, are these yours?" Sarah asked, rubbing the tears from her eyes, trying to collect herself.

"Yes they are. Looks like I've made a mess of things," the man said. Their eyes met again, but this time Sarah saw a light flicker in his eyes. He began shifting boxes around, but his movements were slow, almost deliberate.

Sarah looked quickly at her watch, and then back over her shoulder, as if Paul Connelly were going to walk out of his office at any moment.

"Don't let him get you down," the man said under his breath, as he hefted a box and set it on the floor.

"How's that?" she said, confused.

The man nodded his head in the direction of Paul's office.

"Don't let *him* get you down," the man, repeated, almost inaudibly.

"I'm sorry, do I know you?" Sarah asked.

"No, no, I don't suppose you do. Name's Doc Williamson. Been running this place since before you or your husband were born," he said, his voice rising several decibels.

"My husband?" she asked, her confusion mounting. "Do you...*know* my husband?"

The old man chuckled, his cheeks rising in a sad smile.

"Of course I know him. Darn near everyone in town knows *your* husband."

"I see," Sarah said, painfully. This man knew her husband for the same reason that everyone else knew her husband. When you're accused of trying to convert half the town, news travels fast.

"That's a good man you've married there Mrs. Peterson," Doc said, his voice getting louder.

Sarah's breath caught in her chest, her eyebrows arching upwards in surprise.

"What did you say?" she asked.

"Your husband…John. He's a good man," Doc repeated.

"How could you possibly know that?" she said, a touch of bitterness in her voice. "Have you even met my husband?"

"No, Mrs. Peterson, I've never met your husband. But I've been watching him…from a distance."

A spiteful smile crept across Sarah's face.

"You sure you've got the right guy? Surely you've heard that my husband's a Mormon."

"All the same to me," Doc said, shrugging his shoulders.

"Well, not to everyone else in this town. Been a real deal breaker so far," Sarah said.

Doc laughed softly, and began studying his old, gnarled hands.

"Mrs. Peterson, I would venture to guess that your husband is an even better man than you suspect."

"Oh, is that right?" she said, again surprised.

"You *do* know that your husband had a very legitimate reason for continuing to preach to that congregation, even against your wishes, don't you?"

Sarah's face clouded with confusion. Who was this man and how did he know so much about her family?

"Um, is there something that you know that I don't?" Sarah asked.

"Matter of fact, there is," Doc said, his eyes conveying both warmth and sadness. "Mr. Holler has more than a financial motivation for keeping the doors of that church open."

"Oh really?" Sarah said. The mention of Buddy Holler's name caused a spark of anger to fly somewhere within her. Buddy's appearance in their life had set a chain of events in motion that had turned their lives into a living nightmare.

"Not many people know what I'm about to tell you Mrs. Peterson. Buddy's wife lies in a bed inside a facility in the next county over."

"Buddy's married?' Sarah gasped.

"Oh yes. Married his high school sweetheart. A romance for the ages."

"But you said she's in a facility? What sort of facility? Why?" Sarah said, curious and horrified, all at the same time.

A hint of pain washed over Doc's face as a weathered finger drew up to his chin.

"I reckon it was, oh, going on two years now, Beatrice had a violent reaction to a prescription cough syrup she had taken. Doctors suspect that it somehow interacted with her epilepsy medication. She had a grand mal seizure and never came out of it. It's a long term care facility Mrs. Peterson."

Sarah's hand rose to her mouth in horror.

"She's on experimental drugs. In theory, they keep the effects of the coma from becoming irreversible. It's Buddy's only hope," Doc said, his head inclined with sadness.

"Experimental drugs?" Sarah asked.

"That's right. Not approved by the FDA, and therefore not covered by Medicaid. Sets him back about $8,000 a month. When your husband decided to keep preaching, even in the face of all the risk, he had good reason. He was trying to keep Beatrice alive."

A wave of anguish exploded within Sarah's chest, as fresh tears welled, then spilled over. Her chest heaved up and down as shock and shame roiled within her. Suddenly everything John had done over the last few weeks came into focus.

"Why didn't he tell me Doc?" she said, choking back more tears. "Why didn't he say something?"

"I suspect Mrs. Peterson, that it was his way of respecting Buddy's privacy. Like I said, there aren't too many folks in town that know what that man is going through. Buddy likes to keep it that way."

"Or, maybe I just didn't give him a chance to tell me," she said, more tears streaming down her cheeks.

Doc nodded his head in understanding.

"If Buddy is so private then how, may I ask, did *you* come by this information?" she asked, her voice catching.

A heart wrenching look washed over his face. When he began to speak, he did so slowly, haltingly.

"Well, I've known Beatrice Holler for some time now. We've gotten to be pretty close over the years. You see Mrs. Peterson, Beatrice Holler is my only daughter. That's how I know these things. And that's why I think the world of your husband."

CHAPTER 49

Never before had Paul weathered a verbal onslaught of such pugilistic ferocity. Darkness filled his breast as her angry invective resounded in his mind, "Check, check, check, check...."

It had been one thing to carry out his machinations behind his proxies Steve and Kip or from the safety of Jasper Bickle's email account. But now he he'd been forced to face the real life repercussions of his plan to destroy John Peterson.

As a maelstrom of doubt swirled within him, a divergent thought tried to beat the other ones down. *Stay strong Paul. It's just collateral damage. You must stay strong.* John Peterson *had* attempted to convert an entire congregation. Now he had set his sights on the rest of Mayfield. No matter how much personal devastation he had rained down upon the Peterson family, at the end of the day, they had brought it upon themselves.

Before long, this line of reasoning began to win out, vanquishing the shame and guilt that had begun to gnaw at his conscience. As he began to mentally rebuild his case for what he had done to John Peterson, he heard the faint sound of voices echoing in the hallway. He rolled his chair across the floor, pressed his ear to the edge of the door frame and began to listen. The voices belonged to a man and a woman.

Impelled by his curiosity, he rose from his chair and crossed the hall, pushing himself flat against the opposite wall. As he inched his way down the wall, the voices took on an identity. It was Sarah Peterson and Doc Williamson. Did they *know* each other? He inched closer to the corner, straining for every detail, his body barely obscured by the wall's corner.

After listening in for a few moments, his jaw suddenly fell open, a burst of shame nearly overriding his system. Had he heard it right? John Peterson had decided, reluctantly, to continue preaching at Living Christ Ministries for the express purpose of keeping Buddy's wife alive? Beatrice was *comatose*? Eight thousand dollars *a month*? No, it couldn't be that simple. Surely John Peterson's motivations were far more devious.

And then he heard the crying. It was a deep, anguished cry. Why would Sarah Peterson be crying? Were John's motivations somehow news to her? Surely she knew of Buddy's predicament and her husband's reasons for preaching. *Or had she*? Had *she* miscalculated? Had John Peterson not disclosed the details to his very own wife?

Suddenly it all came into focus, crashing down on him with all the blunt trauma of an enormous sledgehammer. John Peterson had not been preaching to the congregation at Living Christ Ministries for the purposes of converting them. He was preaching at Living Christ Ministries to sustain the streams of revenue required to keep Beatrice Holler alive.

Fresh spasms of pain shot through Paul's torso as he staggered back to his office. Ominous wings of darkness had begun to creep across his field of vision. Just when he thought the darkness would win out, a thought occurred to him. What of the widows? Regardless of John's motivations at Living Christ Ministries, he had still been intent upon converting the widows.

Then he had a flash of inspiration. He started rifling frantically through the drawers of his desk, searching for the Mayfield white pages. He found it and quickly flipped to the listing for Vivian Huxley. He lifted up the receiver on his desk and began frantically punching numbers.

"Hello," came the voice on the other end.

"Sister Huxley, it's Paul Connelly," he said, making no effort to disguise his urgency.

"Why Coach Connelly, what seems to be the problem?"

"Do you remember when John Peterson and his friend came to talk to your group of widows?"

"Why of course I do."

"Do you also remember that you told me that the man that was with him was the leader of a congregation?"

"Yes, that's right."

"Did you ever remember which one?"

"Why yes I did. In fact, I've begun to attend his services."

His suspicions *had* been correct. The two Mormons had already recruited Vivian. Who knew how many of the others were already in their grasp? He felt a fresh burst of vindication mixed with relief.

"And which church is that Vivian?" Paul said, the question a mere formality at this point.

"Well, his name is Ethan Reddick and he's the pastor at a small little church over on Merchant Avenue. It's called the Community Church of Christ."

"What?" Paul said, suddenly confused. "Are you sure?"

"Oh yes, quite sure."

The phone fell out of Paul's hand and spilled onto the floor. If what Vivian was saying was true, then the widow project had been a joint-faith initiative. And if that were the case, then John Peterson's motivations had to be pure.

"What have I done?" he breathed, as a knife of agony plunged into his chest. The principal events of the last four weeks played through his mind like a movie, the two recent revelations putting everything in their perfect context. John Peterson had *not* been intent upon converting the town. He had been intent upon *serving* it.

Paul suddenly felt his appendages tingle with numbness. His whole body felt weak, his heart churning like a runaway locomotive. A layer of sweat broke out all over his body as shame and regret consumed him. Soon the room was spinning. Paul braced himself against the desk in a vain attempt to steady himself. But then his legs crumpled beneath him and he collapsed to the floor with a sickening thud. Soon the darkness returned, closing slowly but inexorably about him.

"Help me!" he gasped, as he attempted to stave it off. But, it was too late. The small portal of light to which he was desperately clinging began to fade and then, darkness.

CHAPTER 50

Dark and morbid thoughts battered John's fragile psyche as he kneeled on the floor of his bedroom, stuffing the contents of his life into small, cardboard boxes. The mindless work of packing had given him ample opportunity to evaluate what might have been. If only he had…if only he had, what, ignored two revelations from God? None of this made any sense. He'd done everything God had asked him to do and what had he gotten in return? His fourth town in as many years? An estranged wife? A mortgage he couldn't afford to pay?

Amid all these tortured thoughts, John heard the front door creak open. He jerked his head up, listening for more sounds.

"Jake?" he yelled out. "Is that you?" But there was no answer.

He rose to his feet, and walked cautiously into the hallway. He turned the corner and stepped into the living room. And there she was. For the first time in nearly two weeks he saw her. His heart thumped within his chest, and his body ached to hold her. He took one step towards her and then caught himself.

"Sarah?" he said, unsure of himself.

He searched her face, looking for some clue, some indication that would explain her presence, but saw nothing. Had she heard of the firing? Was she here to confront him over yet another blown opportunity in a new town? As he stood there in limbo, Sarah suddenly broke across the room, tears rolling down her cheeks, and fell into his arms.

John enfolded her in his arms and hugged her close. For the first time in over two weeks the scent of her hair wafted into his nostrils, intoxicating his senses. He continued to hold her close as her body heaved with tormented sobs, her tears wetting his chest.

"I'm so sorry," she sobbed. "I'm so sorry for what I've done to you."

John held her for a few moments longer, and then pulled away, fixing his eyes upon her.

"What are you talking about?" he said, searching her eyes.

"I know everything," she cried. "I know why you kept preaching. You were trying to tell me, but I wouldn't listen. I've never been so ashamed."

Then she buried her head in his chest again, her shoulders rising and falling as the tears rolled forth.

"That's nonsense," he protested softly. "We had no way of knowing exactly how this was going to unfold. I gave you no choice but to do what you did. I was following a spiritual prompting and had no idea where it would lead us. If I had known it would lead us here, I…"

Suddenly she pulled away and fixed her eyes upon him.

"Don't you dare doubt those revelations. Not now," she pleaded.

"Not doubt them? Look at our lives. All our greatest hopes and aspirations, they're gone. Vaporized. All because of a revelation," John said, making quotation marks with his fingers.

"Revelations," she corrected. "Don't you forget, you received more than one. The last confirming the first. I didn't want to believe it because I was so…afraid. But now I can see it."

John's eyes narrowed with skepticism. Her new found optimism just didn't make any sense. Not in light of all they had lost.

"I know about Buddy and I know about Beatrice," she continued.

"Beatrice?" he said, suddenly confused. "But how?"

"It doesn't matter. What matters is that Buddy needed a blessing in his life, and you heeded the call."

John slackened his grip on his wife and pulled away.

"But don't you get it? Nothing I did ended up helping. Buddy still can't afford the medicine, and now I'm out of a job. Our life is in shambles, and for what? A revelation?"

Chapter 51

Paul's eyes slowly blinked open as a bright whiteness consumed him. He was lying prostrate, but he had no idea where. As his eyes came into focus, the whiteness of his surroundings assaulted his senses. He could now see he was lying in a hospital bed. He was dressed in a white gown, underneath white sheets in a room whose walls were painted perfectly white. A white, fluorescent light buzzed somewhere above him. He seemed to be floating in a sea of whiteness.

He lay motionless in his bed for another ten minutes, lost in a dense fog. Painful images and sequences bandied about in his mind scrambling his thoughts. The silence of the room was suddenly fractured when a door clicked open to his right and a doctor walked in, a clipboard in his hands. Paul trained his eyes upon the doctor's face. He recognized the face, but the name eluded him.

"Welcome back," the man said, smiling down at him. "I'm Dr. Newstrom. You gave us quite a scare there Coach." He leaned over and shined a little flashlight into each of Paul's eyes.

"Can you follow my finger?" the doctor said, dragging his index finger across Paul's field of vision.

"How long have I been out?" Paul mumbled.

"About six hours. Doc Williamson found you collapsed on the floor of your office this morning. He heard the beeping of the phone. Do you remember anything about what happened just before you collapsed?"

"No," Paul said, as the disparate thoughts suddenly distilled into one searingly painful memory. "Not a thing."

He began to revisit the sequence of events that had lead up to his collapse. The pain and memories came roaring back, fresh and vivid.

"You sure?" the doctor prodded.

"Yeah, I'm sure," Paul snapped, still wincing at the memories.

"Good enough," the doctor said, reluctant to press the issue. "Get some rest. I'll be back to check on you in about an hour."

"How long are you going to keep me here?" Paul objected.

"I'd like to keep you at least for another day or two. You're still not well," the doctor said.

"Doc, I can't stay here overnight. This is crazy. I'm fine."

"Paul, you were unconscious for six hours, and nobody knows why. We ran a battery of tests and they all came back negative. It's like your system just blinked out on us. Your body is still reeling from the effects. I'd like to figure out what happened before I release you. I need some time and you need some rest."

"Fine," Paul murmured.

As soon as the doctor left, Paul rose up on his elbows, and began scanning the room. Off to his left, he saw his clothes draped over a chair, his shoes underneath it. He slowly swung his legs over the edge of the bed, pushed himself onto his feet and began a slow, ginger walk towards the chair. Halfway there, his legs buckled, but he caught himself on the bed, steadied himself and then pulled himself upright.

He took a few more tentative steps and then collapsed into the chair. He carefully removed his white apron and then slowly, painstakingly pulled his clothes on.

Paul wasn't going to be staying overnight. There was no medication that could blunt the pain he was now feeling. Paul rose slowly from his chair and began striding cautiously towards the door. Once there, he opened it part way, and poked his head into the hall. A nurse had just disappeared around the corner to his right. To his left, at the end of the hall, he saw a door and an exit sign. He broke towards the door, his gait slow and unsteady. He looked nervously over his shoulder and saw that the hallway behind him was still empty. When he turned back around, a nurse clad in white had appeared and was heading straight for him.

He felt a burst of nerves but he kept walking, his eyes glued to the white tiles beneath his feet. To his relief, the nurse walked right past him without saying a word. He felt his muscles relax, but he hastened his pace nonetheless. After what seemed like an eternity, he made it to the door. He threw his weight against it and felt it lurch open. He looked back over his shoulder one final time, and then stepped out into the gathering dusk, driven by a single burning thought. He had to find John Peterson.

CHAPTER 52

The irony wasn't lost on him. John had finally united his family in their new home, but only in time to pack its contents into boxes and put it back on the market. As John lowered a stack of ceramic plates into a box, he heard a knock at the door. John looked nervously at Sarah, then at the door.

"Well?" she said, nodding her head towards the door.

A small semblance of normalcy had suddenly distilled upon his life, and he was reluctant to let it slip away. He paused for another moment, weighed his decision, and then stepped tentatively towards the door. Once at the door, he paused again, took a breath, and then pulled it open.

Standing before John on the porch, like an apparition, was Paul Connelly. John stood there, frozen in place, his mouth agape, his eyes wide with surprise. Suddenly, a subconscious impulse overrode all his faculties and, in a flurry of anger, John grabbed the door and slammed it shut.

John looked back at his startled wife.

"Why did you do that John? Who was it?"

"It was Paul Connelly," he said bitterly.

"What's *he* doing here?" she groaned.

Before John could answer, he heard three more raps on the door behind him.

"You aren't going to let him in are you?" she said, lines of worry breaking out across her forehead.

John continued to stare at his wife but said nothing. Three more raps, this time louder, sounded on the wood behind him.

He turned slowly, reached for the knob and pulled it open.

"What do you need?" he said curtly.

"I apologize for intruding at your home," Paul said softly. "I was hoping to have a minute of your time."

"I've got nothing to say to you," he said, his voice angrier this time.

"It's urgent. It won't take long," he assured. "I'd just like a word."

John stood there eying his nemesis for what seemed like an hour before nodding his head, ever so slightly, and then stepping away from the door.

"Make it quick and then get out," he demanded.

"You have my word on it," Paul assured him.

Paul stepped past John and into the living room. And then he froze. Standing before him, elbows akimbo, was Sarah Peterson. Her face was a stony, chiseled façade, her brow a map of angry creases.

"Hello," he said meekly, nodding his head in polite deference.

"Why are you in my home?" she said coolly.

"If it's ok, I'd like a word with your husband," Paul said, deflecting her icy rejoinder.

"Have at it," she growled. "We've got nothing left to lose. I'll be in the basement with the children, packing what's left of our lives into tiny cardboard boxes."

She flashed him another icy glare, and then made towards the basement steps.

Paul's face turned red as a tide of prickly shame washed over him.

"Mind if I have a seat?" Paul asked, nodding towards the couch.

John's eyebrows pinched together as he weighed the request.

"Suit yourself," he mumbled.

Paul collapsed onto the couch while John slumped into the chair opposite him, arms and legs crossed defensively. Paul's vacant eyes regarded the flower arrangement on the table before rising to meet John's eyes.

"I'm afraid I've misjudged you," he began, softly.

John made no response, but continued to meet Paul's awkward gaze with a fiery gaze of his own.

"I fear I've miscalculated everything about you," he continued. This time he paused, waiting for some sort of response, if only to gauge how his opening remarks had landed.

"Go on," John said warily.

"I've come by a great deal of information over the course of the last eight hours, information I wish I'd had a long time ago. I know your true motivation for preaching at Living Christ Ministries. I know all about Beatrice and her tenuous condition. That was a heroic act you performed there John, especially given what you knew you were risking."

John's eyes bored into Paul, the only hint of emotion the sharp, downward turn of his eyebrows.

"This little love fest is all great and good Connelly, but it doesn't change the fact that you've dealt my family a major setback. A change of heart would have been great two weeks ago. But it's too late Paul. You just can't un-ring a bell."

Paul's head nodded as he silently absorbed the chastisement.

"I know it John. It *is* too late. I'm afraid that what I've done cannot be undone."

"Then why did you come here Connelly? You got exactly what you wanted. Why don't you just take your victory and go home?"

"Victory? Is that what you think this was?" Paul said, his eyes haunted, his face etched with pain. "This isn't a zero sum game here John. The whole community lost because of what I did to you and your family. I know that now."

John felt his hard features begin to soften by degrees as the picture of what sat before him slowly came into focus. He could see it now. Paul Connelly was a broken man. His head hung in shame, his eyes had lost their focus and his limbs sprawled about him limp and lifeless. This was a shadow of the man who had charged arrogantly into the teachers' lounge, only days earlier, intent upon his destruction.

"Look Paul. There isn't any question that you've turned our world upside down. Thanks to you, we're on our way to our fourth town in four years. Only this time, we're leaving a mortgage behind. Not quite sure how we're going to swing that one."

Paul winced at the mention of the mortgage.

"We just want to pick up the pieces of our broken lives and move on. You have made mistakes and the consequences of those mistakes are very real. But there's no reason to relive them ad infinitum."

John's gaze grew distant, as if he were summoning some previously untapped reserve of strength.

"Whatever epiphany you've had, I can see it's taken its toll. This hasn't been easy on any of us. If it helps…"

John's lips bunched together as he thought about what he was about to do. Then, mustering every bit of willpower he possessed, he looked Paul squarely in the eye and said, "I'd like you to know…that we…forgive you."

Paul blinked, as if awakening from a trance.

"What'd you say?" he said, unsure of what he had just heard.

"We forgive you…for everything you've done to our family," John said, this time more resolutely.

Paul's body went stiff, his eyes wide with disbelief. For a few seconds, he could only sit there, mouth agape.

"Just like that?" he finally managed.

"Just like that," John said firmly.

Paul began to shake his head from side to side.

"After all I've done to you?" he said, the surprise still ringing in his voice.

John nodded his head.

"You see, that's what I don't get about you Mormons. You aren't Christians, yet everything about you, your words, your actions, your attitudes…they're as Christian as anything I've ever seen."

John laughed, a faint smile breaking across his face.

"Are you still laboring under the illusion that Mormons aren't Christians?" John asked.

"Well, no more so than anyone else. I mean, here's what's so hard for me. I can't seem to reconcile what I know about your church with how you live your lives. The two seem to be so inherently at odds with each other."

John turned his head and began scanning the bookshelf off to their right. He stood up, walked over to it and came back with a book in his hands.

"Ok if I share something with you?" John asked.

"Absolutely," Paul said.

John flipped through the pages of the book, found his spot, and began to read.

"For behold, a bitter fountain cannot bring forth good water; neither can a good fountain bring forth bitter water; wherefore, a man being a servant of the devil cannot follow Christ; and if he follow Christ he cannot be a servant of the devil. Wherefore, all things which are good cometh of God; and that which is evil cometh of the devil; for the devil is an enemy unto God, and fighteth against him continually, and inviteth and enticeth to sin, and to do that which is evil continually. But behold, that which is of God inviteth and enticeth to do good continually; wherefore, everything which inviteth and enticeth to do good, and to love God, and to serve him, is inspired of God. Wherefore, take heed, my beloved brethren, that ye do not judge that which is evil to be of God, or that which is good and of God to be of the devil."

John looked up from the book. Paul had lapsed into deep concentration as the words tumbled about in his mind.

"What is this person saying here?" John finally asked.

"Well, he seems to suggest that God has some sort of a litmus test. If something induces you to do good things, to serve God, and to love others, then it has to come from God. If, conversely, something comes from Satan, it would likewise distance you from God. And ultimately, we need to be careful that we don't mistake the one for the other."

A small smile of satisfaction spread across John's face.

"Couldn't have said it any better myself."

"Who wrote that by the way?" Paul said. "It's spot on."

"That was a prophet who lived about 1500 years ago. His name was Mormon."

Paul's mouth fell open.

"That's right Paul. That was a passage from the Book of Mormon."

"But, it can't be," Paul said, suddenly confused.

"Sure it was," John said, turning the book over for Paul to see. "You see Paul, you can't seem to reconcile the fact that I preach a Christian sermon, and render Christian service, yet belong to the Mormon Church. It's no wonder you're confused. Your basic premise violates the very principles of which these verses speak. If the Mormon Church helps me live the teachings of Jesus Christ, to draw closer to him, then it is, by definition, inspired of him. And if it's inspired of him, then the devil can have no hand in it."

A troubled look broke out across Paul's face.

"You see," John continued, "a bitter fountain cannot bring forth good water. Neither a bad fountain good water. If we were really as bad as everything you've heard, then our actions, our very lives would be the most damning evidence of all."

"That's what you'd think," Paul said, still perplexed.

"You've heard this principle before Paul. It's in the Bible. You know, 'By their fruits you shall know them.' Think about the fruits you've observed in our lives, and then draw your conclusions accordingly."

Paul began to nod his head as if a number of competing thoughts were suddenly coalescing into one. He pulled himself upright and then leaned towards John, his eyes bright with understanding.

"It all makes sense," Paul said. "If only I had figured this out two weeks ago before I set this whole mess in motion." Just then, a shadow passed over Paul's face as he latched onto a horrible, agonizing thought. His chin fell to his chest, as if his will for living had been sucked from his very being.

"No, no, no," he cried, his face falling into his hands. "What have I done?"

"What Paul? What is it?" John asked, suddenly unnerved.

"How could I have been so mindless?" Paul said frantically. "I'm so, so sorry John. I'm afraid I've set something in motion that has unspeakable implications. Things are about to get worse for you and your family. Much worse."

Paul leaped from the couch and bolted towards the door. He threw it open, stepped onto the porch and then slammed it behind him. John sat in his seat, too stunned to move, marveling at the sudden truncation of the conversation.

"What's *his* deal?" came a voice from behind him. John turned and saw Sarah standing at the opening of the living room.

"I have no idea. Things were going great and then…something I said flipped a trigger. The blood drained from his face and, before I knew it, he was leaping off the couch and flying out the door."

"I wonder what it was," she said.

"I don't know. All he said before he left was 'things are about to get much worse for you and your family.'"

CHAPTER 53

As Paul sat in John Peterson's living room, it had suddenly occurred to him that the last phase of his anti-Mormon campaign had yet to be fulfilled. Were it to be carried out, the Mormons' reputation in Mayfield would be blighted for years to come.

Paul frantically punched the keys on his phone, sucking in his breath, hoping he wasn't too late. The phone rang several times and then picked up.

"Bickle," came the voice on the other end.

"Jasper, it's Paul. There's been another development with John Peterson."

• • •

Within an hour, the committee had convened. Paul looked out at the semicircle of men, his stomach in knots, his pulse racing.

"Thanks for coming so quickly," he said, rising to his feet. "I've called this meeting because I think we should re-evaluate our strategy with regard to John Peterson. I think it would be an enormous mistake to take our case to these pastors. We've damaged the Petersons enough. They've decided to move on. Mission accomplished gentlemen. I think it's about time we call it a day."

For a few seconds, there was only stunned silence. Then Jasper spoke up.

"Well it's too late for that," he said abruptly. "I've already met with the pastors. Without exception, they have all agreed to help execute the final stage of our plan. Believe you me, come Sunday, there's gonna be fireworks."

Paul's heart pulsed with pain. It no longer hurt for himself. *He* was already beyond the pale. It hurt for the Petersons. The final stage of the plan would be the most devastating of all. And it had already been set in motion.

CHAPTER 54

"*Why you little turncoat*," came a voice from Paul's left. Paul grabbed a warm sheet of paper from the printer in his office and then turned towards the enormous shadow filling his doorway. It was Jasper Bickle.

"What do you want Jasper?" Paul said calmly.

"Did you think those pastors wouldn't call me? I've known those men for 15 years. I had messages in my voicemail the minute you left their offices. We had a plan Connelly. It was well-devised and well-orchestrated, and you've attempted to undermine it completely. Lucky for you, I was able to bring my considerable influence to bear and knock everything back on schedule."

Paul's jaw rippled with anger.

"You have no idea what you've done Jasper. No idea of the implications."

"I'll tell you what I *do* know Connelly. You're getting soft and squishy on Mormonism. Is John Peterson finally getting to you? Is that what's going on here?"

Paul's eyes burned with indignation.

"No Jasper, John Peterson isn't getting to me. It's called listening to my conscience. You should try it sometime."

"You know, I find your shifting allegiance very tragic. You do remember our agreement, don't you Paul? My boy starts that football game on Friday night, or your life gets real ugly, real quick. I'll have Chan Yarber in here so fast it'll make your head spin."

"Don't threaten me Jasper. If you're going to hire a new coach, do it, but don't come around here telling me how to do my job. I'm here to build character and win games, in that order. I'll thank you to leave my office and let me do my job."

Jasper's huge frame began to shake, rocked by another spasm of anger. He raised a meaty hand from his side and stuck it in Paul's face.

"If that Peterson boy so much as sees a glimmer of playing time Friday night, it'll be the last mistake you ever make. I'll bury you Connelly. You hear me, I'll bury you!"

"Get out of my office," Paul said with disgust.

Jasper gave Paul a final, menacing scowl before spinning on his heels and lumbering down the hall. Somewhere Paul heard a door open and then slam shut.

Despite Jasper's threats, Paul was still in the best mood he'd been in all week. He reclined in his chair, his hand drawing warmth from the freshly printed page clenched between his fingers. Soon, the warmth of the page and the smell of fresh ink impelled him onto his feet and into the hallway. Within seconds he was standing in front of the bulletin board in the boys' locker room. He carefully removed the pins from the sheet on the wall, calmly balled it up and tossed it into the trashcan behind him. To the bulletin board he then affixed the newly printed page. He stepped back and admired his handy work. At the top of the page, in bold fresh ink, was the most audacious roster move he'd ever made. He read it out loud just to convince himself he was actually going through with it.

"Starting Quarterback: Jacob Peterson."

Paul felt a wave of peace spread through him as he reflected upon the decision. Jacob Peterson had been restored to the spot that had been rightfully his: starting quarterback for the Mayfield Mustangs.

• • •

As Paul settled back into his office chair, he could hear the locker room begin to bustle with activity. Amid all the chattering of voices, he heard a lone voice ring out.

"Hey you guys, check this out."

Almost instantaneously the noisy clamor reduced to a low rumble. Then Paul heard gasps and whispers as the news of the roster change spread throughout the locker room.

Within seconds, Paul heard the heavy sound of footsteps. The next instant, Trevor Bickle burst through his doorway, anger etched in every line of his face. He had torn the sheet from the wall and had it balled up in his fist.

"You're starting the Mormon," he said in disgust. "Do you have any idea what this means?"

Paul looked up calmly from his keyboard.

"I'll thank you to not raise your voice and return to your locker. I need you fresh and ready to lead the scout team. And…"

"But…," Trevor tried to interject.

"And," Paul continued, "if you do it now without further discussion or histrionics, I'll pretend like this conversation never happened, and you won't have to run hills after practice."

"Just wait 'til my dad hears about this little stunt," Trevor breathed as he threw the balled up roster at the foot of his coach. "You'll be lucky if you last the week." He whipped about and pounded back towards the locker room.

A few minutes later, another face appeared in his doorway. It was Jacob. He looked dazed, as if sleepwalking through a dreamscape.

"Uh, Coach, are you *sure* about this?"

"Have a seat Jacob."

Jacob slid obediently into the metal chair opposite his coach.

"Look Jake, I want to apologize for all of my actions. They've been… inexcusable."

"Um…ok," Jacob said, still trying to get his bearings.

"I know everything about your dad, why he chose to continue preaching…everything."

"Uh, why *did* he continue preaching?" Jacob said, bristling.

"Don't they tell you anything?" Paul asked.

"My dad and I haven't exactly been on the same page these last few weeks," Jacob said with a hint of contempt.

"Look Jake. There's something you need to know about your dad. He's a good man and a true Christian. There was good reason for everything he did at Living Christ Ministries."

Jacob glanced over both shoulders just to be sure his coach was talking to him. There was no one else in the room.

"You're talking about *my* dad right? The guy that turned me into the school pariah? *That* guy?" Jacob huffed.

"The very one. Get a little more information Jake. I think you'll change your tune."

"Uh, if you say so," Jacob said, shaking his head skeptically.

"Now," Paul said, shifting gears, "as of today, you are the starting quarterback of this football team…for now."

"For now?" Jacob asked, confused.

"Yeah, there's a catch. As long as I'm the coach of this football team, you're my guy. However, there are some people in this town that aren't real happy with me right now. These people have the power to replace me at any time. In short, you and I don't have a lot of wiggle room."

"Wiggle room? What do you mean?" Jacob asked.

"We lose a single game, and I'll be gone. If we win convincingly on Friday night, they'll have no choice but to keep me. Hard to fire a coach that's on a winning streak."

"I think I get it," Jacob said, nodding his head.

"So, this makes what happens in practice today all the more critical. Time is of the essence, so we have to make every snap count."

"Alright Coach, tell me what we need to do."

• • •

Jacob looked into the facemasks in front of him, trying to read his teammates' dispositions. What he saw staring back at him gave him little comfort. Their faces were hard, their expressions blank slates.

"Alright gentlemen," Paul said, falling in beside Jacob. "Let's see if we can't stretch the field a little bit with this first one. I want a 90 y go. That's you Dooley. You think you can handle it?"

"Sure coach," Donavan said, without conviction.

Jacob looked into Donavan's facemask. His eyes were cold and empty. Jacob scanned the other facemasks. He was met by stony, dispassionate gazes. Something didn't feel right.

Jacob broke the huddle and walked up to the line. He slipped his hands under center, barked a few signals and then yelled, "Hut!" The leather slapped his hands and Jacob fell into a five step drop, eyeing Donavan as he streaked down the left side of the field. He planted his back foot and then, with a quick flick of his wrist, fired a spiral deep down the left sideline. To Jacob's dismay, however, the ball sailed deep over Donavan's head, landing nearly 15 yards ahead of him.

Jacob's face balled up in confusion. Something definitely wasn't right. Donavan was the fastest guy on the team, by a long shot. There wasn't a pass Jacob could throw that Donavan couldn't run down.

On the very next play, Jacob spotted his fullback Chad Cogan rolling into the flats. Jacob lofted a soft, arching pass towards a spot in the middle of the field. Chad cut towards the football, but at the very last second, the ball glanced off Chad's outstretched fingertips and fell incomplete. Jacob's arms rose to his hips as his confusion morphed into anger. His fullback had been running at three-quarters speed. Jacob was sure of it. First Donavan, now Chad.

Jacob watched in horror as pass after pass was tipped, dropped, fumbled and bumbled. Even Donavan, renowned for his soft hands, managed to drop three more.

After a dozen dropped passes, Jacob looked over at his coach, shrugged his shoulders and turned his palms upward as if to say, "What more can I do?"

Paul blew his whistle and stormed up to the huddle.

"It seems like some of you superstars can't seem to remember how to catch a football. That's a real shame because, now I have to stop practice while the rest of us watch you run hills. Dooley, Cogan, Cutter, Brody, get out of my huddle."

The four players fell out of the huddle and began a slow jog towards the hills that loomed just beyond the sideline where a collection of players now stood. As the four offenders approached, the group slowly parted allowing the players to pass through. Donavan was the last to run by and, as he did, Jacob saw a congratulatory hand reach out to him. Donavan extended his own hand and gave it a slap. Jacob's eyes spread wide with indignation as he honed in on the player's jersey. It was number 15. The hand belonged to Trevor Bickle.

CHAPTER 55

"It would seem that our little strategy is not bringing about the desired results," Jasper said.

The other four members of the committee stared back at him, their faces long and solemn. Jasper continued.

"My boy's got the whole team practically wrapped around his little finger. Today we had receivers dropping balls, slacking on routes, you name it. That practice field was like a zoo. But Connelly's decided to dig in. He's still got the Mormon boy at quarterback. Remember, if this town gets so much as a glimpse of what that boy can do, we're done. This town may not like Mormons, but they hate losing even more."

"Well let's step it up then," said Steve Cattrell. "Let's take this thing public, let everyone know that Connelly is in league with the Mormons. That'll turn the whole town against him. Then you'll *have* to fire him."

Jasper chuckled impatiently as he clasped his hands across his enormous gut.

"Steve, Steve, Steve," Jasper said, shaking his head sadly. "You start trying to get coaches fired because they're partial to this religion or that, you'll have the ACLU all over you like white on rice."

Steve opened his mouth to object but was cut off. It was Kip Welbach.

"Well, how is that any different than what we did to Peterson the other day in the teachers' lounge? Didn't *he* get fired because of his religion?"

Jasper's mirthless eyes fell upon Kip.

"The difference Kip, was that John Peterson was found preaching the Mormon religion within the walls of the school. Using our institutes of learning for the purposes of gaining converts is not, shall we say, good policy. Even the ACLU would agree with that. Besides, he'd been amply warned."

Heads nodded in agreement.

"The good news," Jasper continued, "is that there are other ways to turn public sentiment against Paul Connelly that have nothing to do with Mormonism."

"What do you mean?" Steve asked.

Jasper's face spread in a sadistic grin.

"Paul Connelly was hired to keep those boys out of the headlines and win football games, in that order. This year, he's failed on both counts. Would you agree with that assessment?"

More nodding of heads.

"So, here's how we capitalize. Tomorrow evening at 7 p.m., I'm convening an emergency meeting of the Mayfield school board. The doors *will* be open to the public. Paul Connelly needs to be convicted in the court of public opinion. Brethren, Paul Connelly is no longer fit to be coach of this football team. When I yield the podium, I think you'll find that the public feels exactly the same way."

"But how can you be sure?" Kip asked.

"Oh, don't you worry. There are more than enough people in this town who are willing to testify against Paul. Why, I can count at least four of them in this room alone."

CHAPTER 56

"You have got to be kidding me," Jacob gasped as Arnie nosed his car into the Mayfield High School parking lot.

"Oh yes my friend. Word is, this meeting isn't just a referendum on Paul Connelly. It's a referendum on Mormonism. Half the town's supposed to be here."

"Referendum on Mormonism *and* its sympathizers," added Jacob.

"Exactly," Arnie said, nodding his head.

Arnie drove slowly through the rows of cars until he found a vacant spot on the outer perimeter of the parking lot. He pulled into it and threw his car into park. Jacob grabbed the door handle and began to pull on it when he felt a hand clutching his wrist. He turned and saw Arnie's eyes darting from his rearview mirror to his driver's side mirror.

"What is it?" Jacob said.

"Only about half the football team."

"Trevor?"

"The whole gang."

Jacob released the handle and turned his head slightly to his left, looking out through the back window of the car. He could see a group of five or six boys in shorts and T-shirts. Trevor was in the lead.

Jacob sunk down into his seat.

"Let's lay low for just a minute or two. I'd kind of like to fly below the radar."

"I couldn't agree more," Arnie said.

A few minutes passed, and they pushed their doors open and stepped out of the car. A few stragglers trickled towards the school but, for the most part, the parking lot was empty of people. Heads on a swivel, they made their way cautiously up to the building.

As Jacob pulled on the door he saw, to his relief, that the auditorium lobby was empty. They stepped through the glass doors and into the lobby. Jacob could hear sound issuing from the cracks in the doors directly in front of them. They stepped quietly towards the doors, cracked one open, and then slipped into the darkness of the auditorium. To Jacob's relief, they found two open seats immediately to their right, tucked against the back wall. They folded the seats down and slipped quietly into them.

Jacob took a deep breath and blotted his sweaty hands against his jeans. Within seconds, they heard a gavel pounding at the front of the room.

"This meeting will now come to order," came a booming voice from the center of the stage. Jasper's Bickle's huge body hovered ominously over a lectern in the middle of the stage. To Jasper's right sat four school board members and to his left three more.

"Ladies and gentlemen, members of the community, we hereby convene this emergency meeting of the Mayfield school board," Jasper began. "The purpose for this meeting is to address public concerns that have arisen as to the fitness of this school's head football coach, Paul Connelly."

Jasper paused, as if tamping down a swell of emotion, then continued.

"Let me begin by saying that, as one of Coach Connelly's close friends, I agreed to this meeting only with great reluctance. I have a deep, abiding love for Paul and what he's done for this program. Nevertheless, I could not ignore the growing tide of public requests to provide a forum in which to air this town's grievances."

Jacob squirmed about in his chair, chafing at Jasper's performance. Judging by the audience's rapt attention and solemn countenances, he was striking all the right notes.

"In the interest of time, we ask that you keep your remarks brief and that you dwell only on the facts. I now yield the lectern."

A murmur spread throughout the crowd as Jasper took his place in the empty seat to the right of the lectern. Within a few seconds, a man rose from his seat. He walked down the left aisle of the auditorium and mounted the steps. As the man walked across the stage, the auditorium descended into silence.

Jacob's eyes narrowed as the man turned and stepped up to the podium. It was Steve Cattrell, the instigator from the teachers' lounge ambush. Jacob felt his heart slide into his belly.

Steve looked out at the audience, his face consumed with pain. He grabbed the sides of the lectern as if to steady himself, and began to speak.

"My friends and community members," he began, his voice quavering. "It is with great sadness and disappointment that I feel compelled to address you tonight."

Steve paused, took a sudden interest in his hands, and then resumed.

"Four years ago, this town was blighted by a scandal that none of us will soon forget. Few of us wish to revisit the details of what became known as 'The Mayfield 8'. In the wake of that scandal many folks, understandably, called for the so-called death penalty. However, an agreement was struck that allowed this program to persist under the auspices of a proven disciplinarian. A moral authority, if you will. Paul Connelly *was* that man. When he first arrived, we were asked to have patience. Given the transgressions of the prior coaching staff, it would require time to rebuild the program. The Mayfield 8 were dismissed from the team, the illegal recruits sent back to their home districts. There can be no question that Paul Connelly had to rebuild this program from scratch. However, here we are, four years later. This is now *Paul's* team. His imprint is squarely upon it. And what do we have to show for our patience? Ten wins over four years? Judging by last Friday's performance, we can expect more of the same this season."

Steve paused, as if searching for the courage to go on.

"I know what you may be thinking," he continued. "We may not have victories, but this coach has restored order and discipline to the locker room. That *must* count for something. Well folks, those days are clearly behind us. As many of you know, this program has once again begun to devolve into disorder and chaos. As you may have read in the *Mayfield Standard*, several players were recently arrested for underage drinking, theft, and disturbing the peace.

"Ladies and gentlemen, we hired a man to restore the dignity of this program *and* to win football games. Paul Connelly has proven capable of neither. For the good of our children and for the honor of this program, it's time for a change. It's time for a new leadership. I believe Chan Yarber is the fresh face this program needs. Thank you for your time."

"Hear, hear," yelled someone from the audience as Steve stepped away from the lectern. The rumble resumed as others in the audience murmured their approval.

Over the course of the next 20 minutes, three more men rose, and delivered blistering condemnations of Paul Connelly. As the invectives piled up, Jacob's anger built to its breaking point. Sure his coach had taken his eye off the ball, but he *was* still a good man. His most recent actions had shown it.

When the last man returned to his chair, Jacob felt a surge of energy lift him onto his feet. The chair snapped up behind him as he stepped into the aisle. He took a step towards the stage when, suddenly, he felt a hand latch onto his wrist. He looked down and saw Arnie's bony hand holding him fast.

"Don't do it," he whispered. "It won't end well. A different time and a different place, but not now."

"Let me go," Jacob hissed. "I have to say something!"

Arnie did not respond, but he tightened his grip. As Jacob struggled against Arnie's grasp, he saw a shadow moving in his periphery. He turned to the front of the auditorium and saw another figure stepping up to the lectern. His mouth gaped open, then his legs melted beneath him. Stunned, he collapsed backwards into his chair. Standing before the audience was Ashley Hudson.

She looked out at the audience, her face wistful, her eyes puffy and red. This wasn't a good sign. It wasn't a good sign at all. Jacob felt his stomach tighten as he braced for her first words.

"If there's anyone in this town that can testify of the devastation that comes when a football coach loses his handle on his team, it's me. As many of you know, my family was at ground zero of the Mayfield 8 scandal. I was only 13 when I watched my older sister spend four weeks in a hospital bed, a direct byproduct of the culture of corruption that persisted for years under Frank Bellamy.

"Imagine my skepticism when a new coach showed up with talk of restoring honor—a new era of Mustang football. I didn't exactly buy into his optimism. With the devastation this football program brought to my family, I didn't care who the coach was, or what he preached. But, when Paul Connelly came in that first week and began to clean house, I decided to suspend judgment."

Where was she going with this? Jacob thought. Nervous tendrils of energy grabbed hold of his heart, his foot tapping spasmodically against the floor.

"Well, I think I've suspended judgment long enough," she continued. "You really want to know what Paul Connelly has brought to this town? Look no further than the headlines of our town paper. How many more innocent lives need to be shattered before we realize that this football program is an albatross around this town's neck? If we won't eliminate the football program, then I'll at least settle for a new coach. I move... that Coach Connelly be dismissed from the program. Before it's too late."

As Ashley stepped away from the lectern, a hand drew up to her face, concealing the tears that had begun to stream down it. At the bottom of the steps, she turned to her right, pushed against a door, and disappeared through it.

The cauldron of Jacob's anger now bubbled over. Ashley's harsh condemnation had all but sealed Coach Connelly's fate. This meeting couldn't have gone any worse had Jasper Bickle scripted it himself. Paul Connelly was Jacob's only lifeline to the football field and, with her thoughtless, ill-timed diatribe, Ashley had sliced right through it.

Jasper Bickle's imposing frame rose from its chair and moved behind the lectern. His brow was pinched, his demeanor obsequiously pious.

"While I take no happiness in the words spoken tonight, I respect the opinions that have been shared."

Jasper braced himself against the lectern, his meaty face lined with pain.

"Having heard the voice of the people with regard to Paul Connelly, the school board will now convene privately to discuss your comments and to deliberate over the future of this football program."

CHAPTER 57

"I'm running late Jasper. State your business and be on your way," Paul said sharply, his face partially obscured by the screen door that stood between them.

"Why that's no way to greet an old friend," Jasper protested, a devious chuckle escaping his lips.

"You've got 30 seconds to speak your peace and get off my porch," Paul said.

"You know, for someone whose future hangs so tenuously in the balance, you ought to start showing a little respect."

"I show respect where respect is due," Paul responded, his voice short and crisp.

Jasper's eyes narrowed in contempt.

"Well for starters, I thought you might want to know how you fared in the court of public opinion last night. It wasn't good Paul. It wasn't good at all. This town is overwhelmingly against you. They'd sooner hang you out to dry than let you coach another game in this town."

Paul felt his gut tighten. Jasper was usually all bluster, but this time his words had a ring of truth.

"What's your point?" Paul spat.

"My point is, the pressure to replace you is mounting on all sides. Between the losses and the headlines Connelly, you're practically the second coming of Frank Bellamy. Not a good combination Paul, not a good combination at all."

Paul chafed at the reference to the man he replaced. He was nothing like Frank Bellamy.

"If you're going to fire me Jasper, just do it. But I'm not going to stand here while you gloat."

Jasper stared back at him with an air of condescension.

"The truth is, Paul, I don't know if I'm quite ready to fire you."

"What?" Paul said.

"I came here this morning to extend an olive branch. I think it's time to put all of this behind us," Jasper said, a gleam flickering in his eye.

"What are you talking about?" Paul said, suspiciously.

"I'm willing to let you keep your job, but I've got a condition."

"What kind of condition?" Paul said skeptically.

"I'd like you to dust off the old preacher routine and deliver this town a sermon."

"A sermon? What kind of sermon?"

"Tonight at 7 p.m., you're going to stand before this town, and refute any allegiance you have to members of the Mormon Church. Further, you are to condemn the Mormon religion in the strongest possible terms."

Paul felt dread invading him like a deadly contagion, but he betrayed no emotion. He wouldn't give Jasper the satisfaction. He simply stared back, as if weighing the terms of the deal. After ten seconds he broke his silence.

"Where?" Paul said shortly.

"Living Christ Ministries. I want your statements to have maximum exposure. I want to put this whole Mormon thing to bed, once and for all."

Paul continued to stare back in silence, his face a blank sheet.

"And if," Jasper continued, "I conclude that your sermon is sufficiently contrite, then you'll remain head coach....subject, of course, to periodic review."

"Oh, and another little stipulation," Jasper added. "If you denounce Mormonism, yet Jacob Peterson is still your starting quarterback come

Friday night, then that would not constitute, in my eyes, fruit meet for repentance."

Paul began to object, but Jasper cut him off.

"Further," Jasper continued, "your repudiation of Mormons and their religion is something you've decided to do of your own free will. You've seen the error of your ways and want to square yourself with the people of this town *and* your God. Try to pin it on me and I'll bury you. Got it?"

Paul's chin fell onto his chest as he processed the terms of Jasper's proposal. Everything he had worked for over the last four years was now hanging in the balance. After a long pause, Paul raised his head and fixed his eyes on Jasper.

"Alright Jasper," Paul said with all the gravity of a condemned man. "I'll be there."

· · ·

"Mr. Holler?" came the voice from the other end of the phone.

"Speaking," Buddy said.

"This is Jasper Bickle. It's *so* good to hear your voice."

"What do you want Jasper?" Buddy retorted.

"Well a good morning to you as well," Jasper said, his specious tone undiminished. "Say, I'm not sure if you heard, but my good friend Paul Connelly has decided to walk back his position on the Mormon Church."

"That right? And I'm just positive that he's doing all of this of his own volition," Buddy said sarcastically.

Jasper let out a haughty chuckle. "Do I detect a shade of hostility, Mr. Holler?"

"You're wasting my time Jasper. How can I help you?"

"The better question might be, how can I help you? You see, Paul is currently in search of a venue at which he can, shall we say, deliver the goods. I was thinking that it might very much be in your best interest to host just such a sermon."

"And why exactly would that be in my best interest?" Buddy snapped.

"Well, it helps you in a number of ways. If you play nice and open up your doors, I just may decide to call off any future boycotts of your church."

"Jasper, you're asking me to help you attack the Mormon Church."

"And..," Jasper said, as if waiting for Buddy to make his point.

"And…that seems wrong on every conceivable level."

"Well Holler, we all make choices and, sadly, our choices do have consequences. You just need to decide if you can live with a permanent boycott of your church."

Buddy marshaled all of his willpower to keep from slamming the phone back into its cradle. His options, already bleak, were growing more dire by the second. He stewed in silence for a few moments as he considered Jasper's ultimatum.

"Fine," Buddy said. "I'll play host to your inquisition. But know that this is tantamount to extortion. I…"

Jasper calmly cut him off.

"And by the way," he said, "we are expecting quite a large crowd. Do you mind doing whatever might be required to make room for, oh, say about 2,000 of the good folk of Mayfield? Thanks again. You've been very accommodating. We'll see you tonight."

Buddy began to protest but stopped when he heard the dial tone on the other end of the line. He slammed the phone back down in its cradle.

Buddy spent the next six hours outfitting the outer classrooms and meeting rooms on his campus with closed circuit television in an effort to meet Jasper's demand. It had cost him money that he didn't have, but he couldn't risk raising Jasper's ire. Whether or not he cared to admit it, Jasper Bickle was running this town, and Buddy was hostage to his every whim.

CHAPTER 58

"Get a load of this," Arnie said, waving a piece of paper in Jacob's face.

"What is it?" Jacob asked.

"Says here that practice is canceled. Coach Connelly needs time to prepare for tonight's meeting."

"What meeting?" Jacob asked.

"Have a look," Arnie offered, holding the sheet out.

Jacob snatched the paper out of Arnie's hand and began to read. It was a photocopy of a memo written on Paul Connelly's letterhead. After 30 seconds, Jacob looked up from the page, his eyes filled with disgust.

"Jasper Bickle's behind this," Jacob said.

"Jasper Bickle?" Arnie said skeptically.

"Can't you see Arnie? That kangaroo court last night was all about turning public opinion against Coach Connelly. Now Bickle's got him right where he wants him. With that kind of leverage, he can get Coach Connelly to say just about anything."

"Wow," Arnie responded. "With that kind of insight, you're starting to sound like me."

"I'm totally toast," Jacob said in exasperation. "How am I supposed to play for someone's who's publicly condemned my religion in order to save his job?"

Arnie looked at Jacob ruefully.

"Jake man, I hate to tell you this, but if Paul Connelly is still our coach on Friday, I can pretty much guarantee there's going to be strings attached."

"What are you talking about?"

"If Jasper Bickle lets Coach keep his job, it'll only be if Trevor Bickle is his quarterback."

"What?" Jacob snapped.

"Hey man, don't shoot the messenger. I'm just telling you what I think. Based on what I know about the parties involved, there's no way Jasper Bickle keeps Coach Connelly *and* allows you to play. If Coach stays…you're out."

Jacob slammed his fist against the locker as he let out a groan of disgust.

"Does that surprise you Jake?" Arnie asked.

Jacob's teeth clenched together as the rage burned within him.

"I guess it shouldn't," he breathed.

"Sorry man. Bickle's got his foot on Coach's neck, and he's starting to press."

CHAPTER 59

Jacob *had* dithered about for weeks, unwilling to face the unintended consequences of their burgeoning relationship, but that was no excuse for what Ashley had done. Football had been the last flicker of hope in his otherwise dreary existence, and she had effectively snuffed it out. She owed him answers, and he was going to get them.

He'd rehearsed his line of interrogation a dozen times, but nothing prepared him for the explosion of nerves that was now spreading through his chest. In a flurry of movement, he unbuckled his seatbelt and threw open the car door. If he teetered too long on indecision, he'd talk himself out of it.

He got out of the car and strode purposefully towards the door of the ice cream parlor, his palms damp with sweat. As he pulled the door open, the tinkle of bells, like the first tackle of the game, sharpened his senses. He stepped into the parlor and saw Ashley sitting behind the counter, punching numbers into a calculator. At the sound of the bells, her head rose, and Jacob saw those impossibly blue eyes. He opened his mouth, prepared to launch his first volley, but nothing came out. At the sight of Ashley, his well-rehearsed diatribe had devolved into a jumble of foggy thoughts.

"What are *you* doing here?" Ashley said crisply.

A shimmer of heat shot up his spine and, all of the sudden, his clothes felt just a little too tight. The tenor of her opening salvo had further scrambled his thoughts.

"I…I want some answers," he stammered, struggling to regain his focus.

"Answers? Why do *you* need answers? I'm the one that should be asking the questions," she said.

"What are you talking about?" Jacob said, attempting to press forward with his original plan. "You're the one who single-handedly ensured that I'll never play another down of football in this town. I know I have commitment issues, but that hardly seems justification for the stunt you pulled last night."

"What are you talking about? What I said last night has nothing to do with you."

"You're joking, right?" Jacob said.

"No, I'm not joking. Last night was all about Paul Connelly. I've seen all the same signs. It's Frank Bellamy all over again. I had to say something before someone else got hurt."

Jacob chuckled in disbelief. "You don't get it do you?"

"No Jacob, I *totally* get it. Paul Connelly is losing control of this team. I wasn't the only one at the stage last night that believes that."

Jacob glared back, his eyes brimming with contempt.

"Do you have any idea the damage you did me last night? Do you realize that if Coach Connelly gets fired, my playing days in Mayfield are over?

"What?" Ashley said, her face clouding with confusion.

"Yeah, nice to have all the information before you start piling on, huh? Coach Connelly is the only person in town who still believes in me. If Jasper Bickle fires him, he hires Chan Yarber. Come Friday night, you're going to be looking at Trevor Bickle as your starting quarterback. You can take that to the bank."

Ashley's hand drew up to her mouth in horror.

"I'm so sorry Jacob, I had no idea. If I had known, I would have never…" Ashley lapsed into silence, her eyes falling down to her hands.

"You're telling me you had no idea that Coach Connelly getting fired would negatively impact my opportunity to play?" Jacob said, his voice thick with skepticism.

"Of course not Jacob," she said indignantly. "What do you take me for? Did you think that I was using that forum as…as some sort of payback?"

"Well, can you blame me?" Jacob said defensively.

"Listen to what you're saying. You *have* been incredibly wishy-washy these last few weeks, but that's hardly a reason to have someone fired. Last night had nothing to do with you. How was I supposed to know it would affect you?"

"I just assumed everybody knew."

"Jacob, you have to remember, I don't run in your circles. I make it a point to stay as far away from the football team as possible. I only know what I read in the headlines. And the headlines were starting to read more and more like a Frank Bellamy storyline."

The creases in Jacob's brow began to dissolve as the tension slowly drained from his face.

"So you had no idea?" he asked, his tone a little softer now.

"You know, maybe if you didn't blow me off all the time, we could actually avoid these types of miscommunications."

"Look, my life has been complex these last few weeks, and…"

"Oh please," she said, turning the tables. "I've given you every opening under the sun. I mean, I'm actually a little embarrassed, now that I think about it. Against my better judgment, I finally decide to show some interest in a football player, and all I get is grief and rejection. You know, it really was a good policy. Maybe it would be better if we both just…"

Suddenly, without forewarning, Jacob reached across the counter, cutting her off in mid-sentence. He grabbed her around the shoulders, drew her in, and pressed his lips to hers. To his amazement, she made no attempt to resist.

After about ten seconds, Jacob slackened his grip on her, and slowly pulled away, his heart hammering away in his chest. Ashley's steely countenance had melted, surprise and wonderment competing for control of her face.

"I'm sorry," Jacob breathed. "This is all my fault. I have no excuses for my…"

But before Jacob could complete his sentence, she grabbed him by the front of his shirt and pulled him back across the counter. Her lips fell upon his, her hot breath sending a tingle down his spine. As their lips lingered, another fire ignited inside Jacob's chest, a giddy ecstasy threatening to consume him.

Just when Jacob thought that gravity had relinquished control of his body, he heard a jingle of bells. They turned their heads and saw a young couple with a small child stepping through the front door.

"I *hate* it when that happens," Jacob sighed.

Ashley giggled softly, and bit her lip.

"I have to see you again," Jacob said quickly, under his breath.

"The sooner the better," she whispered.

"When are you done here?" he said restlessly.

"Not until 9. But…I could probably work something out," she said.

"When should I come back for you?"

"How about 7?"

"Way too long to wait," he said grinning, "but it'll have to do."

Chapter 60

At 6:30 p.m., Ashley heard the door of the ice cream parlor jingle to life. She turned her attention to the figure walking through the door and froze. It was Trevor Bickle.

"Ashley? Is that you?" Trevor said, his eyes wide with surprise.

"Uh…hi," Ashley said awkwardly.

She hadn't spoken to Trevor since she'd spurned him in the cafeteria six months earlier. It had been a brutal repudiation, in front of all his teammates no less. To her surprise, he'd reprised his efforts every few months, but Ashley continued to rebuff him with cold, ruthless efficiency.

"I guess I didn't realize you still worked here," he said.

"Every day," she said, struggling to purge the indifference from her voice.

"I'll be darned. How have you been anyway?" he said, as if this were a chance encounter with a long lost friend.

"I've been fine," she said evenly. "You?"

"Never better," he said cheerfully. "Anyway, I can see you're studying there so I'll make it quick," he said, nodding at her open textbook.

"Take your time," she said. She felt pangs of regret as soon as the words came out.

He studied the flavors behind the glass for about 30 seconds before turning his gaze on Ashley.

"If it's not too much trouble, why don't you give me a scoop of rocky road and a scoop of cookies and cream, please."

"No problem," she said, grabbing the scooper and peeling off two balls of ice cream.

"So what's new with you?" Trevor asked breezily.

"Oh you know, work and school, school and work, same old boring routine."

Trevor nodded his head in understanding.

"Same old grind, huh? I know the feeling."

"Yeah," she said, leery of providing fodder for additional conversation.

"Speaking of breaking out of boring routines, you *are* heading over to Living Christ Ministries at 7, right? I hear practically the whole town is going to be there."

"Really?" she said, suddenly curious. "What's going on?"

Trevor's jaw fell open in mock surprise.

"You mean you *haven't* heard?" It was more of a statement than a question. "Coach Connelly is preaching a sermon to condemn Mormonism. Been the talk of the town all day."

"What?" she gasped. "He's going to condemn Mormonism?"

"That's the word."

"What is *wrong* with these people?" Ashley said.

Trevor's face tightened with concern.

"Are you…partial to Mormonism, Ashley?" he asked.

"Well…no, but what if I were? Mormons are some of the best people I know."

Trevor's feigned concern ratcheted up a notch.

"I don't know Ashley. It kind of sounds like you might need to be in that meeting tonight. I'm not sure you know all there is to know about Mormons."

"Like what, for example?" she huffed in protest, her arms drawing up to her chest.

"I don't know, for starters, they believe that their church is the only true church on the face of the earth."

"So they have conviction," she parried.

"But where does that leave the rest of us believers? Is there no room in heaven for the rest of us? I mean, they're not even Christians, for crying out loud."

Ashley seemed baffled by this rejoinder. It didn't seem to make any sense.

"What are you talking about?" she asked, her face twisting up in confusion.

"Or this whole polygamy thing," he said, further stoking the fire.

"What do you mean polygamy?" she said.

"Well, Mormons believe that it's ok to have more than one wife. Seriously, this is news to you?"

She didn't answer, but continued to stare at him, her first seed of panic beginning to sprout.

"Or that their religion was founded by a guy who claimed to have found a bunch of gold plates in the side of a hill and translated them by the power of God. That doesn't ring a bell?"

"No, not at all," she said.

"Yeah, it's called The Book of Mormon. Their version of the Bible."

"They don't believe in the Bible?"

"Like I said, *they're not even Christians.*"

Ashley collapsed onto the stool behind her, shocked at this string of revelations.

"Do I need to go on Ashley?" Trevor pressed.

"No, I think you've made your point," she said, suddenly a world away.

"You know Ashley, maybe you *should* come tonight. Word is Coach Connelly is really going to pull back the curtain on the Mormon Church. You know he's a former pastor right?"

"I think I heard that," she said vacantly.

"Yeah, so this is right in his wheelhouse. Listen, the meeting starts in about half an hour. I was actually on my way over there myself. You could...always tag along."

Ashley's eyes narrowed as she weighed Trevor's offer. Everything he'd revealed about the Mormon Church had been profoundly disturbing. And, according to Trevor, this was only the tip of the iceberg. Within seconds she had made her decision.

"You sure you don't mind?" she asked.

"Nonsense," he smiled. "I'm happy to do it."

CHAPTER 61

Jacob checked his hair in the rearview mirror as he pulled onto Main Street. He'd passed the last two hours as if in a dream, his body infused with a happiness he hadn't felt in months. His life was still a disaster but, in the wake of their kiss, its painful details had begun to fade into the periphery.

Main Street was a ghost town as Jacob pulled the family Suburban to a stop in front of Molly's Ice Cream Shoppe. He threw his car into park, unfastened his seat belt and checked his hair one last time. His whole body tingled as he stepped down from the car and onto the pavement. As he turned to face the ice cream parlor he felt his heart slide into his stomach. The storefront was completely dark, and a closed sign dangled from the window.

He sprinted up to the window, cupped his hands around his eyes and pressed his head to the glass. An arcade of shadows crouched about the interior of the store. He looked at his watch. It was 6:55 p.m.

Now in full-fledged panic, he turned and faced the street, looking one way and then the other. There were no cars in either direction as far as the eye could see. Where *was* she? They'd agreed upon 7 p.m., he was sure of it.

Desperation mounted within him as he felt his life once again veering towards the abyss. Then something vibrated in his pocket. Relief washed over him. It was his cellphone. She was just calling to say she'd be late. But when he pulled his phone out of his pocket he saw, to his disappointment, that it was Arnie. He pressed a button and pushed the phone up to his ear.

"This is Jake," he said, trying to mask his disappointment.

"Peterson, where are you man?" Arnie said.

"I'm standing in front of Molly's Ice Cream Shoppe, where are you?"

"I'm sitting in my car at Living Christ Ministries. The meeting's about to start. I thought you and I were going to meet up."

Jacob suddenly remembered a phone conversation he'd had with Arnie four hours earlier. They had agreed to meet in the parking lot at 6:50 p.m., then slip into the chapel at the last minute.

"Ohhhh!" Jacob groaned. "I totally spaced it man. I made plans to pick up Ashley at Molly's at 7."

"Well, you *aren't* going to find her there. I just saw her walk by. She was with Trevor Bickle."

"What?" Jacob seethed.

"Yeah. They arrived in the same car and walked past me about ten minutes ago."

"Are you serious?"

"Yeah man, totally serious."

Jacob's jaw rippled as the anger swelled within him.

"Anyway, are you coming or aren't you?" Arnie pressed.

"No Arnie, I'm not coming. Don't you get it? She was supposed to meet me here. Now you're telling me she's at the anti-Mormon convention with Trevor Bickle?" He was practically yelling into the phone.

"Look, I don't know what's up with Ashley and Trevor," Arnie said, "but this meeting has huge implications for you, and you're about to miss it."

"I appreciate the concern Arnie, but I don't care about the stupid anti-Mormon meeting. The only thing I care about is getting as far away from this town as fast as I can. I'll see you around."

"But Jake...," Arnie said. But Jacob had already hung up.

CHAPTER 62

As the hour raced towards 7 p.m., Buddy peered out from behind the curtain stage right. In the twelfth row Buddy saw the enormous form of Jasper Bickle wedged into his seat, flanked by his fellow school board members. They sat smugly in their seats, watching the assembly hall fill to capacity with muted satisfaction. Buddy allowed his eyes to drift over the congregation before settling on another figure. He had a haughty smile on his face as his fingers danced across the keyboard of his cellphone. It was Chan Yarber. *What was he doing here?* Buddy thought.

Just then, Buddy saw Jasper's hand reach into his pocket and pull out his own cellphone. He punched a button, and began to read the screen. His face broke into a devious smile and then turned in the direction of Chan Yarber. Chan smiled and nodded his head. Buddy's heart sank as he observed the silent communication.

After the phone call from Jasper that morning, Buddy had suspected that Paul's sermon was about saving his job. But after what he had just seen, he feared that something much more sinister was afoot. Could Jasper really be that devious? Was Paul's firing already a done deal?

Just then a figure stepped through the door to Buddy's left. He wore a tailored blue suit, a pressed white dress shirt with a spread collar, and a red tie with blue stripes. Buddy had to look twice before he realized it was Paul Connelly. The whole town was aware of Paul's vow to never again take to the pulpit. The image that stood before him seemed eerily resurrected from a chapter of Paul's life long since closed.

When Paul drew up to him, Buddy grabbed him by the shoulders and fixed his eyes upon him.

"You look great...how you holding up?"

"Oh, you know, I've seen better days," Paul said, his tone low and subdued.

"Well, you should know that I understand your motivations for being here. Bickle's backed you into a corner."

Paul nodded solemnly. "I only wish I could go back in time and get another crack at this. I'd do everything differently," Paul said.

"I know you would," Buddy said.

The two men shared a quick embrace. Then Paul poked his head around the curtain, and surveyed the packed assembly hall.

"Ah, wonderful, a full house," Paul mused bleakly.

"More than you realize," said Buddy. "I've just been told there are 700 more watching by closed-circuit television in rooms scattered throughout the campus. You'll be addressing 2000 people here tonight."

"2000?" Paul gasped. "That's practically the entire town."

Buddy smiled gravely and nodded his head.

"Listen, it's about that time," Buddy said, glancing at his watch. "Now, I'll start the meeting by introducing you. When I start walking off stage, that's your cue, ok?"

"Good enough," Paul said, blotting his hands against his pants.

With that, Buddy gave Paul a slap on the shoulder and strode out onto the stage. As he settled in at the pulpit, the energy in the hall moved through him like a mighty gale. He cast his gaze over the massive audience and began to speak.

"Today we are blessed to hear from a member of our community we all know and love: Paul Connelly. For the past four years, Paul has been the unwavering leader of our very own Mayfield Mustangs. His leadership has radiated from the locker room, onto the field, and into the community. He is an exemplary citizen, a Christian, and a member of our congregation here at Living Christ Ministries. Brothers and sisters, without further ado, I give you Paul Connelly."

There was no applause. The audience watched with tense anticipation as Paul strode the 20 paces across the stage, then turned to face them. Paul's arms rose to the side of the pulpit as if to steady himself. With the eyes of the entire town bearing down on him, he began to speak.

"I stand before you today, a humbled man," he began contritely.

From behind the curtain, Buddy saw a smile of satisfaction spread across Jasper Bickle's face. Jasper was there to witness the demise of Mormonism, and Paul's opening words had struck just the right note.

"Through my recent actions I have betrayed the responsibility I have to my community, my church, and my God. Regrettably, I have hurt people who had come to rely upon me as an unflinching example of Christian discipleship. I failed to live up to the virtues I once preached from the pulpit, and espoused within my very own locker room. And for that I am truly sorry. For my actions, I will have to pay a steep price. My only hope is that my God will, in time, grant me forgiveness."

A thrill of ecstasy washed over Jasper's face as Paul's recantation unfolded. Mormonism's death knell was only minutes away, and the principal agent in its destruction was rising admirably to the task.

"I became keenly aware of my shortcomings as I observed people within this very community working tirelessly to lift the flagging spirit, to embrace the lonely and the neglected. I saw shining examples of those who rendered selfless service with no thought for remuneration, who sought for no more reward than the satisfaction of knowing they had done the will of God. These selfless Christians radiate goodness, regardless of the challenges with which they are beset. These are the brothers and sisters whose actions are the true hallmark of Christian living.

"Sadly, these examples have contrasted starkly with my own. It pains me to consider how very far I have fallen."

Buddy's eyes trickled back to the twelfth row. The expression on Jasper's face had melted into displeasure, impatience. Some of the school board members were whispering to each other while others had drawn their arms up to their chests.

As Paul's words rolled forth, the vast assembly of people seemed to rise in their seats, their unflinching gazes trained upon the man at the pulpit. They didn't know how these words pertained to the impending denouncement, but they seemed touched by a sense that what was being said was true.

Paul continued: "Through all of this, I've had to redefine the lens through which I understand true Christian discipleship. Let me illustrate with a scripture."

With this Paul pulled a notecard from the side pocket of his suit jacket. He began to read: "Wherefore, a man being evil cannot do that which is good; neither will he give a good gift. For behold, a bitter fountain cannot bring forth good water; neither can a good fountain bring forth bitter water; wherefore, a man being a servant of the devil cannot follow Christ; and if he follow Christ he cannot be a servant of the devil. Wherefore, all things which are good cometh of God; and that which is evil cometh of the devil for the devil is an enemy unto God, and fighteth against him continually, and inviteth and enticeth to sin, and to do that which is evil continually. But behold, that which is of God inviteth and enticeth to do good continually; wherefore, every thing which inviteth and enticeth to do good, and to love God, and to serve him, is inspired of God. Wherefore, take heed, my beloved brethren, that ye do not judge that which is evil to be of God, or that which is good and of God to be of the devil.

"Brothers and sisters," Paul continued, "my great fear is that I have committed that very sin which this scripture warns against. I have judged to be evil that which is of God. I fell into the trap of judging others by their title, by rumor, or by innuendo. In reality, the only true way to get the measure of an individual is by examining their fruits. After all, is it not our fruits by which we shall be known?

"The scripture which I have just shared with you comes from the Book of Mormon, another Testament of Jesus Christ. And it speaks to the heart of the flawed paradigms that are tearing at the very fabric of this community. Can a community that struggles to distinguish that which is of God from that which is of Satan, be on morally firm footing?

"Brothers and sisters, I am not a Mormon. I am a member of this congregation in good standing. But there is a Mormon family in this town who I have judged and measured by the great yardstick of Christian discipleship. I've examined their fruits. And I have not found them wanting.

"The family of whose actions I have spoken is the family of John and Sarah Peterson, a Mormon family with whom many of you are familiar. I have found them to be exemplary citizens and Christian disciples in every way. They may not share our doctrine in every minute detail, but from their fountain flows the purest of water. And I cannot, in good conscience, judge them as anything other than what they really are: true disciples of Jesus Christ."

Buddy's gaze shifted back to Jasper who was squirming in his seat, his bloated face twisted into a scowl. This was no denouncement of Mormonism. This was a denouncement of Jasper Bickle and all who shared in his cruel bigotry.

"Brothers and sisters, the powers that be ordered me to condemn the Mormon Church in order to save my job. To that injunction, may I respond with a scripture: 'What does it profit a man to gain the whole world if he loses his soul?' My friends, I *could* condemn the Mormon Church and *perhaps* keep my job. But for such an act of cowardice and betrayal I would surely lose my soul. As I am unwilling to do so, I hereby resign as head coach of the Mayfield Mustangs effective immediately. May God bless you and may God bless the family of John Peterson."

Paul stepped away from the pulpit and walked briskly offstage, exiting through the same door through which he had arrived only ten minutes earlier. Before the congregation could register what had taken place, Paul Connelly was gone.

CHAPTER 63

Two hours later, Buddy collapsed onto the chair at his wife's bedside. He grabbed the Bible off the nightstand and began flipping through its pages. He stopped somewhere in 1 Corinthians and scanned absently through the verses, searching for some spark of inspiration. After a moment, he raised his eyes to the window across from him, and stared off into the distance. After another moment, his eyes fell on Beatrice.

"Well love, I wish I had better news. We lost Paul Connelly tonight. For good I'm afraid."

Buddy paused, his lips trembling in anguish.

"But that's not the worst of it. We still haven't found a guest preacher. I haven't lost hope, but it's getting harder and harder to come by."

Tears were now curling down his cheeks, cascading onto his shirt. Buddy removed his glasses, and blotted at the tears with the corner of his sleeve. He'd broken down like this before, but never had he felt *this* hopeless. Maybe it was Paul's resignation. Maybe it was the desperate plight of the Petersons. Or, perhaps it was his dwindling bank account. The money was nearly gone and the prospect of replenishment seemed distant and remote.

He laid the open Bible down on the nightstand, his body heaving with great sobs. As his chest rose and fell, he felt his body temperature rise, and his cheeks begin to flush. He dug into his pocket, produced a handkerchief and began dabbing at his eyes, and then his forehead. Still glistening with sweat, he rose from his chair, walked around his wife's bed and pulled the window gently open. The cool air wafted through the opening, bathing him in a soft breeze. Behind him, the pages of the Bible whipped wildly about on the nightstand. Through the window he could see the enormous, lit cross at Living Christ Ministries towering high above the tree line over ten miles away. The sight of it only intensified his despair.

Sufficiently cool, he returned to his chair at Beatrice's side. He grabbed the open Bible from the nightstand and set it gently on his lap. When his eyes returned to the page, he saw that he was no longer in 1 Corinthians, he was now in Matthew 6. He reached down to flip back to his original spot when his eye caught on the first few words of a verse.

"But seek ye first…"

The words sounded eerily familiar. Obeying some involuntary impulse, he started reading the verse from the beginning, this time out loud.

"But seek ye first the kingdom of God, and his righteousness; and all these things shall be added unto you."

He *had* heard the words recently, but he couldn't quite place the context. His brow furrowed as he fished about in his memory for the connection. Suddenly, in a flash of illumination, he remembered. This had been the verse Buddy had thrown out to John Peterson as he walked away after refusing to preach a second sermon. Buddy recalled with wonderment how John had charged into his office only five minutes later prepared to preach indefinitely.

As Buddy reflected upon the exchange, a seed of doubt stirred within him. John Peterson had followed that scripture's injunction with exactness and now appeared to be paying a serious price. He'd lost his job and his home, endured the scorn of an entire town. Had Brother John *not* sought the kingdom of God? Was this John's just reward for bending his will to God's? What exactly *had* been added unto John, after all the dust had settled?

John *had* put God first, yet God had turned a blind eye. There was no justice in what had happened to John Peterson and his family. Was the God of the Bible *not* a God of justice?

The more Buddy explored this contradiction, the more the anger churned within him. But then Buddy was struck by a divergent thought. Maybe God *had* done his part. John certainly had. But what of himself? Had he bent *his* will to that of the Almighty? Oh sure, he had read his scriptures compulsively, and done his best to keep the doors of Living Christ Ministries open after Lester's passing. But had Buddy truly *sought* the kingdom of God?

Over the course of the last two years, Buddy had obsessed over the ministry's finances to such a degree that he could think of little else. The task of keeping his wife alive had pushed everything else to the periphery. Making money had been the order of the day. Every effort, every thought, had been devoted to raising the funds required to keep his wife alive. But had all this been carried out to the exclusion of something far more important? Had his steadfast reliance on the arm of the flesh crowded God out of his life?

This question rattled around in Buddy's mind until a small floret of shame burgeoned within him. As the shame blossomed into full-fledged guilt, Buddy fell to his knees, his hands drawing to his face in contrition. If his wife had any hope of recovery, he would need to turn to the arm of God.

He clasped his hands in front of him and began an anguished plea for help. After nearly an hour of supplication, something began to gnaw at the shame that had metastasized within his breast. The guilt slowly yielded to a pervading warmth that started in his belly and spread upwards into his chest. As a sweet peace consumed him, Buddy began to feel the stirrings of the Holy Ghost.

He stayed on his knees, riveted to the floor as pure intelligence distilled upon his mind, penetrating his heart. After a minute of this, his eyes suddenly sprang open, his face awash with surprise. What God had just told him flew in the face of reason. He staggered to his feet, gave his wife a soft peck on her forehead, and then hurried out of the room.

As Buddy tore down Highway 2, he tried to make sense of the bizarre instruction he had just received. It was completely counterintuitive, yet he couldn't fight the impulse to act upon it. He'd resisted God for long enough. It was time to trust in His plan.

He drove for five more minutes before pulling his car into a gravel parking lot. The sun had set but, judging by the warm glow in the window, he hadn't arrived too late.

Buddy pushed the rickety door open and made for the rectangular outline of light that loomed off to his left. He stepped quietly to the door, knocked lightly and then pushed it open.

"I apologize," Buddy began, "but I had to see you tonight. It couldn't wait."

Ethan Reddick dropped the stack of books he was holding and stared back in shock.

"Mr. Holler?" he said, his eyes spread wide.

"I had to tell you as soon as I found out," Buddy said, dispensing with pleasantries.

"Had to tell me what?" Ethan asked.

"God wants you to preach in my church on Sunday."

"That'll be the day," Ethan laughed. "I didn't exactly light up the pews my first time around Mr. Holler. You know, the whole tongue of fire thing wasn't really happening for me that day."

"Ethan, I don't pretend to understand God's will, but I do know I've ignored it long enough. He just told me, in no uncertain terms, that you are to deliver a sermon at my chapel in three days' time."

Ethan resumed pulling books off his bookshelf and stuffing them into the box on his desk.

"Sorry Buddy. I'm afraid that's impossible. Come Sunday morning, my wife and I will be long gone."

"What? You're leaving?" Buddy asked, suddenly confused.

"That's right. Mayfield didn't quite work out like I'd hoped. I have an uncle in Missouri who's been kind enough to give me a job in his factory. I start first thing Monday morning."

"Look Ethan, I don't know quite how to press this point. God just gave me as specific a revelation as I've ever received. He wants you at my pulpit on Sunday morning at 9 a.m. I'm not leaving here until you tell me yes."

Ethan looked back at him, a sense of exasperation building in his eyes.

"Look Buddy, I don't know what kind of revelation *you* received. What I do know is that *my* revelations have brought me nothing but disappointment and heartache."

"Ethan, I don't pretend to understand what you've gone through. What I can tell you is that God just spoke to me and the message was clear. You are to preach a sermon in my church on Sunday."

Ethan's eyes fell to the stack of books in front of him as he deliberated. After 15 seconds of silence, he raised his gaze.

"Alright Buddy, I'll preach to your congregation, but come 9:30, I'm on the road."

"You have my word on it," Buddy said solemnly.

"Fair enough."

Satisfied, Buddy turned to leave, but before he could reach the door, Ethan stopped him one final time.

"By the way, what kind of crowd are we going to be looking at?"

"That's a really good question Pastor. I haven't the slightest idea."

CHAPTER 64

Paul felt awful that such an important detail had eluded him. He stepped out of the storage unit and into the fading twilight. He walked over to his car, grabbed his cellphone off his dashboard and powered it on. The clock on the phone read 5:45 p.m. He quickly scrolled through his call history, found the right number and pressed call. After a few rings, it picked up.

"Yeah Lou? It's Paul Connelly. I'm afraid I'm calling with a bit of bad news. Yeah, Jacob Peterson won't be playing tonight." A pause. "Yeah, it's complicated. I'm sorry you had to fly into town." Another pause. "No, no I don't know when he'll be playing again. I apologize for all the trouble."

Paul continued to nod his head as he listened. "Yeah, sorry again. Say, if there are any other college recruiters in the hotel with you, would you mind passing along my apologies? I'd appreciate it."

Paul pressed end and then took a deep breath. He'd left messages with recruiters from eight different colleges in the wake of his decision to make Jacob his starter. One had confirmed his attendance, but given the stats he'd left on their voicemails, others would surely arrive. Before returning the phone to his pocket, he took one last look at the screen. And that's when he saw it. There were three new voice mails. He felt his body tense as he pressed a button and pushed the phone to his ear.

"Yeah Paul, hey listen, it's Mike Skinner. It's about 8:30 a.m. and nobody has any clue where you are. You didn't show for your first period class. We're kind of scrambling here."

Paul let out a groan of displeasure. Hadn't they been listening last night? He had resigned. It wasn't a partial resignation. It was an "I can't get out of Mayfield fast enough" resignation. He erased the first message and waited for the second one.

"Hi Paul, Mike again. It's about 1:30. Listen, are you still in town? I stopped by your house during my lunch break and you weren't there. We really need to talk. It's important. Call me."

Paul let out another groan as he erased the message and waited for the third one.

"Hi Paul. Mike Skinner. It's about 4:30. We really need to talk. There are some crazy things happening over here at the school. Where did you go? I really need you to call me."

By the third message Mike's voice had taken on a frantic tone. Paul wavered for a few moments before stuffing the phone into his pocket. Whatever problems they were dealing with were of their own making. Paul had already moved on.

As Paul strode towards a stack of boxes at the back of the storage unit, he felt a faint buzzing in his pocket, followed by a muffled ring tone. He grabbed his phone again and pushed it up to his eyes. It was coming from the school.

"Give it up Mike," he muttered to himself. "It's over."

He pressed the end button and returned the phone to his pocket. As he did, a seed of anxiety worked its way into his gut. Mike had *never* called him on his cellphone. In the aftermath of the Mayfield 8, he'd frequently drop by the office to chat, but he never called. This was four phone calls in one day.

As Paul hefted boxes onto a dolly, Mike's final message began to burrow into his psyche. Why was he so frantic and *so* unbelievably persistent? Sure he'd lost a gym teacher, but Chan Yarber had taught P.E. for years. The transition would be seamless.

Paul had almost succeeded in tamping down his growing angst when his cellphone again began to ring. It was Skinner, for the fifth time. Paul took a deep breath and pressed the button.

"Paul Connelly," he said.

"Thank goodness," came the exasperated voice of Mike Skinner. "Where are you?"

"I'm at the Quick Storage on the south side of town. Why do you…"

"Don't move an inch," Mike said, cutting him off. "I'll be right there."

"Don't bother," Paul said.

But Mike Skinner had already hung up the phone.

• • •

In ten minutes, Paul saw a Chevy Malibu pull slowly around the corner and into his row. Mike Skinner stepped out of the car, relief and worry battling for control of his face.

"You sure disappeared in a hurry last night," Mike said.

"Yeah, well, I didn't have anything else to say," Paul said, grabbing a box off of the dolly and dropping it into the back of the U-haul.

"Were you serious when you said you were resigning last night?"

"Of course I was Mike," Paul said, disappearing into the storage unit.

"Done coaching sure, but done teaching too? Things sure got interesting when 40 students showed up in the gym this morning and there was no Paul Connelly."

"I blew up the bridge behind me last night Mike. That was by design. My days in Mayfield are over. The sooner I get out of here," he said, nodding his head towards the remaining boxes, "the better."

"Yeah, about last night. About the Mormons…about the Petersons… did you *really* mean everything you said?" Mike asked.

"Every last word of it Mike. And if had to do it over again, I wouldn't change a word."

"Yeah, that's kind of what I thought. You know, your little bait and switch created a bit of a stir."

"I wasn't trying to make any friends."

"Well that much was apparent," Mike said chuckling softly. "Listen, you mind getting out of here? I mean, the rest of these boxes can wait, right?"

"Look Mike, I appreciate what you're trying to do here, but I'm moving on. I came for the coaching job, and now the jig is up. Right now, I just want to finish packing and get on my way. The sooner I get this town in my rear view mirror, the better."

"Paul, I'm not here to persuade you to stay," Mike said, bringing his hand to Paul's shoulder. "But a drive *would* do you some good."

Paul looked deep into Mike's eyes, searching for signs of betrayal, but Mike didn't flinch.

"Fine," Paul said.

• • •

They drove without talking for several minutes before Paul finally broke the silence.

"Uh, where are we going?" Paul asked.

"Oh, nowhere in particular," Mike said. "Like I said, just going for a drive."

"I'm trusting you here Mike," Paul said nervously.

"And I appreciate that," Mike said. "You know," he added, "that act you pulled last night...I don't think anyone saw it coming."

"Well if Bickle actually thought I was going to recant, then he doesn't know the first thing about me."

Mike gave a nod.

"You know, the phone calls have been coming all day," Mike said.

"Phone calls?"

"That's right."

"Regarding?"

"I'll let you be the judge of that."

At that precise moment, Mike pulled around the corner, and the high school came into view. And that's when Paul saw them. People were stacked nine or ten deep starting at the boys' locker room and running the length of the high school. They were clad in Mustang maroon and they were clamoring, chanting and pumping signs furiously up and down. As Mike's car pulled into sight, an enormous roar rumbled up over the high school.

"What the...," Paul said, his face flushed with shock.

"Those people that were calling all day? You're looking at 'em. Your sermon last night...well...it struck a chord."

As they pulled into the parking lot, a sea of maroon gave way before them. Some fans slapped the car enthusiastically while others reached through the window, tugging at Paul's arm. When they inched to a stop in front of the locker room door, Paul turned to Mike, a stunned look on his face.

"What's this all about Mike?"

"The people have spoken Paul. The head coaching job of the Mayfield Mustangs is all yours. That is, if you still want it."

Paul's head began to shake slowly. His eyes were downcast, his mood heavy and brooding.

"I can't take this job Mike. Not in good conscience. Not after what this school did to John Peterson and his family."

Mike began to wave his hands in protest.

"No, no, no, Paul. We've taken care of all of it. We've already picked up his option for a second year."

"What?" Paul said, his eyes gaping open.

"If these people have anything to say about it, the Petersons are going to be in Mayfield for a long, long time."

Paul stared back in stunned disbelief.

"And...no restrictions on who I play at quarterback?"

"Paul, you can start Arnie Liebowitz at quarterback for all we care. What you showed last night convinced me, and the rest of this town, that you have the moral judgment and strength of character to be the leader in this locker room for years to come."

"But what about Jasper Bickle?" Paul protested.

"No one's seen Jasper since last night but, word is, he's going to be facing an uphill battle for reelection."

"I...I don't know what to say," Paul stammered.

"Don't say anything Paul. In fact, you've been yapping long enough. Your team's in there waiting for some leadership. So get outta here. The game starts in less than an hour."

Still reeling with shock, Paul pushed the door open, stepped out of the car, and was promptly swallowed up by a sea of maroon.

• • •

When Paul walked through the door, the locker room lapsed into silence, the eyes of the entire team falling upon him. He slowly scanned the locker room, his eyes drifting from player to player, a nervous surge of energy rushing through him. The silence persisted for nearly ten seconds until someone near the back of the room began to clap. It was a lonely, isolated clap, but it was soon joined by another, and then another. Before Paul knew it, the entire locker room had erupted into a chorus of clapping, hooting, and hollering. Paul let out a lungful of pent up air, and a smile of relief crept across his face.

As the chaos began to subside, Paul turned and stepped into his office. He dug his cellphone out of his pocket and began punching numbers.

"Lou, it's Paul Connelly again. It seems Jacob Peterson will be starting tonight's game after all."

Paul smiled and nodded his head.

"Well I'm glad I caught you before you went to the airport. Can you let the others know?"

More smiling and this time a laugh.

"I know they're your competition. But you'd be doing me a huge personal favor."

Another smile.

"Perfect, we'll chat after the game."

Paul stepped out of the office and began to scour the locker room.

"Where's Peterson?" Paul bellowed, to no one in particular.

"No one's seen him," Chad Cogan said. "He wasn't in school today."

CHAPTER 65

"No, sorry Arnie. He's not here. Have you tried over at the locker room?" John asked.

"I just came from the locker room Mr. Peterson. Nobody's seen him all day."

The puzzled look on John's face morphed into concern.

"Were you at least able to give him the good news?" Arnie asked.

"He came home late last night, and was gone by the time I woke up. I presume word got around school though, right?" John asked.

"Mr. Peterson," Arnie said ominously, "Jacob never showed up at school."

"He wasn't at school? Then he still hasn't heard," John said frantically.

"Well that explains it," Arnie groaned.

"We have to find him," John said. "The game starts in less than an hour, and he doesn't know he's the starting quarterback."

"Come on, Mr. Peterson," Arnie said, waving towards his car. "I've got all his equipment in the trunk."

The two sprinted to Arnie's car and then peeled away from the curb.

"He can't have gotten very far," John said, "He's traveling on foot."

"Sure, but he's been gone all day," Arnie pointed out. "He could be anywhere by now. Does he have any old haunts, places he goes when he's down and out?"

"Nothing really comes to mind. I mean, we've only been here a month."

"Think Arnie, think," Arnie said as he slammed his head repeatedly against the steering wheel.

"Uh, you want to keep your eyes on the road," John said motioning towards the centerline.

"Oh, sorry Mr. Peterson," Arnie said, jerking the car back to the right.

"And you tried calling on his cellphone?" John asked, for good measure.

"Sure have. Ever since that little episode with Ashley at the ice cream parlor, it's gone straight to voicemail."

"Ashley?" John asked, suddenly confused.

"Yeah, Ashley Hudson. You *do* know about Ashley, don't you?"

"No. Never heard of her," John said, his eyes narrowing.

"Come on Mr. Peterson, she's only the most gorgeous girl in school. They've had this hot and cold thing going on for over a month. As of yesterday, they were supposed to be hot, but when Jacob went to pick her up from work, she wasn't even there."

"Where was she?" John asked.

"She was at Coach Connelly's sermon…with Trevor Bickle. When Jake found out about it, he went apoplectic. He hung up on me, and I haven't been able to reach him since."

"You're telling me there's a girl in the middle of this?"

"Oh yeah. This isn't just about football Mr. Peterson. There's a girl in the mix."

"Why didn't you tell me that Arnie?" John groaned.

"Uh…didn't think it mattered."

"Turn the car around Arnie," John ordered.

"Huh?" Arnie said, confused.

"Just do it."

Arnie slammed on the brakes, checked his rearview mirror and then pulled his car into a U-turn.

"Head to the movie theatres."

"What?"

"Head to the movie theatres," John repeated.

"What for?" Arnie asked, clearly missing something.

"That's where he goes when he has girl problems."

"He goes to the movies?" Arnie asked, skeptically.

"That's right. When he broke up with his girlfriend last year, he went on an all-day bender. Must have watched six straight movies."

"What, like some sort of escape from reality?" Arnie asked.

"Exactly."

• • •

Thirty minutes before kickoff, they pulled into the nearly deserted parking lot at Movies 8 on the outskirts of Mayfield.

"Kind of empty for a Friday night. Where is everyone?" John wondered aloud.

"They're at the game," Arnie said. "Jake's statistics from last year went viral. The whole town's supposed to be there."

Arnie pulled up to the doors of the theater and John leaped out of the car.

"Wait here Arnie. I'll be right back."

John turned and sprinted up to the ticket window. A teenager sat behind the counter, his body limp, his face devoid of emotion.

"Hi there," John said, forcing a smile. "I'm looking for my son. Ok if I pop in and have a look around? I'll be back in about two minutes."

"Uh, yeah, that'll be $7.50," the boy said in a flat monotone.

"What?" John gasped.

"No one gets in without a ticket," the boy said doing his best impression of an automaton.

"Wait a second. I'm not watching a movie here. I'm looking for my son."

"That'll be $7.50," the boy said, without flinching.

John huffed in exasperation, and then started patting his pockets in search of his wallet. They were all empty. Then he remembered. He'd left his wallet on the bedroom dresser.

He turned to Arnie who sat in his car regarding John's little jig with some degree of amusement.

"Arnie," he hissed. "I need some money."

"What?" Arnie said, his brow crinkling in confusion.

"Just throw me your wallet," John said.

Arnie pulled himself through the driver's side window and threw his wallet over the top of the car and into John's outstretched hands.

John quickly pulled a ten out of the wallet and threw it across the counter to the teenager.

"Keep the change," he muttered, as he sprinted through the door to the right.

"But wait," the boy yelled after him. "You have to choose a movie!"

But John was already through the doors and racing towards the huge electronic marquee on the far wall.

"Action, action, action," he muttered, his eyes scanning the screen as he ran. Whenever Jacob had girl problems, action movies were always the diversion of choice. He narrowed it down to two movies and then sprinted down the hallway.

Halfway down the hallway, he yanked a door open and bolted through it. He snaked through another hallway and came to a second door. He pulled it open and suddenly he was inside. Light streamed from the projector above as the sound of squealing tires and gunshots echoed through the theatre. John quickly scanned the stadium seats but saw only a teenage boy cuddling with his girlfriend in the top row. There was no sign of Jacob. He dashed back to the main hallway, and began scanning in both directions for the second movie. He spotted it on the left at the far end of the hallway.

He broke towards the sign, glancing frantically at his watch as he ran. It was 6:35. Kickoff was less than a half hour away. He got to the door and threw it open. He quickly navigated the hallway, pulled open the final door and then rushed into the viewing area. He turned to his right, waited as his eyes adjusted to the darkness and began a slow scan up the rows of sloped seats. There, in the middle of the top row, slumped deep into his seat, sat Jacob.

"Jacob," his father hissed.

Jacob sprang up in his chair, his eyes straining in the darkness to identify the source of the voice. After a moment, their eyes met.

"How did you find me?" Jacob hissed back.

"Never mind that. You have to come with me right now. We don't have any more time."

"What are you talking about?" Jacob said, irritation sounding in his voice.

"Your game starts in 25 minutes, if you come now, you can make it by kickoff."

"Forget it. I'm not going," Jacob retorted.

"You have to go. The entire town is expecting you."

"What?" Jacob said, rising from his chair.

"Paul Connelly is still coach, and you're starting tonight's game. No time to explain. We gotta go."

Suddenly, understanding leapt onto Jacob's face. He sprang from his seat, sprinted over to the steps and began to take them three at a time.

CHAPTER 66

At 6:58 p.m., Arnie's car screeched to a halt in front of Mustang Stadium. Clad in full Mustang regalia, Jacob threw the backdoor open and stepped onto the pavement. A massive crowd, at least 15 deep, was pressing towards the ticket box at the mouth of the stadium.

"Excuse me, excuse me…pardon me," he said, working his way through the crowd.

"Isn't that Jacob Peterson?" somebody gasped.

"Hey, make way, it's Jake Peterson," another yelled.

Heads whipped about as the buzz around the ticket box began to build. As the crowd became aware of his presence, Jacob saw a tiny pathway open before him giving him an unencumbered path to the field. Within seconds he was on the field, streaking through the west end zone.

As Jacob sprinted towards the home sideline, awareness began to spread through the stadium. Mustang fans sprang to their feet and exploded in a chorus of clapping and cheering that rose up over the stadium. As Jacob approached, he saw his coach standing at midfield, Trevor Bickle at his side.

Through Trevor's facemask, Jacob saw a face that seethed with hatred. As Jacob joined them at midfield, Trevor turned and, in an explosion of anger, launched his helmet against the back fence. He flashed Jacob one last look of contempt and then stormed off down the sideline, cursing as he went.

"Uh, good to have you back, Jacob," Paul said, the shock still ringing in his voice. "A bit of a close shave, but it's good to have you back."

"Yeah, well, remind me not to go into hibernation the next time you decide to give a sermon," Jacob said with feigned exasperation.

• • •

After electing to receive, the Mustangs returned the Saxons' kickoff to their own 28 yard line. Jacob trotted out onto the field and took his position at the head of the huddle. His eyes drifted from facemask to facemask, trying to get a measure of his teammates' fealty.

"We good fellas?" he asked.

He was answered by the enthusiastic nodding of helmets.

"Great. Coach wants us to start this thing off with a bang. 929 waggle, x slant, y post. On two, ready, break."

Jacob stepped up to the line and began barking signals.

"Blue 32, blue 32, hut, hut."

Jacob grabbed the ball, took a five step drop, brought the ball up to his ear, scanned and then launched a rifle shot down the middle of the field. But as Donavan Dooley broke towards the post, the ball sailed high above his head and into the arms of the Saxons' safety nearly ten yards behind him.

The safety tucked the ball away and then shot off in the opposite direction, summoning a wall of blockers as he ran. A channel opened up before him along the Saxons' sideline and he accelerated into it. Several Mustang players gave pursuit, but it was too late. The safety had already put ten yards between himself and the closest Mustang. Five seconds later he streaked untouched into the end zone for a touchdown.

With a surreal numbness invading his limbs, Jacob began a slow trot off the field. Had that *really* just happened? The post pattern Donavan had run had been crisp and perfectly executed, but he'd simply overthrown the ball. His pinpoint precision, the driving force behind 65 touchdown passes and only 7 interceptions in his first two seasons, had suddenly abandoned him. With one over-exuberant flick of the wrist, Jacob was suddenly staring at a 6-0 deficit.

In subsequent series, Jacob tried to subjugate his nerves, but there could be no corralling his wildly exuberant arm. During the rest of the first half, Jacob completed just 2 of 11 passes for 23 yards, and 2 more interceptions. Something was tapping at the back of his mind and he couldn't seem to shake it. It was throwing *everything* off.

What was worse, the defense seemed even more porous than usual. No sooner would Jacob throw an interception, than the Saxons would march right down the field, chalking up first downs seemingly at will. By the time the clock had ticked down to the two minute warning of the first half, the Mustangs were buried in a nearly insurmountable hole: 28-0.

Jacob kneeled on the sideline, leaning on his helmet for support. The stunned crowd had descended into a sea of silence. Jacob couldn't figure it out. The planets had been perfectly aligned only an hour earlier, and now they were spinning off their axes.

Suddenly Jacob heard a whisper in his ear.

"Well Mormon boy, that probably didn't go exactly like *you* planned. Let me know when you need to get bailed out."

Jacob turned to his right and saw Trevor Bickle, a wicked grin smeared across his face.

CHAPTER 67

A shley eyed the group of men in the bleachers to her right warily. With each errant pass, there were frowns, shakes of the head, and muffled exchanges. Armed with clipboards, they assiduously noted each incompletion, each interception...everything. It didn't take long for Ashley to piece it together. These men were college recruiters.

For Ashley, the first half had been as perplexing a game as she'd ever witnessed. She'd googled Jacob on a number of occasions and could recite his stats from memory. He'd thrown only three interceptions all last season. He'd thrown that many in the first half alone. It was like Jacob was there physically, but mentally he was off in some other dimension. By the end of the first quarter, she knew this wasn't just a rusty quarterback acclimating to his first start of the year. Jacob's problems ran far deeper.

With two minutes left in the half, one of the recruiters stood up, and turned to the other men.

"Well gentlemen, I do believe I've seen enough," he said, stepping towards the aisle.

The other men nodded in understanding as the man began descending the bleachers. Ashley's heart tumbled into her stomach as she watched the man go down the steps and disappear into the crowd of people already pressing towards the exit.

In an act of desperation, she took a scrap of paper and pen out of her purse and began to scribble. When she was done, she folded the paper in half, and then worked her way over to the steps. She quickly descended them, hopped onto the landing, and then took another flight of steps to the concrete walkway in front of the players' bench.

There, only ten yards beyond the fence stood Paul Connelly. She called out to him.

"Coach Connelly!"

The coach turned, saw Ashley standing at the fence, and then walked over to her.

"Ashley?" he said, in a tone of surprise. "What's going on?"

Ashley didn't say anything, but handed him the folded piece of paper. He quickly unfolded it and began to read. His eyes darted from the paper to her eyes.

"You sure about this?"

A thin smile spread across Ashley's face.

"Yeah Coach, I'm sure," she said.

• • •

Paul looked out at the locker room full of bedraggled players, the air thick with pessimism. Every ounce of experience told him this game was unwinnable. Yet, there was something in Ashley's note that gave him reason to hope.

After delivering a half time pep talk with all the enthusiasm and motivation he could muster, Paul dismissed his team to the field. The team rose to their feet and began a grim procession out of the locker room. When Jacob passed by, Paul grabbed him by the arm.

"Not you Jake. I want you to hang around for a second."

Jacob hung back, refusing to meet his coach's gaze. His head hung in embarrassment, his shoulders slumped, his body limp and lifeless.

"Look Coach, I know...," Jacob began.

"Take a seat," Paul said, cutting him off.

Resigned and deflated, Jacob collapsed onto the wooden bench. Just as he did, he saw movement off to the coach's right. And then she walked in. It was Ashley.

"He's all yours. I'll see you out on the field, Jacob." Then he turned and disappeared through the door.

"What…what are *you* doing here?" Jacob stammered, a prickly heat rising up his spine.

"The question isn't what am I doing here. The question is, what are you doing out there on that field? You're a total mess out there."

Jacob stared back in disbelief.

"Are you serious?" he said. Her presence in the locker room was insane enough to begin with. And now she was critiquing his performance?

"Two of eleven? You've got to be kidding me. You threw three interceptions all last year. You have three in the first half alone. That's not you out there."

"What do you care?" he said, glowering back at her.

"What do I care? Here we go again. What's with the on again off again thing with you?"

"On again off again? I wasn't the one that didn't show up last night. Where were you when I came to pick you up?"

"I think you know where I was," she said, her eyes falling to her shoes, her cheeks flushing pink.

"Yeah. Matter of fact I do. You were at the little anti-Mormon love fest with Trevor Bickle."

"That's right. I *was* at the chapel with Trevor Bickle. He said some horrible things about Mormons and I had to find out for myself. I wanted to talk to you about it, but you didn't even show up at school."

Jacob folded his arms, refusing to meet her gaze. His eyes were now tracing the contour of the small squares of tile between his feet. Suddenly Jacob got up and started to walk towards the exit.

"Where are you going?" she said, on the edge of exasperation.

"Look, I don't know why you came here," he said over his shoulder.

"I came here…," she said, her voice rising. "I came here because I had to let you know."

"You had to let me know *what*?" Jacob snipped.

"I had to let you know that…" She paused, her body tensing up. "I had to let you know that…I love you."

Jacob's eyes spread wide.

"You love *me*?" he asked skeptically.

"Yes Jacob. Is that so hard to believe?" she said, a pleading look in her eyes.

"After last night, actually, yeah," Jacob countered.

"Well after what I saw in the first half, I thought you needed to get some confirmation."

"That?" Jacob said, pointing in the direction of the field. "You think that was about you?"

"If I'm wrong, I'll walk out of here, and I won't ever come back."

As her words hung in the air, Jacob's pulse quickened. *Don't ruin this Jake*, he said to himself. *Don't drive her away again.* After ten seconds of silence, Jacob spoke.

"You know, when you weren't there last night, my world turned really dark. I was so...so confused, so...angry. I just couldn't figure out why you wouldn't be there. And then when I found out that you were at the anti-Mormon rally, with Trevor Bickle no less, it was like I'd fallen into a deep, dark hole and I couldn't get out."

"And if I could do it all over..." Ashley said.

"I know you would," Jacob said, cutting her off. "I'm just trying to create some context for what you saw out there. It's kind of hard to throw a football when you can't even think straight."

"Well maybe there's something I could do to straighten out those thoughts of yours," Ashley said, taking a step closer to him.

When Jacob raised his eyes to her, she was already reaching for him. Her lips found his, and he pulled her in. As Jacob kissed her, a conflagration started in his chest and quickly consumed him. As he held her in his arms, he had a sudden, strange moment of clarity. Despite the impossible odds, despite the 28 point deficit, there was one thing that seemed strangely clear: the Mayfield Mustangs were going to win this football game.

CHAPTER 68

As Paul walked towards the stadium, he stuffed his hand back into his pocket, found the folded piece of paper and fished it out. He unfolded it and read it again.

"Coach Connelly," it said. "I love Jacob Peterson. But last night I did something that put that in doubt. If you can give me two minutes with him at halftime, I think you'll have a different quarterback for the second half. Oh, and by the way, Trevor Bickle is sandbagging on the right side. You may want to think about benching him."

It was signed, "Ashley Hudson".

Paul shook his head as a soft chuckle fell from his lips. He folded the piece of paper, stuffed it back into his pocket, and then stepped under the bright lights of the stadium.

• • •

As Paul prowled the sideline awaiting Jacob's return, a figure stepped into his periphery. It was Trevor Bickle.

"Hey Coach," Trevor said. "I was just thinking, maybe this would be a good time to put me in. I mean, after that meltdown in the first half..."

Paul looked at Trevor, making no attempt to mask his irritation.

"Bickle, not only are you not going in at quarterback, but I'm starting to have some questions about your commitment on defense. Do me a favor. Find yourself a nice warm spot on the bench, and plant yourself there until I tell you otherwise."

Paul turned and walked away while Trevor stood there, rooted to the ground, his face frozen in shock. Just then, Jacob jogged up to him.

"You ready to play some ball son?" Paul asked.

"I am now," Jacob replied, a huge smile on his face.

"Alright Mr. Peterson. This offense is all yours. Show me what you got."

After the opening kickoff, the Saxons drove down the field until their offense sputtered at their own 40 yard line. After a punt and a short return, Jacob jogged onto the field with the ball at their own 15. Jacob stepped into the huddle, his face brimming with confidence.

"Who are you and what have you done with our quarterback?" Donavan asked, a perplexed look on his face.

"I think it's time to play a little football, gentlemen," Jacob said.

"Better late than never," Donavan retorted.

"Will you relax Donavan and give me a 90 x-y double go on three?" Jacob said winking.

"Coach called that play to start the second half?" Donavan said with skepticism.

"Uh, he didn't actually give me a play."

"So *you're* calling the shots?" Donavan asked.

"I...guess I am," Jacob said with a smile.

"Okaaaay," Donavan said, clearly perplexed.

The huddle broke and the players strode up to the line. Jacob scanned the defense once again, assessing the formation and then leaned over center.

"Blue 18, Blue 18, hut, hut, hut!" he barked.

The two lines crashed together in a flurry of pushing and shoving. Jacob took a five step drop, his eyes looking deep downfield to his left. At the last second, he turned to his right, reared back and launched a tightly wound spiral deep into the night.

By the time the ball reached its apex, Donavan had already created distance between himself and the defender. As he accelerated, both ball and player began converging on the same point. Then, nearly 65 yards from the line of scrimmage, Donavan extended two sinewy arms and plucked the ball from the air. He tucked the ball beneath his arm then sprinted the final 20 yards to the end zone.

For a brief moment, the Mayfield crowd simply did nothing, scarcely able to comprehend what had just transpired. When six points flashed up on the scoreboard, it confirmed the improbable scene that had just played out before them. The stands, now only three-quarters full, exploded into pandemonium.

• • •

As the stands erupted into a frenzy of clapping and screaming, Ashley Hudson smiled inwardly. She glanced over at the two remaining recruiters. One of them conferred briefly with the other, stuffed his hand into his coat pocket and produced a cellphone. He punched a few buttons and then put the phone to his ear. Ashley strained to hear the details of the conversation.

"Yeah Bill? It's Lou. You haven't left yet have you? Good. This kid just threw a 65 yard touchdown pass on the fly. Never seen anything like it."

The man paused and began nodding his head.

"That's right Bill, *on the fly*. It was like a rocket. Something happened to this kid at halftime. I get the feeling this game isn't quite over."

CHAPTER 69

The next morning, Paul stood beside a TV on the gymnasium floor, his team scattered above him in the bleachers. Paul pressed the pause button on the remote control and began jabbing his finger excitedly at the screen.

"There!" he exclaimed. "See that Cogan? That's exactly what I'm looking for. You held the block, and *then* released into the flats. Just like we talked about in practice. That was textbook!"

A broad smile of satisfaction spread across Chad's face.

"This was a tale of two halves, gentlemen," Paul said as he powered down the TV. "Five unanswered touchdowns in the second half. Think of what we could do if we *didn't* have problems with the ladies," he said.

The team burst into laughter as Jacob's face flushed a deep shade of pink. He shook his head in disgust, and then joined in the laughter.

Amid all the giddy euphoria, Arnie brooded by himself, immersed in his own personal rain cloud. A persistent question had been pinging at the back of his mind all morning, feeding his growing sense of disquiet. As his teammates laughed and joked, Arnie kept to himself, his mind a world away. Suddenly he felt a finger jabbing at his ribs.

"Hey space cadet, you missed a great meeting."

Arnie turned his head and saw Jacob standing next to him on the bleachers. Arnie flashed him a halfhearted smile.

"A bunch of us are heading out for a bite. You want to come along?" Jacob asked.

"I'll catch up in a bit. You all go along."

"You sure?" Jacob prodded.

"Yeah, I'll just be a second."

"Good enough," Jacob said as he turned to go.

As the rest of the team filed out of the gymnasium, Arnie remained in his seat, his hands tucked tightly into his armpits.

When the gym was empty, Paul began pushing the TV stand towards his office when he noticed Arnie planted on the bleachers, making no effort to leave.

"Everything alright Arnie?" Paul asked, a touch of concern in his voice.

Arnie lifted his gaze and saw his coach looking up at him from the gymnasium floor.

"Just thinking," Arnie said.

"I can see that."

"You know, there's something about this whole thing that just doesn't add up."

"What's that?" Paul asked calmly.

Arnie's brow furrowed in concentration.

"Well, take John Peterson, for instance."

Paul's eyebrows shot upwards. This was not a subject he was expecting. He scaled the bleacher steps and took a seat just below Arnie.

"What do you mean?" Paul asked.

"Why would John Peterson continue to preach at Living Christ Ministries knowing that disaster was all but inevitable?"

Paul's eyebrows pulled together as he considered the question.

"What are you driving at Arnie?"

"I mean, John Peterson is a smart guy. Certainly he evaluated the risk versus reward quotient before deciding to preach, right? The man preached at Living Christ Ministries for four whole weeks knowing that, at any time, the identity of his religion could be revealed. Why would he do that knowing the price he would pay? There's a missing piece of the puzzle here. I'm usually pretty good at fitting this stuff together. Not this time though," Arnie said, clearly flummoxed.

Paul's eyes narrowed as he considered Arnie's question.

"You know something, don't you coach," Arnie pressed.

"You're right Arnie. There is another piece of the puzzle."

"Well let's hear it," Arnie said.

Paul squirmed uncomfortably on the bench, his mood darkening by the second.

"I'm sorry Arnie. I'm afraid I can't really say."

Suddenly, Paul looked down at his watch as if he were late for an appointment.

"Look, I really need to be going."

"Come on Coach, you can't just leave me hanging like this," Arnie protested.

Clearly agitated, Paul sprang from the bench, took the bleacher steps two at a time, and jogged briskly towards the doors at the far end of the gymnasium.

Arnie watched his coach disappear through the doors with growing anxiety. For some reason, his questions about John Peterson had unleashed a storm of panic upon his coach. Whatever his coach's destination, it might just provide the clue for which Arnie was searching. Arnie sprang to his feet, hurried down the bleachers and sprinted towards the exit.

Arnie slid into the driver's seat just as his coach's car flashed across his rearview mirror. Arnie turned the engine over and threw the car into reverse. He followed his coach from a safe distance until the huge cross at Living Christ Ministries rose into view. Is *that* where he was headed? As his coach turned into the entrance, Arnie slowed to a stop. He watched his coach pull up to the church, get out of his car, hurry over to the entrance and then disappear through the glass doors. Arnie threw his car into gear and pulled down the long, narrow road and up to the building.

Arnie hurried up to the door, pulled it open and stepped through, scanning for signs of his coach. Off to his left he saw a long, dark hallway. Halfway down, he saw light spilling out of an open office door. He walked towards it.

As he drew nearer he could hear the exchange of two voices. One of the voices belonged to Coach Connelly, but he was unsure of the other. He fastened his eyes on the sign to the left of the doorway. In bold white letters against a brown background were the words Church

Administrator. His coach had dropped everything to come see *Buddy Holler?* Arnie pressed his ear up to the doorway, straining for details.

"It just doesn't make sense for you to keep this matter private," Paul said.

"I appreciate your concern here Paul. I really do. But I just don't want my problems bandied all over town. I'm not interested in charity and I don't want to be a burden," Buddy said.

Private matter? Arnie thought to himself. Now we're getting somewhere. He inched closer to the door.

"I understand you like to fly below the radar. We all like our privacy. But you're running out of options here. If you don't raise any revenue soon, the coma will be irreversible. Who's going to pay eight grand a month for your wife's medication if you can't get people into these seats?"

"I just need to find a preacher. Once I find a preacher, we'll right the ship. That's the solution Paul. That's how I want to handle this."

"But you've tried everyone Buddy, there's no one left."

"That's not true Paul. I have a pastor preaching here tomorrow."

"You mean the young guy?" Paul said, cocking his thumb in the direction of the marquee. "If I recall, that didn't go so well last time."

"It'll be different this time Paul. I can feel it. Just promise me you won't say a word about my wife."

Arnie heard only silence for the next 20 seconds.

"Alright Buddy, you have my word," Paul said, breaking the silence.

Hearing these words, Arnie sprinted back down the hallway and through the glass doors through which he had come. He pounded across the pavement, slipped into his car, and tore across the parking lot towards the exit.

As Arnie drove, his thoughts began to race. He had heard that Buddy's wife had slipped out of the public eye a few years ago, but this was the first he'd heard of her coma and the cost of keeping her alive. But it all made perfect sense. John Peterson had risked everything in an attempt to keep Buddy's wife alive. That was the answer!

As the puzzle pieces fell into place, Arnie's eyes narrowed in concentration. Things were desperate for Buddy Holler, and he was refusing to accept outside help. And, while Coach Connelly *had* been sworn to secrecy, Arnie had not been. All at once, Arnie came to a decision. Someone had to finish what John Peterson had started. Things were growing desperate for Buddy's wife, and time was in short supply.

• • •

At 2:30 on Saturday afternoon the phone rang at the Peterson's house. Sarah Peterson took the cooking mittens off her hands and lifted the phone off the cradle.

"Hello, Petersons," she said.

A surprised look came across her face as the caller identified himself.

"Oh…hello," she said.

She nodded her head in silence as she listened to the caller for another 30 seconds before hanging up.

"Who was that?" John asked, looking up from a plate full of spaghetti.

She turned to face him, her eyes wide with shock.

"You're not going to believe this."

"Try me," John said.

"That was Donavan Dooley."

"Donavan Dooley?" John said, his eyebrows arching upwards in surprise.

"Yeah, he was calling on his cellphone from the gymnasium over at the high school."

"What did he want?" John asked.

"The whole team is there. They're…making phone calls."

"Even Jacob?" John asked.

"Well, Arnie picked him up about an hour ago. That must be where they were going."

"Well, what did he say? Why was he calling?" John asked, curiosity building.

"Word leaked out about Buddy's wife. The entire football team is in the high school gymnasium making phone calls. John, they're mobilizing the community."

"Mobilizing the community? To do what?" John asked.

"To show up at Living Christ Ministries."

Chapter 70

"I just don't understand why you agreed to do this," Jenny said as Ethan fired the ignition. "The trip's already going to be tight, and your uncle's expecting you first thing tomorrow morning."

They had spent the previous day stuffing their earthly possessions into the trailer hitched to the back of their station wagon. Ian sat behind them in his car seat wedged between piles of tightly packed boxes.

"Look, we're talking half an hour here. I walk in, give the sermon, and then walk out. Thirty minutes isn't a deal killer here, honey. Besides I gave my word."

"Is there even going to be anyone there?" she asked skeptically.

"Now why would you say a thing like that?" Ethan said, his lips hardening into a line.

"Hon, everyone knows that Buddy's church is on the cusp of financial collapse."

"What?" Ethan said in disbelief. "Who told you that?"

"It's all over town. Ever since John Peterson got banished, Buddy's been scrambling for a replacement."

Ethan shook his head in disbelief.

"Think about it Ethan. Why do you think Buddy came back to you?"

"You know, I really resent what you're implying," Ethan said, a storm brewing in his eyes.

"Well, aren't you even a *little* offended that he would turn to you now?" she countered.

"Why *should* I be offended?"

"Because he's coming to you as a last resort, and frankly Ethan, you're nobody's last resort. *That's* why you should be offended."

"Look, he said God gave him a revelation. I'm taking him at his word."

"Here we go with the revelation bit again. Don't you remember? You had that little revelation telling us to drop out of divinity school and move to Mayfield. Look where *that* got us."

Ethan glared back at his wife, his brow pinched, blood pounding in his neck. But he bit his tongue. He'd long since lost this argument.

"Look, I guess I'm just a little bothered that Buddy would come to you now. You're so much better than this. You proved that these last few weeks."

Ethan's face hardened with resolve. "It's only 30 minutes. I'll be in and out and then we'll be on our way."

"Do what you want," Jenny huffed, folding her arms obstinately against her body. "Your uncle's giving us a chance at stability. I just don't want to blow it by showing up late."

"Look, if this chapel is as desolate as you say it's going to be, I'm sure we won't have any problems slipping in and then slipping out," Ethan assured her.

Jenny turned around to check on the baby.

"Well, the baby's asleep," she said. "If I wake him up now, he'll be up for hours. If it's all the same to you, I'll just wait in the car."

"Are you serious?"

"Yes Ethan, I'm serious."

Ethan turned away from her, the anger building in his eyes.

"Fine," he said abruptly. "I'll make it quick."

They brooded in silence as they turned onto Highway 2 and followed the long, tree-lined road that led to the edge of town.

About 300 yards from the turnoff they saw a startling scene playing out. It was five to nine and cars lined either side of the road as far as the eye could see.

"What the...?" Ethan gasped as they passed the first few cars. "These cars couldn't possibly be...," he said, disbelief swallowing the rest of his sentence.

As they turned into the parking lot at Living Christ Ministries, an even more inexplicable scene awaited them. Hundreds of cars were packed tightly into parking spots in an unbroken sea of metal. Straggling cars were roaming distant rows of the parking lot, searching in vain for the idle, vacant spot. Ethan rolled his traveling caravan to a stop in front of the shiny glass doors at the north entrance.

Ethan glanced over his shoulder at the marquee next to the highway, just to be certain. Sure enough, it read: "This Sunday: Pastor Ethan Reddick".

"It...can't be," Ethan said, his head turning back to the endless rows of parked cars just beyond their windshield.

But then, all at once, dozens of disparate memories began to distill upon his mind. He saw himself kneeling at the side of his bed as God told him to abandon divinity school and start his own ministry. He felt the pain of those chronically empty chapels. Again, he saw the fruitless hours of proselytizing, and countless slammed doors. But, then he saw Brother John at the glass pulpit preaching his very first sermon. Now John was knee to knee with him, expounding on the rudiments of a strong sermon. And then he saw the rapt attention of his own congregation as he spoke with the tongue of fire. Finally Ethan saw Buddy charge into his office and unexpectedly ask him to preach a second sermon.

Ethan tried to process all the isolated images until they slowly coalesced into a single, burning realization.

"*Could* it be?" he wondered aloud.

"Yes, Ethan. Yes it could."

Ethan turned towards Jenny. The hostility in her countenance was gone. Her eyes were glistening and tears were streaming down her face.

"But, there's only one way to find out," she said.

Jenny unlocked her door, pushed it open and stepped onto the pavement.

EPILOGUE: THREE MONTHS LATER

As Buddy gaped from behind the curtain at what was sure to be another packed chapel, the gathering warmth in his bosom conveyed a sense of completeness. Well, near completeness. What he wouldn't give to have Beatrice there with him as half the town descended upon Living Christ Ministries each Sunday.

As had become customary prior to the start of each service, Buddy turned his eyes upon the congregation, scanning for fresh faces. As his eyes washed over the congregation, they settled upon an unexpected sight. On the back row, on the far left side, Buddy saw Paul Connelly. This was nothing out of the ordinary; he'd been a fixture in the congregation for years. But just to Paul's right sat John Peterson. Now this *was* unusual. John had made it a habit of checking in on Buddy at least weekly, but for the last three months, he'd always attended his own church with his family.

Sitting next to John, his hand clutched in her own was Sarah Peterson. Scanning down the row, Buddy saw the Petersons' seven children, with Jacob serving as the bookend. Next to Jacob, his hand in hers, sat Ashley Hudson. Now Ashley was *another* unusual sight. For the last three months, she'd also been attending the Mormon Church. Why she and the Petersons were sitting in his congregation today was anyone's guess.

As his questions compounded, Buddy returned his gaze to John Peterson. When he did, he saw that John had already locked his eyes on him. John flashed him a subtle smile and gave a quick nod of his head. Then Buddy turned his gaze on Paul. He too nodded, and imparted an enigmatic smile of his own.

These unspoken communications did little to quell his mounting curiosity. Just then, out of his periphery, Buddy saw a figure stride across the stage and settle in at the pulpit. The audience lapsed into silence, their eyes fixed upon the stage, their attention rapt. The pastor raised his soft, blue eyes to the congregation and began to speak.

"Welcome to Living Christ Ministries. My name is Pastor Ethan Reddick. We count it an honor and a privilege to worship with you this Sabbath day. Before we begin today's service, I'd like to start by thanking you and the other congregations here in Mayfield who, for the last 24 hours, joined together in a town-wide fast on behalf of Beatrice Holler. As previously specified, the fast will conclude at the end of today's meeting."

Buddy's eyebrows narrowed in confusion, as if his ears had somehow betrayed him. *Town-wide fast? For Beatrice?* Ethan had said nothing of a town-wide fast.

Before proceeding, Ethan paused, turned to Buddy and flashed him a mischievous smile as if to say, "If I had asked, you would have said no. So I didn't ask."

Ethan turned back to the congregation and continued. "While medical advancements can often perform miracles in their own right, there can be no substitute for a town full of Christians who, united in fast and prayer, call down the powers of heaven on behalf of another."

Obscured by the curtain, Buddy staggered backwards against the wall, reeling at this unexpected turn in the meeting. Was it possible, after all the enmity his ministry had engendered, that the other churches in town could unite behind a cause such as his?

Through all the numbness and confusion, Buddy felt a slight tickle in his breast pocket. His hand drew reflexively to his chest and groped for his buzzing phone. He drew it out and pushed it up to his nose. It was a text message. He pressed a button and saw pixilated words flash onto his screen.

It was a message from Dr. Ignacio. He felt a jolt of nerves as his eyes moved slowly across the screen.

"Buddy, you must come quickly. It defies explanation. Something has happened."

Buddy paused, swallowed hard and kept reading.

"It's your wife. She's awake."

THE END

ACKNOWLEDGMENTS

A hearty thanks to the many friends for their feedback and input throughout the entire writing process. I am deeply indebted to Kitty Cone, Jon Mano, Anne McKnight, Paul McKnight, John Morriberon, and Jan and Ray Totzke for their keen insights and useful contributions.

An especially robust thanks goes out to Dave Butler, author and storyteller extraordinaire, for his guiding hand throughout the entire process.

Finally, my deep, heartfelt thanks go out to my marvelous wife Felice, without whose love and support this book could never have become a reality.

boilerplate 18339259R00199

Made in the USA
Lexington, KY
28 October 2012